# SEQUEL

## A Handbook for the
## Critical Analysis of Literature

**Richard C. Guches, Ed.D.**

*Department of English*
*American River College, CA*

PEEK PUBLICATIONS, P. O. Box 50123, PALO ALTO, CA 94303

Copyright 1979

Peek Publications

Second Printing 1980

Library of Congress Catalog Card Number: 79-88953

ISBN: 0-917962-64-8

Manufactured in the United States of America

III

# Copyrights and Acknowledgments

# *Preface*

"And this I believe: that the free, exploring mind of the individual human is the most valuable thing in the world. And this I would fight for: the freedom of the mind to take any direction it wishes, undirected. And this I must fight against: any idea, religion, or government which limits or destroys the individual. This is what I am and what I am about. I can understand why a system built on a pattern must try to destroy the free mind, for this is one thing which can by inspection destroy such a system. Surely I can understand this, and I hate it and I will fight against it to preserve the one thing that separates us from the uncreative beasts. If the glory can be killed, we are lost."

From *East of Eden* by John Steinbeck

# *Dedication*

for

Patti

Jennifer

and

Sean

# Contents

## To the Student:

To write an effective critical analysis you must first possess a basic understanding of sentence structure and paragraphing, as well as the skill to arrange all of the parts of an analysis in a logical and coherent manner. Possessing the skill to organize information and ideas, however, will not result in a successful paper unless you also have a knowledge and understanding of the subject about which you wish to write. While a deficiency in the background of a subject can usually be remedied by the reference sources of a library, sound analytical abilities should not totally rely upon such secondary reinforcement.

SEQUEL is designed to familiarize you with new concepts, with analytical skills, and with new understanding about the nature of literature. However, to become truly skillful and confident in your abilities to analyze fiction, drama, and poetry, you also need to develop a background in literature. SEQUEL has been expressly planned to enhance your understanding, expand your background and promote your appreciation of literature.

The beginning of each chapter has a pretest which should be taken and evaluated prior to reading the chapter's instruction. These pretests enable you to determine which parts of each chapter you already understand. After successful completion of a chapter's instruction, you will be ready to write a critical analysis. Credit for successful completion of a chapter is given only after you have demonstrated mastery in writing a critique, or upon a test that your instructor selects.

Read closely and critically, write clearly and coherently and you will do well— not only in these chapters but also in other courses. In addition, you will feel a personal gain and a sense of accomplishment in being able to understand better what you read and view—and being able to write an effective critical analysis.

# Analyzing Poetry

Many people seem to feel that while they may like novels and movies well enough, poetry is somehow alien to their lives. Usually, however, this is caused by a genuine lack of understanding of what the poet is trying to do and the techniques poets generally employ. A lack of appreciation can stem from either no formal instruction or from overly rigid guides to interpretation. But like the other genres discussed in this book, poetry has its specific characteristics, and to learn these is to enhance one's understanding and appreciation of its forms.

Indeed, through poetry you can see nearly all literary techniques in action. Technical literary devices that would need long passages of prose to demonstrate may be illustrated with but a few lines in poetry. Moreover, the same techniques that are employed by prose writers and dramatists are readily observed in the creations of poets. Observation and identification of these literary techniques will lead you to an understanding and the potential for appreciation. In short, you are not being asked to like poetry (or any literary selections in this book) but rather to understand it and to demonstrate that understanding. If your understanding leads to appreciation and then to real joy in the literature, so much the better. You must remember, however, that it is only the understanding that is required, not the appreciation and certainly not the joy. What is important in this book, and for the rest of your life, is not what specifically you like or dislike but your ability to understand the *"why"* of either—and that is discovered only through the logic of sound critical analysis. A close study of poetry is but a logical first step toward the necessary understanding of analytical technique, because literary techniques are easily illustrated and quickly understood in short poetic selections.

### Objectives:

After completing this unit, you will be able to:
1. Define poetry.
2. Describe allusions and identify referents.
3. Illustrate the use of imagery.
4. Describe the difference between denotation and connotation.
5. Assess the contribution of metaphor to poetry.
6. Interpret symbols as used in poems.
7. Illustrate the three uses of irony.
8. Write an analysis of a poem.
9. Identify the most common figures of speech used by poets.
10. Express confidence in your understanding of poetry and why it has been so popular.

### Pre-Assessment:

Place the letter of the correct answer in the space at the left of each statement.

_____ 1. Most poetry is intended to be (A) spoken (B) heard (C) printed (D) memorized (E) thrilling.

_____ 2. Most poetry involves (A) the feelings of emotional experience (B) the poets' ideas on morality (C) the sense of touch (D) true experience (E) love.

_____ 3. A word's connotation is its meaning (A) as written in a contemporary dictionary (B) to only one character in the poem (C) defined by using only synonyms (D) devoid of emotion (E) beyond its dictionary definition.

_____ 4. When writers employ the technique of imagery they are appealing to readers' (A) logic (B) emotion (C) feelings (D) senses (E) reason.

_____ 5. Readers are able to make reference to events, people, or places in history or previous literature by using (A) metonymy (B) allusion (C) hyperbole (D) irony (E) synecdoche.

_____ 6. Metaphor is a form of comparison which (A) attempts to reveal a relationship between two aspects of life (B) reveals both what it is and something more also (C) shows the intended meaning of the words to be the opposite of their expected meaning (D) contrasts what the audience expects with what is expected by the characters (E) represents abstract ideas as people.

_____ 7. Images, metaphors, and symbols (A) never appear in the same poem (B) are rarely used in normal speech (C) often overlap (D) depend upon dictionary definitions or words (E) belong only to the world of poetry and not fiction or drama.

_____ 8. When writers' meanings are the opposite of what is expected, they are using the technique called (A) tone (B) allegory (C) denotation (D) simile (E) irony.

**2**

_____ 9. When readers of a poem or story or the audience at a play knows something that a character does not know, the writer is using a technique known as (A) verbal irony (B) metaphor (C) dramatic irony (D) allegory (E) tone.

_____ 10. The use of allusion presupposes (A) familiarity with drama (B) course work in literature (C) an interest on the part of readers (D) literate and knowledgeable readers (E) readers' naïveté.

## ANALYZING POETRY

*Learning Activity #1:*

### *Characteristics*

Poetry differs from both prose and drama in its arrangement of words and its expression of experiences, ideas, and emotions. Historically, poetry may be defined as a rhythmical composition, occasionally rhymed, presented in a style that is highly concentrated, very imaginative, and typically more powerful than ordinary prose. Most poetry is intended to be heard—either orally or in the mind's ear as you read it. The arrangement of the words is usually an aid in understanding a poem since it allows the reader to determine the emphasis visually. Some poets have such distinctive visual styles that their work is instantly recognizable. For example:

in Just—

in Just-
spring     when the world is mud-
luscious the little
lame balloonman

whistles     far     and wee

and eddieandbill come
running from marbles and
piracies and it's
spring

when the world is puddle-wonderful

the queer
old balloonman whistles
far     and     wee
and bettyandisbel come dancing

from hop-scotch and jump-rope and

it's
spring
and
    the

        goat-footed
balloonMan     whistles
far
and
wee

—*e.e. cummings (1894-1962)*

**3**

Beyond the obviousness of style, however, there exists the inner meaning of poetry. Poetry, like prose and drama, involves the feelings of emotional experience. Poetry, however, concentrates the experience and compresses the emotion until, with very few words, the compressed feeling is imparted from the poem to the reader.

To understand this concept better you will need to become aware of the experiential idea behind any poem that you wish to analyze. Each poem has an event or idea from which the poet derived inspiration. Often this inspiration comes from a life experience. These life experiences may be as profound as birth, love, or death—but need not be so profound.

Looking at a specific poem should help you begin to see how poetic visions are derived from life events. Robinson Jeffers was a west coast poet whose poetry frequently reflects his rugged Pacific coast environment. Once he found a redtail hawk with a broken wing, and he tried to save it but failed. From this incident, the death of a wild hawk, he fashioned a poem in which he not only shares the experience and his feelings about it, but he also generalizes, based upon the experience, to comment upon some philosophical values that he holds.

## HURT HAWKS

The broken pillar of the wing jags from the clotted shoulder,
The wing trails like a banner in defeat,
No more to use the sky forever but live with famine
And pain a few days: cat nor coyote
Will shorten the week of waiting for death, there is game without talons.
He stands under the oak-bush and waits
The lame feet of salvation; at night he remembers freedom
And flies in a dream, the dawns ruin it.
He is strong and pain is worse to the strong, incapacity is worse.
The curs of the day come and torment him
At distance, no one but death the redeemer will humble that head,
The intrepid readiness, the terrible eyes.
The wild God of the world is sometimes merciful to those
That ask mercy, not often to the arrogant.
You do not know him, you communal people, or you have forgotten him;
Intemperate and savage, the hawk remembers him;
Beautiful and wild, the hawks, and men that are dying, remember him.

I'd sooner, except the penalties, kill a man than a hawk; but the great redtail
Had nothing left but unable misery
From the bone too shattered for mending, the wing that trailed under his talons
     when he moved.
We had fed him six weeks, I gave him freedom,
He wandered over the foreland hill and returned in the evening, asking for death,
Not like a beggar, still eyed with the old
Implacable arrogance. I gave him the lead gift in the twilight.
     What fell was relaxed,
Owl-downy, soft feminine feathers; but what
Soared: the fierce rush: the night-herons by the flooded river cried fear at its
     rising
Before it was quite unsheathed from reality.

—Robinson Jeffers (1887-1962)

4

The poet, obviously, feels deeply about what happened. The depth of his feelings comes through in his words, yet the poem itself is not particularly long. In prose, had the author chosen to use that form, the length of a short story would be much, much longer to convey the same ideas. You can see, then, the compression that has taken place by using the poetic style. This illustrates one of the main characteristics and virtues of poetry. Many feel that this compression of experience enhances the emotions a reader feels about the experiences and ideas expressed in poetry.

EXERCISE #1:

Write a one-paragraph prose summary of the following poem.

### "OUT, OUT—"

The buzz-saw snarled and rattled in the yard
And made dust and dropped stove-length sticks of wood,
Sweet-scented stuff when the breeze drew across it.
And from there those that lifted eyes could count
Five mountain ranges one behind the other
Under the sunset far into Vermont.
And the saw snarled and rattled, snarled and rattled,
As it ran light, or had to bear a load.
And nothing happened: day was all but done.
Call it a day, I wish they might have said
To please the boy by giving him the half hour
That a boy counts so much when saved from work.
His sister stood beside them in her apron
To tell them "Supper." At the word, the saw,
As if to prove saws knew what supper meant,
Leaped out at the boy's hand, or seemed to leap—
He must have given the hand. However it was,
Neither refused the meeting. But the hand!
The boy's first outcry was a rueful laugh,
As he swung toward them holding up the hand
Half in appeal, but half as if to keep
The life from spilling. Then the boy saw all—
Since he was old enough to know, big boy
Doing a man's work, though a child at heart—
He saw all spoiled. "Don't let him cut my hand off—
The doctor, when he comes, Don't let him, sister!"
So. But the hand was gone already.
The doctor put him in the dark of ether.
He lay and puffed his lips out with his breath.
And then—the watcher at his pulse took fright.
No one believed. They listened at his heart.
Little—less—nothing!—and that ended it.
No more to build on there. And they, since they
Were not the one dead, turned to their affairs.

—*Robert Frost (1874-1963)*

## Connotation

Denotation is the dictionary definition of a word. Obviously, a word's definition, what it means according to the "*experts*," is important to everyone. A word, however, often means more than what the dictionary indicates. The meaning of a word beyond its dictionary definition is called *connotation*. The connotative meanings of words are of primary importance to poets, for they want readers to share images and feelings that may be evoked through the emotional value of certain words.

To understand words' connotative values, you should consider how some words cause certain emotional responses whereas other words, meaning nearly the same thing, leave you unaffected. For example, in a romantic ballad, you will never hear of a hero leaping upon his *horse* to race to the rescue of the princess. Neither will he race forth upon his *nag*, *equine quadruped*, or *filly*. Invariably, romantic heroes leap upon waiting *steeds*. The word *steed* has the most romantic connotation; certainly a steed is a horse, but it is the kind of highly spirited horse suitable for a ballad hero.

Think, for a moment, about how connotation is used in our daily lives to reflect our intended meaning. When we are stopped for speeding the person who stopped us is a *cop* but when we want to pursue that occupation ourselves, we wish to become *police officers*.

EXERCISE #2:

For each group of words, circle the one word with the most favorable connotation.

1. female parent, dame, mother, the old lady
2. spy, secret agent
3. average, mediocre, ordinary, commonplace, middling
4. lawyer, shyster, mouthpiece, attorney
5. dwelling, house, abode, residence, home
6. doctor, sawbones, physician, quack

The connotation of a word—its associated meanings, what it implies, its emotional overtones—exists inside people's minds. The more limited denotation exists outside the mind. For instance, you may point to a *mother*—that is outside yourself. Inside, the word mother is associated with the feelings, attitudes, and responses that you have associated with mother since childhood. In another example, *home* denotes that house where you live; however, *home* connotes privacy, intimacy, coziness, perhaps also love, warmth, and security. These connotative elements are what poets wish to emphasize as they attempt to involve their readers in the emotional images they create.

After reading the poem "There is no frigate like a book" complete the exercises that follow.

## THERE IS NO FRIGATE LIKE A BOOK

There is no frigate like a book
    To take us lands away,
Nor any coursers like a page
    Of prancing poetry:
This traverse may the poorest take
    Without oppress of toll;
How frugal is the chariot
    That bears the human soul!

—*Emily Dickinson (1830-1886)*

**EXERCISE #3:**

In two or three sentences, write a prose summary of the poem.

_____

_____

_____

_____

**EXERCISE #4:**

For each of the following words from the poem write a sentence or two explaining the word's *connotation*.

1. frigate

_____

_____

_____

2. coursers

_____

_____

_____

3. chariot

_____

_____

_____

EXERCISE #5:

In line 2, why does the poet use the word *lands* rather than *miles*?

_____

_____

_____

***Learning Activity #3:***

### *Allusion*

Whereas connotation imparts meaning that is beyond denotation, the dictionary definition of a word, so allusion stretches the minds of readers by forcing them to think. Also, like connotation, allusion adds meaning to the literature in which the technique is employed. *Allusion* is a reference to an event, a person, place, or thing in history or previous literature. Through the use of an allusive reference, readers can make connections that greatly enhance their understanding of what they read. Sometimes the allusion is crucial to the understanding of the selection.

### IN THE GARDEN

In the garden there strayed
A beautiful maid
As fair as the flowers of the morn;
The first hour of her life
She was made a man's wife,
And was buried before she was born.

*—Anonymous*

This brief anonymous poem seems, at first reading, to contain a paradox that makes it nonsense. How, after all, can a beautiful maid be married when she is but an hour old and die before she is born? (Have you resolved the paradox?) The allusion is, of course, to Genesis in the Bible where in the story of creation Eve is said to have been created (therefore, never *born*) and immediately married to Adam. The understanding of this poem presupposes a familiarity with the Bible, for without that understanding the seeming paradox can never be resolved.

EXERCISE #6:

Identify the following allusion.

### QUATRAIN

Jack, eating rotten cheese, did say
Like Samson I my thousands slay;
I vow, quoth Roger, so you do.
And with the self-same weapon too.

*—Benjamin Franklin (1706-1790)*

**8**

1. What is alluded to in this poem?

_____

_____

_____

2. Write a prose summary of this poem.

_____

_____

_____

_____

_____

_____

Allusions to previous literature are most frequently to mythology, the Bible (King James Version), and Shakespeare. These are by no means the only references for allusions. Since these are so commonly employed, however, readers must have at least a casual familiarity with them or much literary richness will pass unnoticed.

Some literary allusions are quite subtle and demand critical thinking and a broad background on the part of readers. Here again is Robert Frost's poem. See if you can find the allusion.

### "OUT, OUT—"

The buzz-saw snarled and rattled in the yard
And made dust and dropped stove-length sticks of wood,
Sweet-scented stuff when the breeze drew across it.
And from there those that lifted eyes could count
Five mountain ranges one behind the other                    5
Under the sunset far into Vermont.
And the saw snarled and rattled, snarled and rattled,
As it ran light, or had to bear a load.
And nothing happened: day was all but done.
Call it a day, I wish they might have said                   10
To please the boy by giving him the half hour
That a boy counts so much when saved from work.
His sister stood beside them in her apron
To tell them "Supper." At the word, the saw,
As if to prove saws knew what supper meant,                  15
Leaped out at the boy's hand, or seemed to leap—
He must have given the hand. However it was,
Neither refused the meeting. But the hand!

The boy's first outcry was a rueful laugh,
As he swung toward them holding up the hand                    20
Half in appeal, but half as if to keep
The life from spilling. Then the boy saw all—
Since he was old enough to know, big boy
Doing a man's work, though a child at heart—
He saw all spoiled. "Don't let him cut my hand off—           25
The doctor, when he comes. Don't let him, sister!"
So. But the hand was gone already.
The doctor put him in the dark of ether.
He lay and puffed his lips out with his breath.
And then—the watcher at his pulse took fright.               30
No one believed. They listened at his heart.
Little— less—nothing!—and that ended it.
No more to build on there. And they, since they
Were not the one dead, turned to their affairs.

                                        —*Robert Frost (1874-1963)*

If you spent time looking through the lines of this poem and ignored the title then you missed the allusion altogether. It is all too common to ignore titles and, in this case, it is all-important. You should have noticed, first, that the title is in quotation marks. As you know, quotation marks are used with poetry when writing out the titles in compositions but not when the title is at the head of the poem itself. Consequently, these quotation marks should have tipped you to the fact that the poet is quoting some other source. Since it is a quotation, it is not very likely that the poet would select an obscure source. Where in history or literature is the expression, "Out, out" used? If you were unable to think of any reference with these words then you might consult some secondary source like *Familiar Quotations*, by John Bartlett. In the index section, under "out," the phrase "*Out brief candle*" is listed. On that page, in the middle of a longer quotation is the allusion.

Tomorrow, and tomorrow, and tomorrow,
Creeps in this petty pace from day to day,
To the last syllable of recorded time;
And all our yesterdays have lighted fools
The way to dusty death. **Out, out** brief candle!

Life's but a walking shadow, a poor player
That struts and frets his hour upon the stage
And then is heard no more: it is a tale
Told by an idiot, full of sound and fury,
Signifying nothing.

                    MACBETH Act V, Scene 5, *William Shakespeare (1564-1616)*

The theme of this passage, spoken by Macbeth just after he learns of his wife's death, is the meaninglessness of life and its briefness. The philosophy of this passage coupled with the content of Frost's poem reveals a universal comment about the human condition. The poem's content is a specific incident but the allusion indicates that the poet has broader concerns than the death of one boy on a Vermont farm. Frost is writing about life and death everywhere.

Although Frost's reference is subtle, it illustrates the power of allusion to suggest so much with so few words. Also, it illustrates that the use of allusion presupposes a literate and knowledgeable reader.

EXERCISE #7:

Identify and explain the allusions in the following poems.

1.                          in Just—

        in Just-
        spring    when the world is mud-
        luscious the little
        lame balloonman

        whistles    far    and wee                                    5

        and eddieandbill come
        running from marbles and
        piracies and it's
        spring

        when the world is puddle-wonderful                           10

        the queer
        old balloonman whistles
        far    and    wee
        and bettyandisbel come dancing

        from hop-scotch and jump-rope and                            15

        it's spring
        and
            the

                goat-footed

        balloonMan    whistles                                       20
        far
        and
        wee
                        —e.e. cummings (1895-1962)

_____

_____

_____

_____

_____

_____

_____

2.               FIRE AND ICE

Some say the world will end in fire,
Some say ice.
From what I've tasted of desire
I hold with those who favor fire.
But if it had to perish twice,                                5
I think I know enough of hate
To say that for destruction ice
Is also great
And would suffice.

*—Robert Frost (1874-1963)*

_____

_____

_____

_____

_____

## Learning Activity #4:

### Imagery

When writers wish to share an experience with readers, when they want readers to understand fully what something is like, they appeal to the senses: sight, sound, smell, touch, and taste. The term used for this technique is *imagery*—which seems to suggest that the words form a mental picture. While it is true that it seems primarily a visual image, as used in literature, imagery means an appeal to any of the senses. One of the stronger aspects of Ernest Hemingway's stories is that he so effectively involves the senses. For example, in his short stories, readers can *see* the sun's rays streak through the treetops down into the river; *feel* the icy water and cold, crisp air; *hear* the rippling water and the frying fish; *smell* the early morning dampness and the aroma of cooking fish; and *taste* the breakfast fish. Through this kind of appeal, readers are able to identify with characters and feelings. In poetry, imagery allows readers to experience vicariously the sights, sounds, and feelings that the poet wishes to share.

EXERCISE #8:

Before each line of the following poem write which sense image is used to illustrate the experience.

### MEETING AT NIGHT

1. _____ The gray sea and the long black land;

2. _____ And the yellow half-moon large and low;

3. _____ And the startled little waves that leap

**12**

4. _____ In fiery ringlets from their sleep,

5. _____ As I gain the cove with pushing prow,

6. _____ And quench its speed i' the slushy sand.

7. _____ Then a mile of warm sea-scented beach;

8. _____ Three fields to cross till a farm appears;

9. _____ A tap at the pane, the quick sharp scratch

10. _____ And blue spurt of a lighted match,

11. _____ And a voice less loud, through its joys and fears,

12. _____ Than the two hearts beating each to each!

—*Robert Browning (1812-1889)*

## *Learning Activity #5:*

### *Figurative Language*

Figurative language includes a large number of categories and subcategories; some very important to writers and to readers. Failure to comprehend fundamental language use in poetry can prevent full understanding, thus blocking appreciation. The most common figurative language techniques are included in this learning activity. Other examples of figurative language may be included in your class or researched in the library.

A. Metaphor and Simile

Similes and metaphors are forms of comparison; they indicate some relationship between essentially different things. On a surface level a **simile** states the comparison ("My love is *like* a red, red rose") whereas a **metaphor** implies the comparison ("My love *is* a red, red rose"). In actual use, however, the difference is much more significant. Metaphors tend to be more extensive than similes, but each must make a serious attempt to reveal a relationship between two aspects of life (for example, roses and love). The foundation of much poetry is this metaphoric relationship, whether it is explicit or implied.

### THE EAGLE

*Metaphor:* He clasps the crag with *crooked hands;*
Close to the sun in lonely lands,
Ringed with the azure world, he stands.

The wrinkled sea beneath him crawls;
He watches from his mountain walls,
*Simile:* And *like a thunderbolt* he falls.

—*Alfred, Lord Tennyson (1809-1892)*

**13**

*Metaphor:*

## METAPHORS

I'm a riddle in nine syllables,
An elephant, a ponderous house,
A melon strolling on two tendrils.
O red fruit, ivory, fine timbers!
This loaf's big with its yeasty rising.     5
Money's newminted in this fat purse.
I'm a means, a stage, a cow in calf.
I've eaten a bag of green apples,
Boarded the train there's no getting off.     10
        *—Sylvia Plath (1932-1963)*

*Simile:*

## A VALEDICTION: FORBIDDING MOURNING

As virtuous men pass mildly away,
  And whisper to their souls to go,
While some of their sad friends do say,
  The breath goes now, and some say, "No,"

So let us melt, and make no noise,     5
  No tear-floods, nor sigh-tempests move,
'Twere profanation of our joys
  To tell the laity our love,

Moving of th' earth brings harms and fears,
  Men reckon what it did and meant,     10
But trepidation of the spheres,
  Though greater far, is innocent.

Dull sublunary lovers' love
  (Whose soul is sense) cannot admit
Absence, because it doth remove     15
  Those things which elemented it.

But we by a love so much refined,
  That ourselves know not what it is,
Inter-assurèd of the mind,
  Care less, eyes, lips, and hands to miss.     20

Our two souls therefore, which are one,
  Though I must go, endure not yet
A breach, but an expansion,
  Like gold to airy thinness beat.

If they be two, they are two so     25
  As stiff-twin compasses are two,
Thy soul the fixed foot, makes no show
  To move, but doth, if th' other do.

And though it in the center sit,
  Yet when the other far doth roam,     30
It leans, and hearkens after it,
  And grows erect, as that comes home.

Such wilt thou be to me, who must
  Like other foot, obliquely run;
Thy firmness makes my circle just,     35
  And makes me end, where I begun.
        *—John Donne (1572-1631)*

The simile in "The Eagle" compares, from a bird's eye view, the dive of an eagle with the speed of a thunderbolt. This hyperbole (intentional exaggeration for effect) allows the reader to identify with the bird, to feel its dive toward earth and to experience the rush of the dive as compared to a thunderbolt. The power of the simile rests with this ability to compare experiences explicitly.

The more powerful literary technique, metaphor, employs more subtlety and requires more thoughtful contemplation. The figures of speech in "Metaphors" make several comparisons, some of which may be humorous. The poet has compared a pregnant woman with a riddle, an elephant, a house, a melon, a fruit, a loaf, a purse, a means, a stage, and a cow; yet in her humorous metaphors the poet recognizes a resigned finality in the condition of pregnancy: having boarded the train, she writes, "there's no getting off." Through this series of metaphors, we can recognize the poet's observation about the experience of pregnancy; we can both see the physical awkwardness and share the feeling of resignation. In this example the author achieves an intensified statement by representing each of the poem's images by a metaphor.

On a more complicated level, the similes of "*A Valediction: Forbidding Mourning*" begin with a comparison of the impending separation of a pair of lovers with the death of a virtuous man. Since a virtuous man has nothing to fear after death, he anticipates no afterlife punishments; his passing is peaceful. Likewise, the lovers should as easily and peacefully part thereby not cheapening their love nor fearing the separation.

In his next simile, the poet compares the lovers' separation with the movements of the planets. If movement is detected in the lowest sphere, as with earthquakes, then people are worried and fretful, but if the movement is in the highest spheres, as with the movement of other planets, it goes unnoticed. Since their love is in the highest spheres, the parting should not cause trepidation. The poet also compares the lovers' separation to a stretching of gold as it is beaten into foil, and last, to the movement of a compass; while one leg remains at home the other leg moves away yet around. Even so, the two legs remain attached at the top; their love binds them forever together.

A metaphoric comparison of two things often strives toward a closer definition of some human emotion. The poet accomplishes this by transferring the meaning of a known thing or experience, called a *referent*, to something else. For example:

> **l(a**
>
> l(a
>
> le
> af
> fa
>
> ll
>
> s)
> one
>  l
>
> iness     —*e.e. cummings (1894-1962)*

In Cummings' poem, "a leaf falls" is the referent with which everyone is familiar, while the emotion of loneliness is compared to the falling leaf. The poet expresses loneliness as a falling leaf, as well as conveying both the emotion and the image in the poem's shape. This poem is a very compressed metaphor and is highly effective.

EXERCISE #9:

List each metaphoric comparison contained in the following poem.

### TO SEE A WORLD IN A GRAIN OF SAND

To see a world in a grain of sand
And a heaven in a wild flower,
Hold infinity in the palm of your hand
And eternity in an hour.

—*William Blake (1757-1827)*

_____

_____

_____

_____

_____

EXERCISE #10:

List five examples of metaphoric use of language from your reading, viewing, or conversations outside of class.

1. _____

_____

_____

_____

2. _____

_____

_____

_____

3. _____

   _____

   _____

   _____

4. _____

   _____

   _____

   _____

   _____

5. _____

   _____

   _____

   _____

   _____

**EXERCISE #11:**

Is the following poem an example of the use of metaphor or simile? Circle one.

Metaphor          Simile

### UPON MISTRESS SUSANNA SOUTHWELL, HER FEET
Her pretty feet
Like snails did creep
A little out, and then,
As if they played at bo-peep,
Did soon draw in again.

—*Robert Herrick (1591-1674)*

B.   Symbolism

Images, metaphors, and symbols often overlap and are occasionally difficult to distinguish. Generally, however, an image means nothing more than what it is. (*The small brown bear rubbed its backsides against the rough bark of a large sugar pine tree.*) A metaphor means something other than what it states. (*The alert Oregon bear rushed from behind a camouflage stand of pine and wrote me a speeding ticket.*) A **symbol** means both what it is and other things as well. In fact, symbols often have multiple meanings. (*You can lead a horse to water, but you can't make it drink.*) In this example we can see the image of a horse, and we can also visualize a stubborn person. An image does not stop being an image simply because it is used in a metaphor or a symbol. This may be seen in some of the many objects that we regard as

**17**

symbols. The flag is a symbol, so is a backyard swimming pool. VW buses, Cadillacs, and Harley Davidson motorcycles are all symbols, too. All symbols are subject to interpretations.

In literary use, symbols depend upon their context for meaning. Some symbols are generally accepted as universal and give few problems in their interpretation: water=life; sleep=death; winter=old age=death; dove=peace; sunrise=birth; sunset=death.

Occasionally, a poet employs personal symbols, and these depend entirely upon their use in context for interpretation. As with most analysis, this contextual use and emphasis directs the reader from an imagematic or metaphoric interpretation to the symbolic intent of the poet.

Consider the following poem:

### THE ROAD NOT TAKEN

Two roads diverged in a yellow wood,
And sorry I could not travel both
And be one traveler, long I stood
And looked down one as far as I could
To where it bent in the undergrowth;          5

Then took the other, as just as fair,
And having perhaps the better claim,
Because it was grassy and wanted wear;
Though as for that the passing there
Had worn them really about the same,          10

And both that morning equally lay
In leaves no step had trodden black.
Oh, I kept the first for another day!
Yet knowing how way leads on to way,
I doubted if I should ever come back.          15

I shall be telling this with a sigh
Somewhere ages and ages hence:
Two roads diverged in a wood, and I—
I took the one less traveled by,
And that has made all the difference.          20

—*Robert Frost (1874-1963)*

In the first three stanzas Frost's poem describes a place in the woods where two roads forked and the narrator ponders which one to take. The imagery is vivid; consequently, the mental picture of the roads and their appearance is quite clear. Also the narrator's dilemma is clear: the narrator wishes to experience both roads but realizes that for now a choice must be made. The visual imagery includes the following from the first three stanzas:

> the yellow wood
> the undergrowth
> grassy
> leaves

**18**

Frost begins to develop the symbolic nature of the poem at the end of the third stanza. Here the narrator suggests that, while he wishes to save the road not taken for another day, he realizes that *"way leads on to way,"* that is, each road leads to other divisions and these lead to yet others, on and on. This is true of roads and also true of other experiences. This is the point at which alert readers begin to realize that the poet has something more in mind than a word painting. This preliminary judgment is confirmed in stanza four where the narrator reveals that the result of the choice *"has made all the difference."* You might well ask *"made all the difference"* in what? The answer will not become clear, however, until you realize that the roads diverging in the woods is a symbol. Everything the poem states about roads in the woods is true but the observations are also true about any of the great decisions in life. We can all look back upon decisions that we have made and feel that the decisions, the road we chose, *has made all the difference*. You should see clearly that Frost's poem is symbolically both about roads diverging in the woods and about decisions. From neither can we return to explore what it would have been like to travel the other way.

The use of symbols is not unique to poetry, of course. Much of the world's great literature is filled with symbolism. Perhaps that is, in part, what makes it great. Certainly, it is the symbolic nature of the work that makes such novels as Herman Melville's *Moby Dick* live for generations. In any case, the multiple meanings that symbols possess is partly what makes good literature rewarding to experience again and again. It is possible to find new meanings and different interpretations each rereading, even with old and loved literary favorites.

EXERCISE #12:

Read the following poems and complete the exercises.

### A WHITE ROSE

The red rose whispers of passion
  And the white rose breathes of love;
Oh, the red rose is a falcon,
  And the white rose is a dove.

But I send you a cream-white rosebud,
  With a flush on its petal tips;
For the love that is purest and sweetest
  Has a kiss of desire on the lips.

*—John Boyle O'Reilly (1844-1890)*

For the above poem, write what is symbolized by each of the following:

the white rose _____

the red rose _____

the rosebud _____

## THE TIGER

Tiger! Tiger! burning bright
In the forests of the night,
What immortal hand or eye
Could frame thy fearful symmetry?

In what distant deeps or skies          5
Burnt the fire of thine eyes?
On what wings dare he aspire?
What the hand dare seize the fire?

And what shoulder, and what art
Could twist the sinews of thy heart?        10
And when thy heart began to beat,
What dread hand? and what dread feet?

What the hammer? what the chain?
In what furnace was thy brain?
What the anvil? what dread grasp          15
Dare its deadly terrors clasp?

When the stars threw down their spears,
And water'd heaven with their tears,
Did he smile his work to see?
Did he who made the Lamb make thee?        20

Tiger! Tiger! burning bright
In the forests of the night,
What immortal hand or eye,
Dare frame thy fearful symmetry?

—*William Blake (1757-1827)*

For the above poem what are a few of the things that might be symbolized by each of the following?

the Tiger _____

the Lamb _____


## THE NOISELESS PATIENT SPIDER

A noiseless patient spider,
I mark'd where on a little promontory it stood isolated,
Mark'd how to explore the vacant vast surrounding,
It launch'd forth filament, filament, filament, out of itself,
Ever unreeling them, ever tirelessly speeding them.

And you O my soul where you stand,
Surrounded, detached, in measureless oceans of space,
Ceaselessly musing, venturing, throwing, seeking the spheres to connect them,
Till the bridge you will need be form'd, till the ductile anchor hold,
Till the gossamer thread you fling catch somewhere, O my soul.

—*Walt Whitman (1819-1892)*

In two or three sentences identify the symbol in the above poem and explain its meaning.

**20**

_____

_____

_____

_____

_____

_____

_____

_____

_____

## C. Irony

Often the freshness of literature comes from a unique observation of an experience or idea. The freshness may be achieved overtly but the most successful employ a subtlety of expression that forces readers to think. One of the most subtle kinds of expression is **irony**, a technique that may be humorous or sarcastic in which the intended meaning of the words or the situation is the opposite of their expected meaning. We use **verbal irony** frequently when we wish to emphasize a point humorously or sarcastically. (Trying to look out into a valley filled with smog she says, "What a lovely view.") From the context the real meaning is clear, though the meaning is the opposite of what is said. A famous example of verbal irony, laced with sarcasm, occurs in Shakespeare's play, *Julius Ceasar*, when Mark Antony, orating over the body of the murdered Julius Ceasar, says of one of the chief assassins, "Brutus is an honorable man." The crowd (and the audience) soon see that Antony means just the opposite.

*Verbal Irony:*

### OF ALPHUS

No egg on Friday Alph will eat,
  But drunken he will be
On Friday still. Oh, what a pure
  Religious man is he!

*Sixteenth Century—Anonymous*

A kind of irony with which you may be less familiar but which is often used in literature is **situational irony**. In situational irony a discrepancy exists between what is expected and what actually happens.

**21**

## OZYMANDIAS

I met a traveller from an antique land
Who said: Two vast and trunkless legs of stone
Stand in the desert . . . Near them, on the sand,
Half sunk, a shattered visage lies, whose frown,
And wrinkled lip, and sneer of cold command,      5
Tell that its sculptor well those passions read
Which yet survive, stamped on these lifeless things,
The hand that mocked them, and the heart that fed:
And on the pedestal these words appear:
"My name is Ozymandias, king of kings:      10
Look on my works, ye Mighty, and despair!"
Nothing beside remains. Round the decay
Of that colossal wreck, boundless and bare
The lone and level sands stretch far away.

*—Percy Bysshe Shelley (1782-1822)*

The situational irony lies in the discrepancy between what Ozymandias expects (that we will despair) and what actually occurs (that nothing is left).

Another kind of irony, **dramatic irony**, is usually found in drama, where the audience knows something a character does not. A classic example of dramatic irony occurs in Sophocle's play *Oedipus* when Oedipus curses whoever it is that caused the plague in the city of Thebes; however, the audience knows, as Oedipus does not, that he has cursed himself.

Dramatic irony may be also used in poems and stories.

*Dramatic Irony:*

## THE WORKBOX

"See, here's the workbox, little wife,
    That I made of polished oak."
He was a joiner*, of village life;      *carpenter
    She came of borough folk.

He holds the present up to her      5
    As with a smile she nears
And answers to the profferer,
    "Twill last all my sewing years!"

"I warrant it will. And longer too.
    'Tis a scantling that I got      10
Off poor John Wayward's coffin, who
    Died of they knew not what.

"The shingled pattern that seems to cease
    Against your box's rim
Continues right on in the piece      15
    That's underground with him.

"And while I worked it made me think
    Of timber's varied doom:
One inch where people eat and drink,
    The next inch in a tomb.                        20

"But why do you look so white, my dear,
    And turn aside your face?
You knew not that good lad, I fear,
    Though he came from your native place?"

"How could I know that good young man,            25
    Though he came from my native town,
When he must have left far earlier than
    I was a woman grown?"

"Ah, no. I should have understood!
    It shocked you that I gave                      30
To you one end of a piece of wood
    Whose other is in a grave?"

"Don't, dear, despise my intellect,
    Mere accidental things
Of that sort never have effect                     35
    On my imaginings."

Yet still her lips were limp and wan,
    Her face still held aside,
As if she had known not only John,
    But known of what he died.                      40

                    —*Thomas Hardy* (*1840-1928*)

The dramatic irony in "The Workbox" occurs with the growing knowledge that the wife in the poem obviously knew John Wayward much better
than she admits to her husband, who has only limited knowledge. (Note also
the verbal ironies in lines 25 to 28 and in line 34.)


EXERCISE #13:

Identify and describe the irony in each of the following poems. (Note there may
be more than one in each.)


                    EPIGRAM

As Thomas was cudgeled one day by his wife,
He took to the street, and fled for his life.
Tom's three dearest friends came by in the squabble,
And saved him at once from the shrew and the rabble,
Then ventured to give him some sober advice.        5
But Tom is a person of honor so nice,
Too wise to take counsel, too proud to take warning,
That he sent to all three a challenge next morning.
Three duels he fought, thrice ventured his life,
Went home, and was cudgeled again by his wife.       10

                    —*Jonathan Swift* (*1667-1745*)

_____

_____

_____

_____

_____

_____

_____

## FORMAL APPLICATION

*The poets apparently want to rejoin the human race.* TIME

I shall begin by learning to throw
the knife, first at trees, until it sticks
in the trunk and quivers every time;

next from a chair, using only wrist
and fingers, at a thing on the ground,      5
a fresh ant hill or a fallen leaf,

then at a moving object, perhaps
a pieplate swinging on twine, until
I pot it at least twice in three tries.

Meanwhile, I shall be teaching the birds      10
that the skinny fellow in sneakers
is a source of suet and bread crumbs,

first putting them on a shingle nailed
to a pine tree, next scattering them
on the needles, closer and closer      15

to my seat, until the proper bird,
a towhee, I think, in black and rust
and gray, takes tossed crumbs six feet away.

Finally, I shall coordinate
conditioned reflex and functional      20
form and qualify as Modern Man.

You see the splash of blood and feathers
and the blade pinning it to the tree?
It's called an "Audubon Crucifix."

The phrase has pleasing (even pious)      25
connotations, like *Arbeit Macht Frei*,[1]
"Molotov Cocktail,"[2] and *Enola Gay*.[3]

             —*Donald W. Baker (b. 1923)*

_____

[1]Labor liberates—Nazi party slogan.
[2]Homemade firebomb.
[3]The name of the airplane that dropped the atomic bomb.

_____

_____

_____

_____

_____

_____

_____

_____

_____

## MY LAST DUCHESS

### *Ferrara*

That's my last Duchess painted on the wall,
Looking as if she were alive. I call
That piece a wonder, now; Fra Pandolf's hands
Worked busily a day, and there she stands.
Will 't please you sit and look at her? I said        5
"Fra Pandolf" by design, for never read
Strangers like you that pictured countenance,
The depth of passion of its earnest glance,
But to myself they turned (since none puts by
The curtain I have drawn for you, but I)             10
And seemed as they would ask me, if they durst,
How such a glance came there, so, not the first
Are you to turn and ask thus. Sir, 'twas not
Her husband's presence only, called that spot
Of joy into the Duchess' cheek; perhaps             15
Fra Pandolf chanced to say, "Her mantle laps
Over my lady's wrist too much," or, "Paint
Must never hope to reproduce the faint
Half-flush that dies along her throat." Such stuff
Was courtesy, she thought, and cause enough         20
For calling up that spot of joy. She had
A heart—how shall I say? too soon made glad,
Too easily impressed; she liked whate'er
She looked on, and her looks went everywhere.
Sir, 'twas all one! My favor at her breast,         25
The dropping of the daylight in the West,
The bough of cherries some officious fool
Broke in the orchard for her, the white mule

She rode with round the terrace—all and each
Would draw from her alike the approving speech, 30
Or blush, at least. She thanked men—good! but thanked
Somehow—I know not how—as if she ranked
My gift of a nine-hundred-years-old name
With anybody's gift. Who'd stoop to blame
This sort of trifling? Even had you skill 35
In speech—which I have not—to make your will
Quite clear to such a one, and say, "just this
Or that in you disgusts me; here you miss,
Or there exceed the mark"—and if she let
Herself be lessoned so, nor plainly set 40
Her wits to yours, forsooth, and made excuse—
E'en then would be some stooping; and I choose
Never to stoop. Oh, sir, she smiled, no doubt,
Whene'er I passed her; but who passed without
Much the same smile? This grew; I gave commands; 45
Then all smiles stopped together. There she stands
As if alive. Will 't please you rise? We'll meet
The company below, then. I repeat,
The Count your master's known munificence
Is ample warrant that no just pretense 50
Of mine for dowry will be disallowed;
Though his fair daughter's self, as I avowed
At starting, is my object. Nay, we'll go
Together down, sir. Notice Neptune, though,
Taming a sea-horse, thought a rarity, 55
Which Claus of Innsbruck cast in bronze for me!

—*Robert Browning* (*1812-1889*)

*It is easier to write a mediocre poem than to understand a good one.* —Montaigne

# Other Literary Techniques

1. **Allegory**—a metaphoric device in which abstract ideas or concepts are represented as people, objects, or situations.

### MATTHEW 13: 24-30

24  Another parable put he forth unto them, saying, The kingdom of heaven is likened unto a man which sowed good seed in his field:

25  But while men slept, his enemy came and sowed tares* among the wheat, and went his way.

26  But when the blade was sprung up, and brought forth fruit, then appeared the tares also.

27  So the servants of the householder came and said unto him, Sir, didst not thou sow good seed in thy field? from whence then hath it tares?

28  He said unto them, An enemy hath done this. The servants said unto him, Wilt thou then that we go and gather them up?

29  But he said, Nay; lest while ye gather up the tares, ye root up also the wheat with them.

30  Let both grow together until the harvest: and in the time of harvest I will say to the reapers, Gather ye together first the tares, and bind them in bundles to burn them: but gather the wheat into my barn.

*Bible—King James Version*

---

*weeds

2. **Apostrophe**—addressing an object as though it were living—or speaking to a person as though the person is present.

### THE TIGER

Tiger! Tiger! burning bright
In the forests of the night,
What immortal hand or eye
Could frame thy fearful symmetry?

In what distant deeps or skies          5
Burnt the fire of thine eyes?
On what wings dare he aspire?
What the hand dare seize the fire?

And what shoulder, and what art
Could twist the sinews of thy heart?     10
And when thy heart began to beat,
What dread hand forged thy dread feet?

What the hammer: what the chain?
In what furnace was thy brain?
What the anvil? what dread grasp         15
Dare its deadly terrors clasp?

When the stars threw down their spears,
And water'd heaven with their tears,
Did he smile his work to see?
Did he who made the Lamb make thee?      20

Tiger! Tiger! burning bright
In the forests of the night
What immortal hand or eye,
Dare frame thy fearful symmetry?

—*William Blake (1757-1827)*

3. **Personification**—a form of metaphor which gives the characteristics of humans to animals, objects, or ideas.

### THE EAGLE

*He clasps the crag with crooked hands*;
Close to the sun in lonely lands,
Ringed with the azure world, he stands.

The wrinkled sea beneath him crawls;
He watches from his mountain walls,
And like a thunderbolt he falls.

—*Alfred, Lord Tennyson (1809-1892)*

28

4. **Metonymy**—a word used in place of another that is closely associated with it.

### SPRING

When daisies pied* and violets blue,
  And lady-smocks all silver-white,
And cuckoo-buds of yellow hue
  Do *paint* the meadows with delight,
The cuckoo then, on every tree,     5
Mocks married men; for thus sings he,
          "Cuckoo!
Cuckoo, cuckoo!" O word of fear,
Unpleasing to a married ear!

When shepherds pipe on oaten straws,    10
  And merry larks are ploughmen's *clocks*,
When turtles tread, and rooks, and daws,
  And maidens bleach their summer smocks,
The cuckoo then, on every tree,
Mocks married men; for thus sings he,    15
          "Cuckoo!
Cuckoo, cuckoo!" O word of fear,
Unpleasing to a married ear!

      —*William Shakespeare (1564-1616)*

---

*patches of two or more colors.

5. **Paradox**—a contradiction that is nevertheless true.

### MY LIFE CLOSED TWICE

*My life closed twice before its close;*
  It yet remains to see
If Immortality unveil
  A third event to me,

So huge, so hopeless to conceive,
  As these that twice befell.
Parting is all we know of heaven,
  And all we need of hell.

      —*Emily Dickinson (1830-1886)*

6. **Hyperbole**—the use of overstatement for effect.

### THE EAGLE

He clasps the crag with crooked hands;
*Close to the sun* in lonely lands,
Ringed with the azure world, he stands.

The wrinkled sea beneath him crawls;
He watches from his mountain walls,
And like a thunderbolt he falls.

      —*Alfred, Lord Tennyson (1809-1892)*

**29**

7. **Synecdoche**—a signficant part represents the whole.

### SPRING

When daisies pied and violets blue,
  And lady-smocks all silver-white,
And cuckoo-buds of yellow hue
  Do paint the meadows with delight,
The cuckoo then, on every tree,           5
Mocks married men; for thus sings he
                   "Cuckoo!
Cuckoo, cuckoo!" O word of fear,
Unpleasing to a *married ear!*

When shepherds pipe on oaten straws,     10
  And merry larks are ploughmen's clocks,
When turtles tread, and rooks, and daws,
  And maidens bleach their summer smocks,
The cuckoo then, on every tree,
Mocks married men; for thus sings he,     15
                   "Cuckoo!
Cuckoo, cuckoo!" O word of fear,
Unpleasing to a *married ear!*

           *—William Shakespeare (1564-1616)*

8. **Understatement**—(the opposite of hyperbole) stating less than what is meant.

### MY MISTRESS' EYES ARE NOTHING LIKE THE SUN

My mistress' eyes are nothing like the sun;
Coral is far more red than her lips' red:
If snow be white, why then her breasts are dun:
If hairs be wires, black wires grow on her head.
I have seen roses damasked,* red and white,     5
But no such roses see I in her cheeks;
And in some perfumes is there more delight
Than in the breath that from my mistress reeks.
I love to hear her speak, yet well I know
That music hath a far more pleasing sound:     10
I grant I never saw a goddess go,—
My mistress, when she walks, treads on the ground.
    And yet, by heaven, I think my love as rare
    As any she belied with false compare.

           *—William Shakespeare (1564-1616)*

---

*of different colors

9. **Tone**—the writers' or narrators' attitudes toward their subject, their audience, or themselves.

## LOVE

There's the wonderful love of a beautiful maid,
  And the love of a staunch true man,
And the love of a baby that's unafraid—
  All have existed since time began.

But the most wonderful love, the Love of all loves,
  Even greater than the love for Mother,
Is the infinite, tenderest, passionate love
  Of one dead drunk for another.

*—Anonymous*

10. **Alliteration**—the repetition of sounds in the beginning of words (usually consonants) that are similar.

He clasps the crag with crooked hands;
Close to the sun in lonely lands,
Ringed with the azure world, he stands.

The wrinkled sea beneath him crawls;
He watches from his mountain walls,
And like a thunderbolt he falls.

11. **Onomatopoeia**—the deliberate use of words whose pronunciation closely resembles the sound of the event or thing named.

Examples: buzz, cackle, whirr, sizzle, hiss, murmur

12. **Other Types of Irony**—
    A. Socratic Irony:

    Pretense of ignorance in a discussion to expose an opponent's fallacious logic.
    B. Romantic Irony:

    Writers creating a serious mood only to make light of themselves.
    C. Irony of Fate:

    The difference between what a human's hopes and expectations are and what is decreed by the gods.

# Traditional Analysis

Frequently the understanding of a work of art may be enhanced by venturing outside the work itself to see what others have to say about it, to see what insights may be gained by examining the history of the times, or to see what the author's biographical information may offer. These kinds of concerns are traditional ways of looking at all art. Readers, in particular, often want assistance in analyzing books, poems, and plays and turn to critics, those who have made a specialty of literary study, for insights. Moreover, the historical milieu out of which something is written often aids in seeing it in a new perspective. The historical point of view is especially helpful when the author's own background can be seen as a contributing factor in the creation of the literature. The insights available by examining an author's life have long been recognized as important. Traditional analysis is, then, a series of analytical methods employed by students, teachers, and scholars which looks outside the work to help understanding it.

## Objectives:

After completing this unit, you will be able to:

1. Identify the main elements of traditional analysis.
2. Define linguistic connotation.
3. Distinguish between biographical and historical analysis.
4. Analyze a short work for its genre characteristics.
5. Assess the contribution of an author's biographical data to his writing.
6. Appraise the value of history to the theme or setting of a work.
7. Evaluate a work's ethical considerations.

_____ 1. As used with literature, didacticism means (A) to dictate (B) to teach (C) to analyze (D) to enjoy (E) to fool.

_____ 2. Great literature achieves its greatness (A) through subtlety of expression (B) by teaching a moral lesson (C) by its creation by a famous author (D) through uplifting characters (E) by being very popular.

_____ 3. The three main categories of literature are (A) short stories, novels, and fiction (B) short stories, plays, and prose (C) poetry, novels, and movies (D) fiction, poetry, and novels (E) prose, poetry, and drama.

_____ 4. Genre means (A) film types (B) ethical consideration (C) play casts (D) literary categories (E) poetic meter.

_____ 5. Linguistic connotation is concerned primarily with (A) today's meanings of the words in a story (B) the meanings of the words in a selection at the time they were written (C) the denotation of the words in a story (D) how emotional the words are in a selection (E) why certain words were chosen for a story.

_____ 6. In older works textual authenticity is often important because (A) we are not always certain we have all the words as the author wrote them (B) we want to test a work's impact upon the readers of its day (C) no one can tell what an author intended (D) the words are usually faded (E) we need to verify that the printers used the right manuscript.

MATCHING:

_____ 7. Connotation

_____ 8. Ethics

_____ 9. Linguistics

_____ 10. Universality

(A) the dictionary definition of a word

(B) the implied meaning of a word beyond its dictionary definition

(C) a system to investigate the validity and reasoning of arguments

(D) the study of speech and writing

(E) that which appeals to all people during all times in all places

(F) a set of values or principles by which human actions are judged

## TRADITIONAL ANALYSIS

Traditional analysis is the critical approach of most library research papers. Prior to the 1930s, traditional analysis was the *only* approach and led, some have charged, to an overemphasis upon the background of an author's life or the historical context in which a work was created. Later critics, reacting to what they viewed as the excesses of traditional analysis, refused to consider anything outside the literature itself as relevant. By maintaining perspective, however, traditional analysis can contribute considerably to your understanding of much literature.

## Ethical Considerations

Of all the ways literature may be viewed, ethical considerations are perhaps the oldest. From classical times (ancient Greece and Rome) critics viewed literature's primary purpose as teaching ethics or morality. These ethics may or may not be religious in precept, but they must instruct. Consequently, all good literature, early critics felt, must teach some ethical lesson. The word that is used to characterize those works that teach is **didacticism**. It is taken from the Greek work, *didaskein*, meaning 'to teach.'

As used in contemporary literature, however, didacticism frequently has a negative connotation. The term is used to describe those literary selections which attempt to teach in such an overbearing way that the enjoyment and art are diminished or lost altogether. For example, read the following didactic verse and poem:

*Didactic verse —*

"Early to bed and early to rise
    makes a man healthy, wealthy, and wise."

*Didactic poem —*

### A PSALM OF LIFE
#### What The Heart Of The Young Man Said To The Psalmist

Tell me not, in mournful numbers,
    Life is but an empty dream!—
For the soul is dead that slumbers,
    And things are not what they seem.

Life is real! Life is earnest!                    5
    And the grace is not its goal;
Dust thou art, to dust returnest,
    Was not spoken of the soul.

Not enjoyment, and not sorrow,
    Is our destined end or way;                10
But to act, that each tomorrow
    Find us farther than today.

Art is long, and Time is fleeting,
    And our hearts, though stout and brave,
Still, like muffled drums, are beating         15
    Funeral marches to the grave.

In the world's broad field of battle,
    In the bivouac of Life,
Be not like dumb, driven cattle!
    Be a hero in the strife!                        20

Trust no Future, howe'er pleasant!
    Let the dead Past bury its dead!
Act,—act in the living Present!
    Heart within, and God O'erhead!

—*Henry Wadsworth Longfellow* (*1807-1882*)

While "Psalm of Life" was greatly enjoyed in its day—1838—modern readers usually feel that Longfellow's purpose, to teach or preach, was obviously more important to him than the art of his poem. While it is true that great literature often teaches, it achieves its greatness through subtlety of expression and format; the arrangement is fresh and the author does not overstate the point.

For example, the following poem might also be said to teach, or at least contain, a strong theme:

OZYMANDIAS

I met a traveller from an antique land,
Who said: "Two vast and trunkless legs of stone
Stand in the desert . . . Near them, on the sand,
Half sunk a shattered visage lies, whose frown,
And wrinkled lip, and sneer of cold command,                                5
Tell that its sculptor well those passions read
Which yet survive, stamped on these lifeless things,
The hand that mocked them, and the heart that fed:
And on the pedestal, these words appear:
My name is Ozymandias, King of Kings:                                        10
Look on my Works, ye Mighty, and despair!
Nothing beside remains. Round the decay
Of the colossal Wreck, boundless and bare
The lone and level sands stretch far away."

—*Percy Bysshe Shelley* (*1792-1822*)

EXERCISE #1:

In one or two sentences describe the point of the above poem.

_____

_____

_____

_____

_____

If you noticed a considerable difference between "Psalm of Life" (1938) and "Ozymandias" (1817), you have probably begun to see what didacticism is and how it detracts from an appreciation of literary art. The poet Shelley is obviously much more concerned with his poem's artistic impact on the reader in "Ozymandias" than is Longfellow in "Psalm of Life." Yet, Shelley's poem can be said to have an ethical lesson—a moral. But the poem's moral is discovered by the reader. Longfellow, on the other hand, states his ethical conclusions directly. Essentially, that is the difference between didactic writers and those who are not.

During the twentieth century, some writers have written novels so didactic that, while the story may be otherwise interesting, the propagandistic characterizations and plots detract from the other merits the works may possess. Some critics, for example, feel Frank Norris' *The Octopus*, an anti-railroad story, and John Steinbeck's *Grapes of Wrath*, the plight of depression era migrant farmers, to be didactic.

EXERCISE #2:

Define didacticism in the space below and explain why modern writers avoid it.

_____

_____

_____

_____

_____

EXERCISE #3:

Compare the following two poems.

## THE EAGLE

He clasps the crag with crooked hands;
Close to the sun in lonely lands,
Ringed with the azure world, he stands.

The wrinkled sea beneath him crawls;
He watches from his mountain walls,
And like a thunderbolt he falls.

—*Alfred, Lord Tennyson* (*1809-1892*)

## THE OAK

Live thy Life
  Young and old,
Like yon oak,
Bright in spring,
  Living gold;                                    5

Summer-rich
  Then; and then
Autumn-changed,
Soberer-hued
  Gold again.                                     10

All his leaves
  Fall'n at length,
Look, he stands,
Trunk and bough,
  Naked strength.                                 15

—*Alfred, Lord Tennyson* (*1809-1892*)

1. Which of the above poems might be considered didactic? _____

**37**

2. Explain the reasons for your choice.

_____

_____

_____

_____

_____

_____

   Didacticism aside, ethical consideration offers readers a vast mirror in which they may view the soul of humanity. Through literature we can all see the questions with which human kind has struggled for centuries. Basic ethical-philosophical questions have remained virtually unchanged since the dawn of recorded history, and literature is but one avenue of discovery. If you read the dramas of ancient Greece, you will discover that ethical musings were the same then as they are today: Is there a god? If there is does he/she have control over the lives of humans? What happens after death? Why are we here? How did life begin? These are all universal questions. It is fascinating to note that while the universality of these questions remains virtually the same, the answers differ among different peoples and different times.

   The ethical debate is the concern of not just literature but all the humanities. Painting, sculpture, music, dance, and photography, as well as literature, offer answers to universal questions. It was through the postulating of ethical answers to the universal questions of the humanities, in particular literature, that classical Greeks and Romans came to feel that good literature must teach. The ancient Greek Philosopher Plato (427-345 B.C.) emphasized literature's moralism and utilitarianism, and the Roman critic Horace (65-8 B.C.) stressed *dulce et utile*—delight and instruction.

   Consider again Shelley's classic poem "Ozymandias." Traditional critics who emphasize ethical consideration along the lines espoused by Plato and Horace are likely to point out the statement of excessive pride Ozymandias had inscribed upon his memorial. The delight is in the poetic irony—the fact that the old king asks us to look at all his accomplishments and to despair because we are so puny by comparison, yet nothing of his works remains. His accomplishments are in actuality puny in comparison with the forces of wind and sand. The lesson, of course, concerns human pride and one's influence in so short a span of time on earth as a lifetime—or even the time-span of a civilization.

   Ethical considerations are, then, a major emphasis of traditional analysis. Traditional critics do not, however, totally neglect other aspects of literature, such as form, use of language, and artistic merit; rather, these are but secondary concerns—subordinate to the moral and philosophical lessons of ethical consideration.

**38**

EXERCISE #4:

After each of the following selections write two or three sentences in which you list its major ethical consideration.

### RICHARD CORY

Whenever Richard Cory went down town,
We people on the pavement looked at him:
He was a gentleman from sole to crown,
Clean favored, and imperially slim.

And he was always quietly arrayed,                                    5
And he was always human when he talked;
But still he fluttered pulses when he said,
"Good-morning," and he glittered when he walked.

And he was rich—yes, richer than a king—
And admirably schooled in every grace:                               10
In fine, we thought that he was everything
To make us wish that we were in his place.

So on we worked, and waited for the light,
And went without the meat, and cursed the bread;
And Richard Cory, one calm summer night,                             15
Went home and put a bullet through his head.

—*Edwin Arlington Robinson* (*1869-1935*)

_____

_____

_____

_____

### THE SICK ROSE

O Rose, thou art sick.
The invisible worm
That flies in the night
In the howling storm

Has found out thy bed
Of crimson joy,
And his dark secret love
Does thy life destroy.

—*William Blake* (*1757-1827*)

_____

_____

_____
_____
_____
_____
_____

## THE WORLD IS TOO MUCH WITH US

The world is too much with us; late and soon,
Getting and spending, we lay waste our powers:
Little we see in Nature that is ours;
We have given our hearts away, a sordid boon!
This sea that bares her bosom to the moon;                    5
The winds that will be howling at all hours,
And are up-gathered now like sleeping flowers;
For this, for everything, we are out of tune;
It moves us not.—Great God! I'd rather be
A Pagan suckled in a creed outworn;                          10
So might I, standing on this pleasant lea,
Have glimpses that would make me less forlorn;
Have sight of Proteus rising from the sea;
Or hear old Triton blow his wreathèd horn.

*—William Wordsworth (1770-1850)*

_____
_____
_____
_____
_____
_____
_____

*Learning Activity #2:*

## Genre Characteristics

Since each literary type, or genre, has particular standards by which it is judged, a traditional student of literature needs to determine carefully into which category a work might best be placed. Overall, literature has three genre categories: *prose, poetry,* and *drama.* Each of these types may be further divided, however, into subtypes. For example, prose is characterized as *short story, novel,* or *nonfiction.* Poetry, even more than prose, has a plethora of forms: *lyric, narrative, dramatic, symbolic, epic, sonnet,* and *ballad* are but a few. Each type has its adherents and each attempts to communicate according to a particular, predetermined structure. It is important, therefore, to establish accurately a selection's form in order to determine the standards by which it is to be analyzed. For example, in reading a poem like "Ozymandias" you should either recognize that its genre is a sonnet, or you should research the poetic types until you do recognize it. A sonnet is a fourteen-line verse that in Old French means *little song.* Since "Ozymandias" fits this form, you should further research what special criteria might be employed in an analytical judgment of Shelley's poem as representative of the sonnet genre.

For another genre characteristic example, consider the difference between the novel and the short story. It is not, for instance, a great defect for a short story to have weak character development, provided it has other strong elements. A short story is usually too short to depict fully a human character. With the longer novel form, however, the failure of a writer to develop his characters is a serious deficiency.

EXERCISE #5:

Analyze the following poem by emphasizing its genre characteristics. Use the library if you need to.

### LORD RANDAL

"Oh where have you been, Lord Randal, my son?
Oh where have you been, my handsome young man?"
"Oh, I've been to the wildwood; mother make my bed soon,
I'm weary of hunting and I fain would lie down."

"And whom did you meet there, Lord Randal, my son?        5
And whom did you meet there, my handsome young man?"
"Oh, I met with my true-love; mother, make my bed soon,
I'm weary of hunting and I fain would lie down."

"What got you for supper, Lord Randal, my son?
What got you for supper, my handsome young man?"        10
"I got eels boiled in broth; mother, make my bed soon,
I'm weary of hunting and I fain would lie down."

"And who got your leavings, Lord Randal, my son?
And who got your leavings, my handsome young man?"
"I gave them to my dogs; mother, make my bed soon,        15
I'm weary of hunting and I fain would lie down."

"And what did your dogs do, Lord Randal, my son?
And what did your dogs do, my handsome young man?"
"Oh, they stretched out and died; mother, make my bed soon,
I'm weary of hunting and I fain would lie down."          20

"Oh, I fear you are poisoned, Lord Randal, my son.
Oh, I fear you are poisoned, my handsome young man."
"Oh, yes, I am poisoned; mother, make my bed soon,
I'm weary of hunting and I fain would lie down."

"What will you leave your mother, Lord Randal, my son?          25
What will you leave your mother, my handsome young man?"
"My house and my lands; mother, make my bed soon,
I'm weary of hunting and I fain would lie down."

"What will you leave your sister, Lord Randal, my son?
What will you leave your sister, my handsome young man?"          30
"My gold and my silver; mother, make my bed soon,
I'm weary of hunting and I fain would lie down."

"What will you leave your brother, Lord Randal, my son?
What will you leave your brother, my handsome young man?"
"My horse and my saddle; mother, make my bed soon,          35
I'm weary of hunting and I fain would like down."

"What will you leave your true-love, Lord Randal, my son?
What will you leave your true-love, my handsome young man?"
"A halter to hang her; mother make my bed soon,
For I'm sick at my heart and I want to lie down."          40

*—Anonymous*

_____

_____

_____

_____

_____

_____

_____

_____

_____

_____

*Learning Activity #3:*

## *Linguistic Connotation and Textual Authenticity*

A.   Textual Authenticity

Textual authenticity, while quite closely related to linguistic connotation, is not primarily concerned with simply the connotation of a word. The first concern for the critic interested in authenticity is whether or not contemporary readers have the correct or exact word as originally penned by the author. Often in older works, and occasionally even in newer ones, the text which comes to the publisher is imperfect. Sometimes words are smudged, misspelled, omitted, or in some way lost. Publishers are then forced to repair or guess at an author's original intention. This practice makes the accuracy of a publisher's choice debatable as new interpretations are placed upon the text, or as later evidence either confirms the publisher's judgment or refutes it in favor of yet another interpretation. For example, scholars are still debating what Andrew Marvell really intended in line 34 of his poem "To His Coy Mistress." As it is printed in the book, lines 33 and 34 read as follows:

> "Now therefore, while the youthful hue
> Sits on thy skin like morning dew."

The problem is that the first edition has the last word as not "*dew*'" but "*glew.*" "*Glew,*" however, was a seldom used spelling of glue, a word that simply does not fit at all well in the context of the poem. Some critics have suggested that Marvell meant "*hew*" which means warmth; unfortunately, this term had drifted out of use and is, therefore, doubtful as a choice. Originally some publisher selected "*dew*" and the choice has become so well accepted that it is a rare text indeed that bothers to footnote the word to point out that it was not Marvell's word.

With the advent of modern printing and reproduction techniques, fewer and fewer of these textual authenticity problems occur. However, some modern writers repeatedly revise their work. These revisions later become the focal point of study to determine not only which of a text's variations is the author's final intended version but also which is the best version.

B.   Linguistic Connotation

Linguistic connotation and textual authenticity, while closely related analytical interests, are distinct tools of criticism. **Linguistic connotation** concentrates upon the meanings of words at the time they were written. While it is usually not too difficult to determine the denotation (the definition of a word based upon dictionaries and other documents available from the period of interest) the word's connotation is the main interest of those who are concerned with linguistics.

Sometimes the meaning of a line may be lost or misinterpreted if you are unfamiliar with the connotation a word had at the time it was written. For example, in Shakespeare's play *Hamlet*, Prince Hamlet, upset with his mother's hasty marriage after the death of her husband (Hamlet's father), takes out his bitterness upon Ophelia, a young woman of whom he is ordinarily quite fond. Seeing his mother's actions as indicative of all women he tells Ophelia in Act III, Scene 1,

> "Get thee to a nunnery. Why wouldst
> thou be a breeder of sinners?"

Some sources have suggested that the term "nunnery" means that Hamlet is suggesting to Ophelia that she remove herself from temptation; that is, if she were to enter a religious convent she would not produce sinners as his mother has become, nor what he feels he has become. The imagery of a "nunnery" as a convent is an effective way to explain Hamlet's growing misogyny, but it totally fails to impart the viciousness that has begun to cloud his thoughts. Nor will "nunnery," as a convent, explain Ophelia's revulsion at such a suggestion. However, upon analysis of the slang of Shakespeare's day, you will discover that while the denotation of "nunnery" did mean convent, the common connotation of "nunnery" during Elizabethan times was that of a brothel.

Most people would agree that "nunnery" as brothel changes the imagery of the lines dramatically. This meaning is not only indicative of Hamlet's state of mind but is also in keeping with Hamlet's other comment that Polonius, Ophelia's father, is a fishmonger. In Elizabethan slang, a fishmonger is not a seller of fish but of women—a pimp. This imagery fits the play well if you see that Hamlet believes his mother's sin to be a sexual one—marrying without a suitable period of mourning. In fact, she waits only a few days after the funeral, and incestuously marries her brother-in-law.

While this is only one example, it illustrates what most interests one who is concerned about the accuracy of linguistic connotation.

EXERCISE #6:

Read the following poem.

### SPRING

When daisies pied and violets blue,
  And lady-smocks all silver-white,
And cuckoo-buds of yellow hue
  Do paint the meadows with delight,
The cuckoo then, on every tree,                    5
Mocks married men; for thus sings he,
                    "Cuckoo!
Cuckoo, cuckoo!" O word of fear,
Unpleasing to a married ear!

When shepherds pipe on oaten straws,          10
  And merry larks are ploughmen's clocks,
When turtles tread, and rooks, and daws,
  And maidens bleach their summer smocks
The cuckoo then, on every tree,
Mocks married men; for thus sings he,          15
                    "Cuckoo!
Cuckoo, cuckoo!" O word of fear,
Unpleasing to a married ear!

—*William Shakespeare* (*1564-1616*)

44

As one interested in linguistic connotation, answer the following questions in a sentence or two. The poem ends each stanza by stating that the cuckoo is "unpleasing to the married ear."

a. Why would the cuckoo bird's *behavior* be unpleasant to the "married ear?"

_____

_____

_____

_____

_____

b. Why should the *sound* the bird makes, "Cuckoo," be unpleasing?

_____

_____

_____

_____

_____

*Learning Activity #4:*

*Sociology*

Sociological analysis, one of the oldest critical points of view, is concerned with the intellectual and social environment out of which literature is produced. Sociological critics do not think that authors can create in an intellectual vacuum; consequently, even those who write in lonely isolation must be greatly influenced by the world in which they live and write.

For critical purposes, the traditional sociological approach may be divided into two distinct areas of interest: (A) the immediate environment, **biography**; and (B) the larger environment, **history**.

A. The Immediate Environment—Biography

Authors' biographies are often quite helpful in attempting to understand their work fully because they usually write about what they know. For example, the knowledge that John Milton was blind is an invaluable aid to understanding his poetry. Furthermore, a familiarity with other writings by the same author can offer insight. Characters and settings occasionally recur in subsequent works, and the fuller development that this practice occasions

**45**

allows you to appreciate writers more fully by referring to previously written works. Both Kurt Vonnegut, Jr. and William Faulkner are famous for taking minor characters from one book and developing them into major characters in other books. John Steinbeck did this with a character from the short story, "The Snake," located on page 218 of this book.

Here is a section from part of a student paper that analyzes Steinbeck's other writing as it relates to "The Snake."

John Steinbeck was born in Salinas, California, in 1902. The early history of his family, until he was into his pre-school years, is outlined in the epic novel East of Eden as a subplot. Young Steinbeck grew up in the Salinas Valley, Monterey Peninsula, area in which so many of his works are set. The Long Valley, in which the story "The Snake" first appeared, is the Salinas Valley. Another of his short stories, "Flight," is set just south of Carmel on the Monterey Peninsula. Of Mice and Men is set in the farmland along the Salinas River. Finally, two novels, Cannery Row and Sweet Thrusday, are set in the community of Monterey, California, the same locale as in "The Snake." The most important of these works in its relationship to "The Snake" is Cannery Row, for "The Snake," published in 1938, introduces the character Dr. Phillips, who in 1944 becomes the central character Doc of Cannery Row.

The character of the doctor serves Steinbeck as a commentator for his philosophical view of life. Through the doctor in "The Snake," as well as the doctors in Cannery Row, In Dubious Battle, and The Moon Is Down, he views life biologically. Steinbeck views human life in what may be called a "tide pool." That is to say, human life may be viewed objectively as a biologist might examine the living creatures in a seashore tide pool. It is independent and self-contained, and it is animalistic.

Humans viewed in this respect take on the qualities of animals. Steinbeck seems to feel that humans must be viewed first animalistically before they can be understood as humans. In order to accomplish this, they must be objectively viewed as biological specimens by observing both their physical and psychological reactions within their environment.

John Steinbeck is indeed qualified to use the frame of reference he does in this story. Prior to entering upon a literary career, he studied marine zoology at Stanford University and later worked in a marine biology laboratory. Thus, he is able to detail realistically the duties and functions of the marine biologist, Dr. Phillips.

While some critics object to what they view as overdependence upon matters extraneous to the literature itself, it is hard to dispute the idea that some familiarity with an author's life, and other writing, can aid in the understanding of a particular piece of literature.

**46**

EXERCISE #7:

Read the following poem.

## WINTER

When icicles hang by the wall,
    And Dick the shepherd blows his nail,
And Tom bears logs into the hall,
    And milk comes frozen home in pail,
When blood in nipped and ways be foul,          5
Then nightly sings the staring owl,
        "Tu-whit, tu-who!"

A merry note,
While greasy Joan doth keel* the pot.

When all aloud the wind doth blow,          10
    And coughing drowns the parson's saw,
And birds sit brooding in the snow,
    And Marian's nose looks red and raw,
When roasted crabs** hiss in the bowl,
Then nighly sings the staring owl,          15
        "Tu-whit, tu-who!"

A merry note,
While greasy Joan doth keel the pot.

---

*skim
**crab apples

1. What would you like to know about the above poem to enhance your understanding of it?

_____

_____

_____

_____

_____

_____

    a. When do you think it was written? _____

    b. Who do you think might have written it? _____

    _____

**47**

EXERCISE #8:

Read the following poem.

### THE WORLD IS TOO MUCH WITH US

The world is too much with us; late and soon,
Getting and spending, we lay waste our powers:
Little we see in Nature that is ours;
We have given our hearts away, a sordid boon!
This Sea that bares her bosom to the moon;      5
The winds that will be howling at all hours,
And are up-gathered now like sleeping flowers;
For this, for everything, we are out of tune;
It moves us not—Great God! I'd rather be
A Pagan suckled in a creed outworn;      10
So might I, standing on this pleasant lea,
Have glimpses that would make me less forlorn;
Have sight of Proteus rising from the sea;
Or hear old Triton blow his wreathèd horn.

1. What personal statement is the author of the above poem making about his life?

_____

_____

_____

_____

2. When do you think this poem was written? Why?

_____

_____

_____

_____

### B. The Larger Environment—History

While the immediate environment or biographical data of authors is concerned with the personal information about their lives and the other things that they have written, the larger sociological concern is with the historical context out of which authors germinate their ideas. In other words, many critics are very interested in what influence the historical events of a period

**48**

might have either upon writers or upon the characters they create. For example, Nathanial Hawthorne wrote his popular novel, *The Scarlet Letter*, long after the Puritans, about whom the novel was written, lived. Your familiarity with the historical influence of Puritan times can greatly enhance your understanding of the book. Likewise, one who knows something about the French Revolution will better understand Charles Dickens' novel, *A Tale of Two Cities*.

One should remember the statement that no writer creates in an intellectual void; all people, including writers, are influenced by the times in which they live. Of the many issues of the contemporary world, one might reflect upon the recent changes in attitude toward such issues as abortion, capital punishment, or feminism. It is difficult to see how any contemporary writer could write about those subjects and not be greatly influenced by current attitudes and recent historical events.

Historical influences are particularly important for such works as *The Octopus*, by Frank Norris (railroad expansion); *The Jungle*, by Upton Sinclair (the meat-packing industry); or such propagandistic novels as *Uncle Tom's Cabin*, by Harriet Beecher Stowe (slavery); and *Grapes of Wrath*, by John Steinbeck (migrant farm workers). Sometimes the historical influence is more subtle, but it can offer insight nonetheless. Even such recent works as *Jonathan Livingston Seagull*, by Richard Bach, is more meaningful when viewed against the backdrop of the recent interest in mysticism and parareligion.

EXERCISE #9:

Read the following two poems:

### THE MAN HE KILLED

Had he and I but met
By some old ancient inn,
We should have sat us down to wet
Right many a nipperkin!*

But ranged as infantry,         5
And staring face to face,
I shot at him as he at me,
And killed him in his place.

I shot him dead because—
Because he was my foe,         10
Just so; my foe of course he was;
That's clear enough; although

He thought he'd 'list, perhaps,
Off-hand-like—just as I—
Was out of work—had sold his traps—         15
No other reason why.

Yes; quaint and curious war is!
You shoot a fellow down
You'd treat, if met where any bar is,
Or help to half-a-crown.         20
—*Thomas Hardy (1840-1928)*

---

*half-pint cup

# DULCE ET DECORUM EST

Bent double, like old beggars under sacks,
Knock-kneed, coughing like hags, we cursed through sludge,
Till on the haunting flares we turned our backs,
And towards our distant rest began to trudge.
Men marched asleep. Many had lost their boots,        5
But limped on, blood-shod. All went lame, all blind;
Drunk with fatigue; deaf even to the hoots
Of gas-shells dropping softly behind.

Gas! GAS! Quick boys!—An ecstasy of fumbling,
Fitting the clumsy helmets just in time,        10
But someone still was yelling out and stumbling
And flound'ring like a man in fire or lime.—
Dim through the misty panes and thick green light,
As under a green sea, I saw him drowning.

In all my dreams before my helpless sight        15
He plunges at me, guttering, choking, drowning.

If in some smothering dreams, you too could pace
Behind the wagon that we flung him in,
And watch the white eyes writhing in his face,
His hanging face, like a devil's sick of sin,        20
If you could hear, at every jolt, the blood
Come gargling from the froth-corrupted lungs
Bitter as the cud
Of vile, incurable sores on innocent tongues,—
My friend, you would not tell with such high zest        25
To children ardent for some desperate glory,
The old lie: *Dulce et decorum est*
*Pro patria mori.* *

        —*Wilfred Owen (1895-1918)*

*Latin, from the Roman poet Horace, meaning, "It is sweet and becoming to die for one's country."

1. Write a paragraph explaining why one poem may be better understood through historical analysis than the other.

_____

_____

_____

_____

_____

_____

The following student paper is a traditional analysis of "Lady Lazarus" by Sylvia Plath. Read the poem first (page 168), then read the analysis.

Sonja Gorman
English 1B
Dr. Guches
March 10, 1979

TRADITIONAL ANALYSIS OF

SYLVIA PLATH'S "LADY LAZARUS"

In her poem "Lady Lazarus," Sylvia Plath employs a situational irony lamenting death.  Along with the biblical Lazarus, Plath always seems to want to accomplish the imponderable.  However, her life was filled with situations that left her in constant turmoil, therefore never quite attaining the miracles she was prophesying in her mind. Like the title, several of the stanzas in "Lady Lazarus" are analogous to Sylvia Plath's life, as she uses irony to express her attitudes toward death, toward her career, and toward the men in her life.

Sylvia Plath rarely wrote about anything but herself, reflecting her inclinations, usually toward death.  This theme became stronger in her later works as seen in "Lady Lazarus," written during the last month of her life and indicative of her feelings at that time.  As the poem relates, she is attempting suicide a third time at age thirty, "Once each decade."  The first, apparently an accident at age ten, was followed by an attempt in her early twenties.

> The second time I meant
> To last it out and not come back at all.
> I rocked shut
>
> As a seashell.
> They had to call and call
> And pick the worms off me like sticky pearls.

Plath had just completed a month as guest editor at Mademoiselle maga-zine.  Unable to adjust to "the dead summer world of a suburban Boston,"[1] after her exciting month in New York, she crawled into the cellar of her home and swallowed some pills.  Rocking, shut into an embryonic position, she had to undergo shock treatments along with psychiatric care to be "called back" to life.  Her fascination with

death is further illustrated in her book <u>The Bell Jar</u>.  On the opening
page, she writes of the execution of the Rosenburgs.  Plath is upset
not with the political background of the case and its injustice but
with the process of electrocution and how it must feel to be "electro-
cuted all along your nerves."[2]  The irony seen throughout the poem is
that although she speaks of experiencing death three times, the poet
is still alive.

Sylvia Plath primarily wanted to be notable as a poet; however,
she did everything with a restless excitement.  In letters to her
family, she wrote expressing a desire to be a fantastic mother;[3] she
went into motherhood with the same fascination she attached to her
marriage in its early stages.  Plath was often consumed with energies
towards various projects.  She lived on the highs that each new endea-
vor gave her.  Examination of her life shows a preoccupation with herself and a compulsion for overachieving.  A friend once said of Plath,
"It was as if Sylvia couldn't wait for life to come to her . . .. She
rushed out to greet it, to make things happen."[4]  However, she could not
make things happen all the time.  As much as she wanted to do well in
all things, she often was depressed by failure when she had to contend
with normal everyday life:  housework, pregnancy, babies, cooking, ill-
ness.  Her occasional collection of literary prizes and awards were
laurels to maintain motivation because of this inability to adjust to
ordinary daily living.  However, Plath did believe in herself as a
writer, and when she wrote in "Lady Lazarus,"

> Dying
> Is an art, like everything else
> I do it exceptionally well.
>
> I do it so it feels like hell
> I do it so it feels real
> I guess you could say I've a call.

she really believed she did everything well.  But the irony is she
really was not doing well at all.  Her marriage was a failure, with
the probability of failing as a mother and her success as a poet in
question.

The two major relationships Plath had with men were both acutely
emotional, creating intense, odious feelings.  Her father's untimely

death when she was ten years old was seen as a sign of weakness in
him.   Therefore, she always looked for strong men, "physically wanting
a Colossus, with a great soul; it would be sinful to compromise."[5]
The intensity of this alienation with her dead father was magnified
when her husband abandoned her and the children for another woman.
Plath was devastated because in her husband she thought she had found
"the intelligent, loving, liberal father I have always longed for."[6]
These inner feelings can be seen in "Lady Lazarus" as she addresses
the men in the poem as Herr Doctor and Herr Enemy (because of her
father's German background) before she mockingly writes, "Do not think
I underestimate your great concern."  Indignantly she ends the poem
with

> Out of the ash
> I will rise with my red hair
> And I eat men like air.

In all probability, it was the unhappy relationships with her father
and husband that consumed her in life because of her unrealistic expectations of what men should be.  Consequently, these expectations
contributed to her confused state of mind and thus her death, another
discrepancy between what was actually happening in Plath's life and
what she indicates in her poem.

Sylvia Plath succeeded in her third attempt at suicide; however,
through her poems she has become a "Lady Lazarus" and performed a
miracle.  She has risen from the grave to become renowned.  Through
the posthumous publication of her poems, she is remembered, although
many critics believe only because of her death is she notable; otherwise, her poems would be unwarranted of the praise given them.  Ironically, by completing her self-fulfilling prophesy displayed so many
times in her poems, Sylvia Plath has reconciled her death wish, noto-
riety, and feelings towards men from her tomb.

FOOTNOTES

[1]Lois Ames, "Biographical Notes" in Sylvia Plath's The Bell Jar (New York:  Harper and Row, 1971), p. 286.

[2]Sylvia Plath, The Bell Jar (New York:  Harper and Row, 1971), p. 1.

[3]Mary Cantwell, "On Her Love and Marriage, " Mademoiselle, July 1975, p. 82

[4]Cantwell, p. 82.

[5]Cantwell, p. 82.

[6]Saul Maloff, "The Poet as Cult Goddess," Commonweal, June 4 1976, p. 372.

BIBLIOGRAPHY OF SOURCES CITED

Ames, Lois.  "Biographical Notes" in Sylvia Plath's The Bell Jar.
          New York:  Harper and Row, 1971.

Cantwell, Mary.  "On Her Love and Marriage."  Mademoiselle, July 1975.

Maloff, Saul.  "The Poet as Cult Goddess."  Commonweal, June 4, 1976.

Plath, Sylvia.  The Bell Jar.  New York:  Harper and Row, 1971.

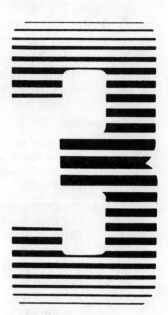

# Analyzing Fiction

Of all the literary genres, fiction is the most widely read and enjoyed. People read fiction—short stories and novels—to enjoy or to be entertained, to escape, and to learn. Occasionally a fictional story will seem to catch the imagination of nearly the whole reading public. These works become, almost overnight, "best sellers"; they sell out quickly, generate long waiting lists at the library, and become conversation topics at cocktail parties and on television talk shows. All this attention, of course, catapults their sales into the millions. Beyond their popularity, or perhaps because of it, readers derive a great sense of satisfaction from reading fiction. It seems to appeal to some inner feelings—feelings that bring joy from vicarious experiences. To derive the most enjoyment possible from a work of literature, however, one needs to understand it. Fiction, like any other genre, has its characteristics, and to know them is to enhance one's understanding and appreciation of the form.

Fiction is, then, a literary genre that appeals to both casual readers and to serious students of literature alike. People who make the effort to learn the characteristics and techniques of fiction enhance their own critical, analytical skills.

*Objectives:*

After completing this unit, you will be able to:
1. Define the basic elements of fiction.
2. Identify fictional elements in a literary work.
3. Distinguish between romanticism and realism, primitivism and naturalism.

**55**

4. Interpret a work's point of view and discuss its effectiveness.
5. Write an analysis of a short fictional work.
6. Relate the theme of a short story.
7. Assess the contribution of a story's setting to the plot, atmosphere, and ideas expressed.
8. Appraise the value of a story's use of foreshadowing.
9. Evaluate a story's exposition, climax, and resolution for credibility.
10. Express greater confidence in your understanding of fiction.

*Pre-Assessment:*

_____ 1. Romance may be characterized by an interest in (A) the true to life, (B) the cause and effect principles of science, (C) objective presentation, (D) fate determined by the environment, (E) nature and a return to the simple life.

_____ 2. Which of the following is not a characteristic of primitivism?
(A) Glorification of the primitive
(B) Celebration of natural beauty
(C) Emphasis upon scientific detail
(D) Idealization of childhood
(E) Desire to return to a simple life

_____ 3. Naturalists (A) revolted against romance, (B) believe all phenomena is a result of the cause and effect principles of science, (C) deny the existence of anything miraculous or supernatural, (D) feel that humans are controlled by their passions and by their environment, (E) all of the above.

_____ 4. Which of the following is NOT a basic area of conflict in fiction?
(A) The individual against nature
(B) The individual against history
(C) The individual against the individual
(D) The individual against self
(E) The individual against the gods

_____ 5. Foreshadowing can (A) prepare the reader for the final outcome, (B) substitute for a plot, (C) never be used in realistic fiction, (D) cause a story to lose probability, (E) make characters resemble real people.

_____ 6. In literature a *foil* is a character who (A) spoils the main character's plans, (B) duels constantly, (C) is a fool, (D) is intended to be contrasted with a main character, (E) functions as a listener.

_____ 7. Theme is concerned with (A) a story's plot, (B) a story's purpose, (C) propaganda, (D) the overemphasis of ideas, (E) entertaining diversions.

_____ 8. The omniscient point of view (A) gives the narrator god-like powers of seeing and knowing all, (B) gives the narrator no clear view of all the characters, (C) is objective, (D) tells only what characters look like and what they do, (E) is stream of consciousness.

_____ 9. First person narrator (A) sees all and reports what characters think, (B) reports what is on only one other character's mind, (C) refers to himself as "I," (D) is objective, (E) uses the pronoun "you" frequently.

_____ 10. Stream of consciousness (A) is omniscient, (B) is objective, (C) is a nineteenth century technique, (D) links thought patterns together subjectively, (E) refers to the setting.

***Learning Activity #1:***

## *Romanticism, Realism, Primitivism and Naturalism*

When asked why they prefer fiction to other literary genres, most people state that they feel fiction to be more realistic to read than either drama or poetry. This desire for the true to life in literature can be deceptive for the unwary, however. No short story or novel actually portrays truth or reality because the very nature of the printed word leads to some distortion.

Fiction can promote distortion in two obvious ways. Experience can appear to be better than it actually is, or it can appear to be worse. When fictional experience appears to be better than reality, we refer to that experience as *romantic*; when the experience is an accurate description of reality, we refer to it as *realistic*; when the experience appears worse than reality, we refer to it as *naturalistic*. Romance, realism, and naturalism are three ways that we can relate fiction to our lives. Each is a different perception of what is real, and each has, at one time or another, become so popular in literature and in art that whole periods of time have been called by these terms.

### A. **Romanticism**

Romanticism is a term that has been applied to the principles and characteristics of the romantic movement (1770-1850). The main emphasis of the movement in both literature and art was the promotion of imagination, sentiment, and individualism in artistic expression. Since the Old French and medieval historical romances of the seventeenth century dealt exclusively with fanciful and far-fetched adventures that were distant from familiar and ordinary life, such as the tales of King Arthur and the Knights of the Round Table, the term romantic itself came to denote things that were unreal or opposed to fact. During the next century the term came to mean that which was extravagantly fictitious in creating scenes that are pleasing but far from an accurate depiction of truth.

The interests of the romantics were characterized by a concern for nature and a return to the simple life. Related to this was a renewed interest in the nostalgic past. As a result, writers chose subject matter for their fiction that was unfamiliar, remote, and out of doors. Passion and imagination, along with a great interest in the horrible and supernatural, were emphasized.

> Characteristics of Romantic Fiction
> 1. Distant settings
> 2. Adventures among strange people
> 3. Mystery
> 4. Emphasis upon the unfamiliar
> 5. The unnatural and the horrible
> 6. The past

The readers' appetite for romance stimulated writers to produce even more romantic fiction. Nathanial Hawthorne, for example, wrote of the puritans of the seventeenth century from his vantage point in the mid-nineteenth century (e.g. *The Scarlet Letter*, 1850). Herman Melville's novels *Typee* (1846), *Omoo* (1847), and *Mardi* (1849), are all set in French Polynesia among primitive peoples, and the books made their author hugely popular. Only later, after 1851 and the publication of *Moby Dick*, a symbolic novel, did his popularity wane. The public loved him for his early novels but did not seem to understand the symbolic quality of his later work because they desired more romance with less serious intent.

Today, there is a renewed interest in romanticism. Modern publishing companies have found financial success in publishing a plethora of new titles according to a very strict romantic formula. Names such as Violet Winspear (e.g. *The Sin of Cynara*, 1976), Janet Dailey (e.g. *The Homeplace*, 1976), and Anne Mather (e.g. *Wild Enchantress*, 1977) are very popular in America. Also, many new novels, as well as television programs and movies, have exploited a renewed interest in the past (e.g. *Little House on the Prairie, The Waltons*). Furthermore, horror and the unnatural, fundamental romantic elements, are ever popular as witnessed by the success of the novels and the movies *Jaws* and *The Exorcist*. Romanticism is alive and flourishing in today's world.

## B. Primitivism

Primitivism, a subbranch of romanticism, is concerned with the idea that natural or very early conditions of society are the very best situations for human life. Those who subscribe to this view conclude that primitive humans, living close to nature in their tribal villages in the forests and jungles, do not suffer the evil influences of urban society. Primitive humans are, accordingly, more nearly perfect, thus nobler than civilized humans. Moreover, since gods reveal themselves more completely in nature, primitives are essentially moral; they are not confronted with the evils of self-imposed limitations on freedom that exist for city dwellers. Human behavior, the primitives believed, is naturally prone to be good. Savages, by this reasoning, are quite superior— *Noble Savages*. Part of the enchantment with noble savages was created from the accounts of voyaging and by the discovery of the South Seas; consequently, primitive life became the theme of many romantic fictions.

Like savages, children were idealized as being closer to gods than adults. Children at birth are, of course, as close to nature as they can or will ever be. Thus the more educated and the more conformistic children become, the less natural they are and the farther they drift from the gods. Civilization, in this view, is inherently unnatural and therefore evil. Pearl, in *The Scarlet Letter*, for example, is a primitive child who seems to be far more uninhibited and natural in the forest than when she is in the civilized, Puritan village.

Romantic Primitivism

1. Glorification of the primitive
   (*Typee*—Herman Melville)
2. Celebration of natural beauty and the simple life
   (*Walden Pond*—Henry David Thoreau)
3. Idealization of the child and childhood
   (*Uncle Tom's Cabin*—Harriet Beecher Stowe)

EXERCISE #1:

Read the short story "The Masque of the Red Death" (page 214) by Edgar Allan Poe and list in the space below the characteristics of romance that appear in Poe's story.

1. _____

2. _____

3. _____

4. _____

5. _____

EXERCISE #2:

Write a paragraph in which you contrast, in your own words, romanticism and primitivism.

_____

_____

_____

_____

_____

_____

_____

_____

_____

_____

_____

_____

_____

_____

_____

## C. Realism

After decades of romantic literature, writers became interested in achieving **versimilitude.** Versimilitude, a word of Latin roots, meaning true - like, represented a shift in the way people thought about fiction and the way writers treated it. Writers, like Stephen Crane in "The Open Boat" and *The Red Badge of Courage*, wished to incorporate within their work the semblance of truth by using realistic detail. Beginning as a movement in the late nineteenth century, the emphasis in fiction became accuracy, especially in dealing with background information. Viewed in one way, the realistic movement was a reaction to the flights of imagination that characterized romantic writing. Realists wanted to portray an image of life as it really is.

The main emphasis of the realists, a reaction to conservative Victorianism, became the presentation of events so specifically that the details were nearly photographic. Quite the opposite of imaginary conception of experience which was used by the romantics, realists became concerned with social and psychological problems. Therefore, the characters in realistic fiction suffered frustrations from an environment which was often presented as sordid and depraved, as in Upton Sinclair's *The Jungle*, a novel set in the Chicago stockyards. While romance emphasizes beauty and order, realism emphasizes the actuality of the ugliness and disharmony that exists in the world—thus, their themes differ markedly.

On a scale from pure fantasy to actual history, realism and romaticism might look like this:

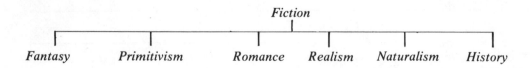

While the differences between romance and realism seem quite substantial, they share important qualities when they are compared with history or journalism. What makes realists different from reporters is emphasis. A realist's actuality is more generalized or typical than a reporter's factual account of actual events. Frequently, the realistic writer's fictional experiences are more vividly memorable than a newspaper account of a similar event. A comparison of Stephen Crane's newspaper account of his boat's sinking with his short story "The Open Boat" on the same subject is indicative of this difference in vividness.

Neither romance nor realism is, after all, absolute truth. Realism is closer to the romantic than to historical accounts, and, looking at the graph, one sees romance is closer to realism than pure fantasy. As a matter of fact, much of the most successful fiction is a very skillful merging of romance *and* realism. The works contain sufficiently accurate detail to give the reader the feeling of authenticity while the subject and characters are remote, exotic, adventurous,

**60**

mysterious, deal with the unfamiliar and emphasize the imagination. Such works as William Golding's *Lord of the Flies* or Antony Burgess's *Clockwork Orange* demonstrate this combination of romance and realism.

## D. Naturalism

Naturalism represents an extreme form of realism. In complete revolt against romance, naturalists take the philosophical position that all phenomena can and should be presented as the natural cause and effect principles of science, especially those of chemistry and physics. Naturalists deny the existence of anything miraculous or supernatural. In art and especially literature, naturalists believe that the methods of scientific transcription of nature should be employed. Fiction should become, then, little more than a series of objective reports.

Particularly influenced by the theories of biological determinism espoused by Charles Darwin or the economic determinism of Karl Marx, literary naturalism strives for a treatment of natural humans with scientific objectivity. From the writer's or reader's point of view, then, naturalistic fiction includes more details and is less selective of details than realism. Humans, in this view, are controlled by their instincts and passions and by their economic and social environment. Accordingly, humans lack free will; therefore, a naturalistic writer may make no moral judgments. Consequently, most naturalistic fiction is pessimistic as in Norman Mailer's *The Naked and the Dead*.

Whereas romanticism was the emphasis during the eighteenth and most of the nineteenth centuries, primitivism reached its zenith in the late eighteenth century and realism was influential during the late nineteenth and early twentieth centuries. Naturalism has been the dominant literary movement of the twentieth century.

Leaders in the Naturalistic Movement:

### Scientists—Philosophers
Charles Darwin (1809-1882, British)
Thomas Huxley (1825-1895, British)
Herbert Spencer (1820-1903, British)
Karl Marx (1818-1883, Prussian)

### Writers
Emile Zola (1840-1902, French)
James Joyce (1882-1941, Irish)
Theodore Dreiser (1871-1945, American)
William Faulkner (1897-1962, American)
Ernest Hemingway (1899-1961, American)
Robinson Jeffers (1887-1962, American)
Eugene O'Neill (1888-1953, American)
Henrik Ibsen (1828-1906, Norwegian)
Frank Norris (1870-1902, American)
Jack London (1876-1916, American)
John Steinbeck (1902-1968, American)
Norman Mailer (1923-      , American)

EXERCISE #3:

Write a paragraph in which you contrast realism with naturalism.

_____

_____

_____

_____

_____

_____

_____

_____

_____

EXERCISE #4:

Read the short story "To Build a Fire" by Jack London (on page 205) and list in the space provided the characteristics of realism and naturalism that appear in London's story.

_____

_____

_____

_____

_____

_____

_____

_____

_____

_____

## Plot

Plot is probably the easiest element of fiction to understand, and many unsophisticated readers tend to see it as the whole story, failing, as a result, to see any of fiction's other rewarding elements. On the other hand, analyzing plot is a good place with which to begin understanding any fictional work. On its simplest level, plot may be only a sequence of action that embodies some sort of *conflict*, one force opposing another. The plot's action is composed of the changing balance of forces in the story's events. The reader's interest in a story is centered first on this struggle. Conflicts may be divided into four chief types:

1. The individual against nature—
   Ernest Hemingway's *Old Man and the Sea*
   Peter Benchley's *Jaws*
   Herman Melville's *Moby Dick*

2. The individual against another individual—
   William Shakespeare's *Hamlet*
   Alexandre Dumas' *The Three Musketeers*
   (most stories of action and love)

3. The individual against self—
   Victor Hugo's *Les Miserables*

4. The individual against the gods—
   Sophocles' *Oedipus*

EXERCISE #5:

What is the conflict in the short story "To Build a Fire"?

_____

_____

_____

_____

The ancient Greek philosopher, Aristotle, stated that every story must have a beginning (before which nothing matters), a middle, and an end (after which nothing matters). Simple sounding though this is, it insures readers' interest, and it makes sense with regard to a story's plot. A story's beginning, called the **exposition**, introduces characters and their relationship to their environment. Even though they may be involved in actions or events with which we are unfamiliar, the situation quickly develops into a hint or promise of conflict. Once the conflict begins to develop, the largest section of a story begins: the **complication**. The complication continues until, through what is called the **climax**, it becomes apparent where the plot's action is headed. The

**63**

final portion of the story indicates the conflict's settlement in the **resolution.** In some formula stories these plot elements are quite easy to identify; for example, the typical western may be organized as follows:

| | |
|---|---|
| **Exposition** | Nearly seventeen-year-old Nell, planting seeds in her garden on her father's ranch, is startled when several cattle crash through the barbwire fence to drink from the spring near the new corn, while Bart, the foreman from a neighboring cattle ranch, looks on without any visible concern for either the broken fence or the trampled corn. |
| **Complication** | Despite the fact that Dalton Bradley has vowed to wipe out every sheepherder in the valley, his son, Dalton, Jr., has fallen in love with Nell. She shyly returns his affection even though her father is organizing all the sheepmen to lead a raid on the cattle ranches. |
| **Climax** | The young couple, caught in the crossfire between the opposing sheep and cattlemen, are seriously injured when trampled by stampeding cattle. |
| **Resolution** | The chagrined fathers, meeting outside the room where their children may be dying, agree to divide the valley between sheep and cattle and live peacefully together. The young couple recover and marry, thus uniting the two families and forever ending the conflict. |

As trite and full of western clichés as the above plot outline is, it represents how a basic plot structure works. Sometimes, simply understanding the plot's structure is all we want from a book or a movie; we want only some entertainment and escape. For analysis, however, plot structure does not tell you very much about the story, but it does give you a place to start a discussion or an analysis. What is helpful and leads toward a deeper understanding is an analysis of a story's probability.

EXERCISE #6:

In one sentence each, summarize the exposition, the complication, the climax, and the resolution of "To Build a Fire."

Exposition  _____

_____

_____

Complication  _____

_____

_____

Climax _____

_____

_____

Resolution _____

_____

_____

## Probability

Since we know that fiction is only a representation of life and not really life itself, we—the audience—demand that writers make their stories seem probable. We want to believe in the events and characters. However, we are inclined to disbelieve anything that seems excessively fantastic or implausible. Writers can, though, rely upon a uniquely human capability as they write their stories: **the willing suspension of disbelief.** This works through our unique ability to pretend that the events we read in a book or view in a drama or a film are actually happening right there before our eyes. This phenomenon allows us to cry, to be horrified, to fear, or to love, in short, to be affected by what we read or view. We want to really care for, to really fear for the characters. We want to fear for the young man as we wonder whether he will be able to rescue his love before the train crushes her on the tracks where the villain has tied her. Of course, we are likely to grant writers of romantic fiction somewhat more leeway than we would grant to realistic writers, but in either case, or even in fantasy, a writer must take pains to create within the plot the feeling of truth. This may be accomplished through his handling of chronology, motivation, and foreshadowing.

## Chronology

**Chronology**, the arrangement of events in time, is an important element in establishing a story's credibility. If the events seem to progress too swiftly, a story will not seem to portray truth. In actuality it is not the clock or calendar that is of most importance, but rather the effect of the passage of time. We have all seen thirty-minute situation comedies on television during which a young couple meet, fall in love, become engaged, survive an ordeal, marry, and leave on their honeymoon. These events might seem credible for a ninety-minute program, perhaps even sixty minutes, but thirty minutes leaves us not only breathless but unconvinced. The same situation is true in fiction. Sufficient time must *seem* to pass for the story's events to seem probable in our minds.

Several techniques for movement of time are available to writers. The most important of these is the manner in which the author unfolds the story. For example, simple narration—story telling—covers considerable ground swiftly; therefore, if a writer wishes to create the impression of the passage of time, some other writing style should be employed. Dramatized narration, which includes dialogue, moves a plot much more slowly; consequently, the reader, having to take more time to read the passage, feels that the story time has also been extended. The plot action of a story stops altogether when a writer employs pure analysis and description. Even though time stands still for these passages, the writer must engage in analysis sparingly because there is a danger that readers will feel these sections dull or tedious and skip them altogether. The creative use of these writing styles, these "delaying tactics," controls the fictional chronology, thereby making the characters and events more probable.

## Motivation

Why do characters in a story behave as they do? Readers not only want to know what happens in a story but why it happens. Unless a story reveals the motivation behind the events and character behavior in a story, it will seem quite improbable. There are several ways for writers to present motivation.

1. Analysis —the writer tells the reader why.
2. Dialogue—characters themselves or other characters may report motives.
3. Character personality—characters behave appropriately to the personality types they represent.

In any case, a character's motivation must come from within the story. The fiction must be an entity unto itself and not depend upon any outside justification for the motives inherent in the plot. If a reader must search for motivation outside the story, the story's probability is greatly diminished. To make the characters in a story resemble real people, their behavior must not be questioned: readers must feel that if they knew real people like the fictional people, they would react and behave in a similar manner; otherwise, the story loses probability.

## Foreshadowing

Surprise, Samuel Taylor Coleridge concluded, is not nearly as satisfying as is expectation. By this, Coleridge meant that readers sincerely enjoy the fulfillment of the expectations that a story has created, for example, when the protagonist and the woman marry. Expectations, or suspense, is created by a plot device known as **foreshadowing**—hints about what will happen later in a story. If we have been led to expect something, we feel satisfaction when it occurs. Foreshadowing occurs in the movie *Jaws*, for instance, when viewers are shown several pictures of sharks attacking small boats early in the film. This prepares them for the shark's attack on the boat later, so that even though the shark's size and the scope of its destruction are quite fantastic, within the movie's context it is plausible. This result is satisfying to us not because of

**66**

the characters' fate but because our expectations are realized. A story's probability is enhanced when foreshadowing hints at the final outcome. Critical readers are those who are alert for foreshadowing hints and thus are the most rewarded and satisfied for discovering them.

Another useful function of foreshadowing is the preparation of the reader for the final outcome. Without this preparation the conclusion to the story might be quite confusing. In *Moby Dick*, for instance, the mechanics of a whale boat's operation are described early and in detail. This allows the reader to understand fully just what is occurring in the story's final chapters as Captain Ahab becomes tangled in the harpoon line. Without the earlier foreshadowing detail, either the action would have to be interrupted for explanation or the readers would be totally confused about how Ahab's end came. Also this foreshadowing in *Moby Dick* allows the action, at its most exciting point, to move forward uninterrupted and with complete probability.

EXERCISE #7:

Summarize in two or three sentences the foreshadowing used in "To Build a Fire."

_____

_____

_____

_____

_____

_____

_____

_____

_____

_____

_____

*Learning Activity #3:*

*Setting and Character*

**Setting**

The setting in fiction is the *place* where the events occur and the *time* or *age* of the action. But more than that, the setting establishes the atmosphere which helps create the mood. You might note, for example, how important setting is to certain types of stories. Ghost stories are often set in old castles or ancient houses, isolated from suburbia, preferably located on cliffs over-looking barren and rocky shorelines. The atmosphere, established by the setting, plays a dominant role in the fiction of certain writers—for instance, "Heart of Darkness" by Joseph Conrad or many of the stories of Edgar Allan Poe.

Notice how the setting establishes an atmosphere of impending doom in the following excerpt:

> The room in which I found myself was very large and lofty. The windows were long, narrow, and pointed, and at so vast a distance from the black oaken floor as to be altogether inaccessible from within. Feeble gleams of encrimsoned light made their way through the trellissed panes, and served to render sufficiently distinct the more prominent objects around; the eye, however, struggled in vain to reach the remoter angles of the chamber, or the recesses of the vaulted and fretted ceiling. Dark draperies hung upon the walls. The general furniture was profuse, comfortless, antique, and tattered. Many books and musical instruments lay scattered about but failed to give any vitality to the scene. I felt that I breathed an atmosphere of sorrow. An air of stern, deep, and irredeemable gloom hung over and pervaded all.
>
> "The Fall of the House of Usher"
> *by Edgar Allan Poe*

Setting may also reveal to readers something about the fictional characters in a story. The details of setting can reveal their personality traits, their personal habits, their social status, and their interests. This subtle development of characters through the setting is especially effective because the traits and interests are implied rather than explicit. This makes the characters seem all the more real, since in life we gain opinions about people and their habits through impressions.

In some stories the setting is so closely related to the plot that the events appear to be a direct result of the setting. For instance, the Mississippi River virtually determines Huckleberry Finn's actions. Likewise, stories that have a very limited environment, such as *Robinson Crusoe*, are often inseparable from their settings. Moreover, the setting may take on a symbolic function that is much beyond simply a realistic description of where and when the story takes place. In "The Open Boat" by Stephen Crane, the great, impersonal, superior sea is a natural power that is objectively indifferent and unfeeling about the four men in a small dinghy who are desperately trying to reach shore after a shipwreck. The philosophical nature of the story is symbolized by the setting. Setting, then, may be simply where a story takes place, or the setting may relate to the characters, plot, or the ideas on symbolic levels.

**EXERCISE #8:**

In two or three sentences describe how the setting in "To Build a Fire" contributes to each of the following:

1. Plot _____

_____

_____

_____

2. Atmosphere _____

_____

_____

_____

3. Ideas _____

_____

_____

_____

_____

## Character

Characters are, of course, the people of fiction, the author's cast. However, there are several ways that a writer may reveal his characters to readers, and understanding the techniques of revelation can show you not only how to look at characters but how the author intended for you to see them. Some characters are revealed through the same techniques that people are revealed in life. First, we come to know characters by what others think of them. Second, we make judgments about them based upon what they look like. Third, we learn about them by how they speak in the dialogue, and fourth, we learn a good deal about them based upon what they do or what they do not do.

We also learn about characters based upon what they themselves think. This last method is not a method by which we can learn about real people. It is a fictional technique only. Usually, writers reveal their characters through a variety of these devices, but the method or methods that are employed are determined to a large extent by the story's point of view.

After you understand how characters are revealed, it is important to understand each individual character's function in a particular story. (What did each give the story? Why is each included in the story?) It is not difficult to answer these questions for main characters, but you need to ask the same questions of minor characters as well, since minor characters are there for a purpose also. Occasionally, minor characters are present in fiction simply to create the illusion of a populated setting. Often, they are important in successfully moving the plot forward. Sometimes minor characters serve an essential role in the environment because their presence can help shed light on the main character's personality. Once in a while, a character is the sympathetic *confidant* or *confidante* who listens and who is necessary to draw the main character into conversation, thereby allowing the reader to learn more about the plans or events of the story.

Another function of a minor character is that of a *foil*. A foil is a character who is intended to be contrasted either in behavior or attitudes to the main character. This term, for example, derives from the custom that dueling foils come in matched pairs that appear to be the same on the outside but may be quite different upon exceptionally close analysis. In Shakespeare's *Hamlet*, for example, the young courtier Laertes is contrasted to Prince Hamlet. The personality and attitude of Hamlet are made all the more clear through the contrast.

EXERCISE #9:

In a sentence or two, state how the main character is revealed in "To Build a Fire."

_____

_____

_____

_____

_____

_____

_____

_____

**70**

**EXERCISE #10:**

Briefly explain in what way the dog in "To Build a Fire" is a foil.

_____

_____

_____

_____

_____

_____

*Learning Activity #4:*

*Theme and Point of View*

## Theme

*Theme* in fiction is the generalization that is either stated or implied and holds a story together. Sometimes referred to as a *controlling idea* or a central insight, theme is concerned with a story's purpose. Of course, not all stories have themes beyond a simple attempt to intrigue, to frighten, or to excite—in short, to give vicarious experience. Mysteries, horror stories, and adventures are quite entertaining, but they are not significant beyond what they are: entertaining diversions that are pleasurable but of no lasting importance. Theme is present in fiction only when there exists a serious effort on the author's part to create a unified work and to explore some universal truths about it. Occasionally, writers will incorporate some life theory or concept as the central idea and construct a story that is intentionally designed to illustrate its truth as in Charles Dickens' *Hard Times.*

While it is informative to isolate a story's theme in order to examine and discuss it, theme is never the *only* meaning, for whole meaning is the sum total of all a story's elements. When a writer dwells excessively on a theme in fiction, he runs the risk of overemphasizing his ideas: the result is a fiction that appears didactic—written solely to teach. Didactic fiction often preaches and, as you should remember, is generally regarded as inferior literature. Moreover, didactic fiction typically enjoys a relatively short popularity. For example, Harriet Beecher Stowe's *Uncle Tom's Cabin* is today only a historical document, relating to the American Civil War; almost no one reads this fictional propaganda any longer. Even great writers may occasionally lapse into fiction that, because it is so concerned with the moral message, preaches rather than illustrates. John Steinbeck's famous *The Grapes of Wrath*, while still close to us, will probably not be regarded by future generations as among his best works because it propagandizes and preaches excessively.

Theme and moral are not terms that may be employed synonymously. Their meanings are different. If you view the term "moral" narrowly, it becomes simply a value judgment about what you consider to be good or bad, right or wrong. Using this narrow definition of moral one might, for example, condemn a work's characters for "immoral behavior" and thus condemn the work as not being moral. Most critics, however, believe that any work of art, if it is worthwhile at all, is essentially moral. This apparent contradiction can best be understood by a broader definition of moral as applied in literature. Lacking the narrow, restrictive definition of what is right or wrong, moral in its broad sense is an expressed precept or general truth; consequently, if a writer has been successful in accurately illustrating life—word-painting a true picture of life's conditions—then his fiction is moral. In this broad sense, moral and theme, while still somewhat different, may be closely related, and no work may be pejoratively classified as lacking in moral content simply because we do not approve of the behavior of the characters. All serious works of literary fiction are essentially moral because the harmonious combination of the fictional elements of plot, setting, character, and theme attempt to illustrate life's truths.

Sometimes it is difficult to recognize a story's theme, but there are two obvious ways available to examine a work for the author's meaning. (1) Sometimes our estimation of a theme can be confirmed by reading an author's other writings. This would be quite helpful, for example, in discovering Ernest Hemingway's recurrent theme of man illustrating his virtue by facing death alone and bravely. (2) More often, however, theme must be determined by closely analyzing the characters' conflicts—what they are and how they are concluded.

**EXERCISE #11:**

Read the very short story "Birthday Party" by Katharine Brush. In no more than two or three sentences, write out the theme of "Birthday Party." Then, briefly discuss the hints or clues which lead you to the theme.

_____

_____

_____

_____

_____

_____

**EXERCISE #12:**

In no more than two or three sentences, state the theme of "To Build a Fire." Then discuss the hints or clues that lead you to the theme.

_____

_____

_____

_____

_____

_____

_____

_____

_____

_____

_____

_____

_____

## Point of View

Another way to begin to examine the theme in fiction is to determine a story's point of view. In its technical sense, point of view means the way the story's narrator relates to his fictional characters and to his story. Sometimes referred to as a story's *angle* or *focus*, point of view is not an arbitrary method used by an author to reveal his character or plot; it is, rather, a very carefully planned and special viewpoint. If a story is told completely in dialogue or we see a play, there is no one between the action and the viewer. However, if we read a play, or a story that contains any descriptive material whatsoever, that stage direction or story description has a point of view. For example, in "Birthday Party" we are told that the man had a "self-satisfied face," and his wife was "fadingly pretty." These are not objective qualities of people; they are subjective observations of the story's narrator. As a result, they are spoken from a particular, biased point of view.

Since all stories, except those of pure dialogue, need a teller, a narrator from whose viewpoint a story's elements unfold, the point of view must be chosen by an author very carefully. This choice of point of view will determine to a large extent the effect of a story and, depending upon the story's purpose, how successful its impact will be upon the reader. As a reader you must be very careful yourself that you do not confuse the narrator's view of his fictional world with the author's view; they are not the same even when the narrator refers to himself with the first person pronoun "I." No matter how well Hamlet speaks nor what opinions he may hold upon acting, it is not necessarily Shakespeare speaking nor his opinions.

Whenever we begin a piece of fiction, we expect to be able to see clearly how narrators relate to the content of the story and into which characters' minds they can see. To accomplish this an author may choose from four basic points of view:

1. **First Person Narrator**—One of the characters tells the story. Referring to himself as "I," the narrator can tell the reader what is thought and felt about the events but is unable to relate the inner feelings of any other characters. A variation of this technique has a narrator, who is completely outside the action, relate the events. Even though not a participant, the narrator, likewise, cannot see into the minds and true motives of anyone.

Character as Narrator
e.g. *Lord Jim* by Joseph Conrad
(Seems natural—character tells us what happened to him—very intimate)

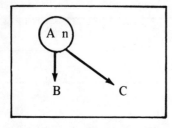

or

Narrator only observer—not a participant
e.g. *Huckleberry Finn* by Mark Twain

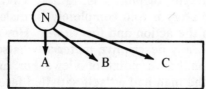

2. **Limited Omniscient**—Someone, other than a character in the story, tells the reader the story. The narrator refers to the character with the pronouns "he" and "she" and can see inside characters' minds but chooses to reveal the innerworkings of only one character; therefore, while the reader is told what one character thinks and feels and what the others say and do, the reader sees the events from only a limited viewpoint.

e.g. *Barn Burning* by William Faulkner
*Madam Bovary* by Gustave Flaubert

Narrator, who is an observer, has knowledge of the inner mind of only one of the characters (concentrated subjectivity).

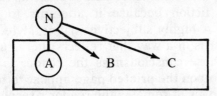

3. **Omniscient**—The narrator apparently has god-like powers of seeing and knowing all and chooses to tell everything to the reader. The omniscient point of view allows the reader into the minds of all the characters so that their thinking and feelings are quite clear.

e.g. *1984* by George Orwell

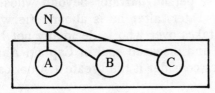

4. **Objective**—The narrator, who is outside the story, reveals the characters externally only. The reader is told what the characters look like and what they say but never what they think or how they feel. All matters of the subjective, thought and feelings, are impossible from the objective viewpoints.

e.g. *The Killers* by Ernest Hemingway

Narrator, totally objective, reports only what is seen and what is said without revealing opinions in any way. (Most lifelike—presents story the way we would know about it in life.)

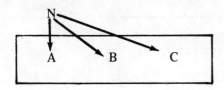

Occasionally, writers employ techniques that are somewhat different from these standard four points of view. One quite rare form is the second-person viewpoint. In this instance, the pronoun "you" is used throughout. (Early one morning, you walk along the winding trail overlooking an isolated beach when you notice a small, orange object just outside the crashing breakers. You tense as you realize that, just maybe, you had found the long missing life raft.) The "you" point of view is rare because it was not found to be particularly effective in involving the reader in the action.

Another fictional point of view that has been especially popular during the twentieth century is *stream of consciousness*. This represents the greatest effort to involve the reader in fiction because it attempts to express a character's unconscious thought. A highly subjective writing style, stream of consciousness links thought patterns in a way that reflects the actual thought process. When the character, whose consciousness the reader is within, is incoherent or retarded, the words upon the printed page appear to be irrational, unfocused, and illogical. Moreover, it remains the reader's responsibility to make sense out of the apparent jumble. But perseverance and close analysis will usually bring logical sense to it; the insights that you gain make the effort more than worthwhile. (*The Sound and the Fury* by William Faulkner; *Ulysses* by James Joyce.)

Sometimes, point of view shifts within a week. For example, in *Moby Dick* the story begins with a first person narrator beyond whose vision we cannot see: "Call me Ishmael." Later, after he is aboard the whaling ship *Pequod*, an omniscient narrator takes over who is decidedly not Ishmael and who can see into the very heart and diseased soul of Captain Ahab. Yet the work is effective, and some critics consider it the greatest American novel.

EXERCISE #13:

In two or three sentences, analyze the point of view of "Birthday Party."

_____

_____

_____

_____

_____

_____

_____

_____

**EXERCISE #14:**

What is the point of view in "To Build a Fire?"

_____

_____

_____

_____

_____

# Formalistic Analysis

A work of literature, if it is worthwhile at all, ought to be able to stand by itself. Readers should be able to enjoy literature without having to rely upon some prior knowledge of an author's work, the history of the era in which it was written, or the psychologies of Sigmund Freud or Carl Jung. Readers should be able to understand, to analyze, and to appreciate a work without having to do library research and without having to read what other critics have had to say about it. The real joy of reading for students of literature comes through their own critical abilities, developed through wide experiences in reading and through an understanding of literature as a form of art—a structure that stands by itself. The formalistic approach to the interpretation of literature is a method that emphasizes readers' critical abilities and encourages the acquisition of analytical skills even for casual readers.

*Objectives:*

After completing this unit, you will be able to:
1. Describe the formalistic approach to literary interpretation.
2. Define the literary terms that form the basic vocabulary of formalistic analysis.
3. Identify the concerns that are irrelevant to the formalistic approach.
4. Follow a step-by-step procedure in planning a formalistic analysis.
5. Write a formalistic analysis of a literary selection.
6. Evaluate a story's use of formalistic elements.
7. Assess the value of the "new criticism" for contemporary literature.

8. Express greater confidence in your ability to perform your own analysis of literature without assistance.
9. Evaluate a story's allusions and appraise their effectiveness.

*Pre-Assessment:*

_____ 1. Which of the following is NOT of concern to formalists?
   A) imagery  B) irony  C) metaphor  D) biography  E) symbol

_____ 2. Which of the following IS a concern of formalists?
   A) the relation of a literary work to its age
   B) the relation of the meanings of words in the story to the story's imagery
   C) the relation of a literary work to other works of the same type
   D) the relation of the work to other works by the author
   E) the relation of a literary work to the biography of the author

List 5 of the most important literary techniques of the formalistic approach:

3. _____

4. _____

5. _____

6. _____

7. _____

_____ 8. The primary concern of the formalistic critic is the viewing of a literary work as
   A) a work of art
   B) a work of social significance
   C) a work of deep philosophical thought
   D) a work of psychological importance
   E) all of the above

_____ 9. The formalistic critic looks for
   A) the anthropological significance of the recurring words
   B) the important events from an author's life that may appear in his story
   C) evidence that the work has or will become a "classic"
   D) the unifying patterns that shape a work and give its parts a relevance to its whole
   E) all of the above

_____ 10. Literature that is art differs from a newspaper story by
   A) having universal appeal
   B) having hidden meanings
   C) avoiding sex and violence
   D) not being true
   E) being written in a higher level of English

# FORMALISTIC ANALYSIS

*Learning Activity #1:*

## The New Critics

After World War I, a group of scholars came together at Vanderbilt University where Professor John Crowe Ransom (born 1888) was teaching. Ransom, along with three of his students—Allen Tate (born 1899), Robert Penn Warren (born 1905), and Cleanth Brooks (born 1906)—developed a philosophy of analysis that became known as *the New Criticism*. During the decades of the 1930s and the 1940s the ranks of the *New Critics*, as they became known, grew with the addition of Kenneth Burke (born 1897), Yvor Arthur Winters (born 1900), and Richard Palmer Blockmur (born 1904). By 1941 Ransom had written *The New Criticism*, and what the New Critics called *formalistic analysis* was launched. Although formalist analytical philosophy is still popular, the above-mentioned names are the dominant influences on formalism in literature.

Examining the biographical information of an author and the historical context in which the writing took place is frequently very interesting. The New Critics took the position, however, that the really important or valuable information can be derived only from the text of the work itself. Everything else, according to their theories, is peripheral, extraneous, and distracting. For example, a reader who concentrates upon Herman Melville's extensive voyages throughout the South Pacific rather than reading, rereading, and closely examining the text of *Moby Dick* will never truly understand the fullest significance of Captain Ahab's conflict with the great white whale. It is through an examination of a work's *form*—the structure or pattern of a work such as the short-story form or the ballad form—that one may derive a deep understanding of it as a form of art or a work of art.

The central focus of the formalistic approach is, then, to discover what a work expresses and what it means without any other reference to the work such as biographical data on the author or the history of the times. One must examine a piece of literature closely enough to begin discovering its structure; one must look for the unifying patterns that shape the work and give its parts a relevance to the whole. For example, a reader of an epic poem begins to analyze by closely examining the text to discover how closely the poem is structured like other epic poems. This approach can lead one to different levels of meaning, which, in turn, leads to greater understanding. For example, William Golding's *Lord of the Flies* may be read as (1) a novel of adventure about the struggles of some English school boys to secure their rescue from an island, and although they have some hardships and must fight to survive the forces of superstition and nature, they are ultimately successful; (2) a story about the passage of a group of youngsters from childhood toward maturity and adulthood; (3) an examination of guilt and responsibility between the rights of the individual and the power of the mass; (4) a criticism of world power politics and the use of force as an instrument for the settlement of disputes; or (5) an analysis of philosophical and idealogical concepts in conflict with one another. How the different levels of meaning are interwoven and assist one another and how they are linked with the action in the story has to do with the work's structural form: its art form. The form is the concern of formalistic analysis, and a formalist tries to discover what a work means by first discovering *how* the work expresses its meaning through its structural form.

## What Do Formalists Look For?

Formalistic analysis emphasizes certain language devices as a means toward understanding form. Actually these language devices are many of the same ones that are considered important in other analytical approaches (which you studied previously) but the formalist concentrates upon them with an intensity that is not shared by the others. By way of review, the major language interests of formalistic analysis follow:

### 1. Semantics

Semantics, the study of word meanings in language or the study of communication processes themselves, belongs at the head of any list of formalistic interests. Semantics, for instance, is concerned with topics like the ritual use of language, fallacious reasoning, and connotation and denotation. Although formalists are interested in each of these semantic topics, they seem most interested in connotation, the meanings that words have in addition to their dictionary meanings.

A.  Denotation

A word denotes that which the dictionary states. In other words, denotation is the dictionary meaning of a word. Formalists use denotation to establish the connotation of words.

Example: mother = a female who has borne a child

B.  Connotation

Connotation is the meaning of a word *beyond* its dictionary meaning. Words acquire their connotations through their past histories, their associations, and the emotional responses they elicit.

Example: mother = beyond a female who has borne a child, mother may mean security, affection, home, selflessness, and love.

### 2. Imagery

Imagery represents sense experience through language. Words or phrases that explain how something looks (sight), feels (touch), tastes, sounds (hearing), or smells appeal to the senses.

Examples: golden poppies, cold showers, sour lemons, chirping birds, sulfur outhouses

### 3. Metaphor

Metaphor is an implied comparison between things that are essentially unlike. A metaphor implies that something *is* something else. The technique is

**82**

particularly useful for its power of suggestion in explaining or clarifying people, objects, ideas, or occurrences.

Examples: He is a pig; The boat sliced through the bay's chop; Freedom should soar on a warm summer's thermal; The early rising assassin prepared a mourning omelet of grief.

### 4. Symbolism

A symbol is anything in literature that means more than what it is. Often the meaning of an abstract idea may be represented in a story or poem by some object.

Examples: Youth and beauty are frequently pictured as a rose in poetry; In his novel *Moby Dick*, Melville used the whiteness of the whale to suggest many different meanings.

### 5. Irony

Irony is an apparent contradiction between what is said and what is meant or between what is done and what was intended.

Examples: A snow storm in May—what great weather for water skiing; The Bolshevik Revolution of 1918 was fought to free the working class from the oppression of the Tsars—now the workers are oppressed by the communist dictators.

### 6. Allusion

Allusion is an incidental reference, often brief, to other literature, previous history, mythology, or even an earlier part of the same work. An author uses allusion to make his ideas more easily understood by calling something familiar to the readers' attention. The most frequently used sources of allusions refer to Greek mythology, the King James Version of the Bible, and Shakespeare.

Example: George discovered, much to his displeasure, that by continuing his romance with Dawn, he was reaching for forbidden fruit. (The allusion is to Genesis where Adam and Eve have been forbidden to eat of the fruit of the Tree of Knowledge.)

### 7. Tone

Tone represents a writer's or a speaker's implied attitude toward his or her subject, audience, or self. Tone is the writer's point-of-view in expressing mood in a literary work.

Example: See "Apparently with no surprise" by Emily Dickinson on page 86.

EXERCISE #1:

_____ 1. The New Critics came together
A) after World War II
B) after the stockmarket crash of 1929
C) after World War I
D) after John Kennedy was elected president
E) after the Spanish-American War

_____ 2. The New Critics developed an approach to literature that became known as
A) symbolic analysis
B) archetypal analysis
C) structural analysis
D) traditional analysis
E) formalistic analysis

_____ 3. The New Critics took the view that the really important or valuable information may be derived only from
A) the text
B) the author
C) the era
D) the psychological symbols
E) linguistic authenticity

_____ 4. For a formalist it is through an examination of a work's _____ that its art may be discovered.
A) religious significance
B) form
C) psychic aura
D) mood
E) irony

_____ 5. Which of the following is NOT a concern of new criticism?
A) semantics
B) imagery
C) metaphor
D) Freudianism
E) allusion

Identify the figure of speech or literary device used in each of the following lines:

_____ 6. "A tap at the pane, the quick sharp scratch and blue spurt of a lighted match,"

_____ 7. "It is with words as with sunbeams—the more they are condensed, the deeper they burn."

_____ 8.  "In the garden there strayed
A beautiful maid
As fair as the flowers of the morn;
The first hour of her life
She was made a man's wife
And was buried before she was born."

*Anonymous*

_____ 9. Some dirty dog took my parking place.

_____ 10. "When blood is nipped and ways be foul,
Then nightly sings the staring owl,"

**84**

*Learning Activity #2:*

## What Formalists Ignore

If you look closely at the analytical devices of formalistic analysis, they are an attempt to understand and explicate a literary work's structure and texture by isolating its parts to see how they relate to the form of the whole. The complete emphasis is upon the work itself. Therefore, formalistic analysis ignores the following:

1. the relation of a work to its historical age
2. the relation of a work to any other works of the same type
3. the relation of a work to any other works by the same author

No matter how interesting authors' lives may be or how intriguing the social significance of their works, these details are irrelevant to the formalist. Thus, formalists deal solely with the work itself. Consequently, one who wishes to employ the formalistic approach should not be tempted to become sidetracked by dealing with the fact that, for instance, Kurt Vonnegut, Jr., author of *Slaughter-House Five*, was a prisoner of war in Dresden, Germany when that city was firebombed by the Allies just as was Billy Pilgrim, the main character of his novel. Samuel Clemens' boyhood along the Mississippi River is interesting, but hardly necessary to an understanding of his book, *The Adventures of Huckleberry Finn*. Likewise, the speculation that the poet Walt Whitman may have been homosexual or that Samuel Taylor Coleridge was addicted to drugs or that Shakespeare's sonnets were written to some "dark lady" are all, while interesting sidelights for speculation, without importance to any formalistic explication of their writing. What is important is what can be found within the literature itself.

## Universal Appeal

Putting aside the esoterica of sociological, biographical, and historical information, the formalist concentrates upon the work—the poem, the short story, the drama, or the novel—as a pattern of words. Because they are set down on the page in a particular and precise way, they form a structure that has a meaning of its own—a structural form that is art. Unlike the newspaper story that simply reports an event, the work of art has built into it the form that gives it *universal appeal*, an appeal that touches almost everyone who reads it—today as in the past and, undoubtedly, into the future.

Emily Dickinson's poems have that element of universal appeal. No journalistic report, "Apparently with no surprise" appeals to most everyone with its comment upon the apparent contradiction between faith and beauty and an approving, indifferent Almighty.

## APPARENTLY WITH NO SURPRISE

Apparently with no surprise
To any happy flower,
The frost beheads it at its play
In accidental power.
The blond assassin passes on,
The sun proceeds unmoved
To measure off another day
For an approving God.

*—Emily Dickinson*

While the formalist never confuses the plot summary or prose paraphrase of literary art works with an in-depth critical analysis, summary may still be quite useful as a preliminary technique to discover a work's meaning. Beyond these preliminary efforts, however, lies the hard work of discovering the underlying principles by which the form of the work is shown to be an integral part of the content. This relationship is discovered by a close textual examination of the imagery, the tone, word and phrase connotations, irony, and allusion employed by the writer. It is this concentration upon words and form that keeps the reader concerned with art rather than background, with art rather than philosophy, sociology, or psychology.

### *Learning Activity #3:*

#### *Writing the Formalistic Analysis*

First, read "The Snake" by John Steinbeck (see page 218). Do not go any further in this unit until you have read the story. Reread "The Snake" several times until you are quite familiar with all of its parts. Begin to ask yourself questions about it as you become more and more familiar with the story's events. Concentrate upon what happens and why. Think about the characters, the setting, and the language. Following are some questions that you might ask about this story.

1. What is Dr. Phillips' attitude toward his work?

   Dr. Phillips sees himself as a scientist: objective, clinical, and unaffected by emotions. He seems to have constructed for himself a little world of his own, isolated and separate from the world of human contact. He seems to feel that what he is doing is important; he seems to feel a bit superior to others. The story is clearly seen through his eyes.

2. Why does the woman come to the laboratory?

   The woman wants to purchase a snake. Her reasons are ambiguous; at least we do not see her motives clearly because the story is not through her eyes. We only become acquainted with her through Dr. Phillips' perceptions of her.

3. Why is Dr. Phillips so irritated with the woman's visit?

   Dr. Phillips has very carefully isolated himself from the world of humans; therefore, he finds any outside intrusion unwelcome. Moreover, his scientific, clinical, objective domain is challenged by his emotional overtones to the woman and her purpose. Dr. Phillips' emotions seem to be in conflict, for he is both attracted to and revolted by the events of the evening.

**86**

4. Why does not Dr. Phillips simply ask the woman to leave?

Dr. Phillips seems uncertain of himself. He does not wish to be rude yet he seems to lack the diplomatic social skills necessary to be either graceful as a host or polite in requesting her to return at a time more convenient for him.

5. How does Dr. Phillips treat the woman?

Dr. Phillips, unsure of his own feelings, attempts cruelly to shock his guest. He first impolitely lectures on the biological reproduction of starfish then prepares the cat he has just executed for examination by students in biology classes. He is plainly upset that his work neither disturbs the woman nor even interests her.

6. What is Dr. Phillips' reaction to the evening's events after the woman leaves?

Dr. Phillips has had his snug little world disturbed. He has been unable to deal with his emotional responses to what has occurred, nor, for that matter, to the woman herself.

7. Why is Dr. Phillips so increasingly disturbed by his guest?

Dr. Phillips is apparently proud of his work and his knowledge. He is accustomed to awed, respected treatment, and his guest's indifference bothers him. Furthermore, as the visit continues, he begins to notice certain physical peculiarities in the woman that cause her to look more and more snake-like in the doctor's eyes. This accelerating visual image reaches its most profound impact upon the doctor when he refuses to look at the woman for fear she is opening her mouth just as the snake is opening its mouth to consume the rat.

8. Why are there repeated references to the sound of waves under the laboratory?

First, the waves repeatedly remind us of both the story's setting and of the physical and emotional isolation of the little laboratory, and of Dr. Phillips. Second, the sound of the water grows louder as the story's tension accelerates in intensity. After the tention of the immediate events subsides, the sound of the water is reduced to a gentle whisper.

9. What language devices or techniques are used in the story?

The answer to this question is, of course, many. You should have discovered several by simply rereading and asking questions about what is happening in the story. The following is not an exhaustive list of techniques you could find in the story. It is, rather, only a suggestion to start you on your analysis:

A. Imagery—Sound is an important part of the setting. The kettle on the stove hums, the rats scramble, and cats mew. Underneath, the waves lap against the piles while the snakes hiss. What other imagery can you find in the story?

B. Metaphor—"The person is the rat." People as animal metaphors are central to the theme of the story. Can you find other metaphors?

C. Symbolism—Dr. Phillips is himself a symbol of a modern scientific attitude of professional objectivity.

D. Irony—It is ironic that Dr. Phillips' clinical professionalism leaves him helpless in the presence of the woman.

E. Allusion—"If I knew—no, I can't pray to anything," alludes to the popular notion that scientists do not believe in supernatural beings, such as gods; therefore, his scientific background leaves him without any emotional support.

F. Tone—The story is seen only through Dr. Phillips' eyes, and we share in his loneliness. We understand his philosophy and his professional bias. The tension that we feel as the mood of the story becomes uneasy, even fearful, is the doctor's fear and his mood. The tone, then, is one of fear; the doctor's attitude toward himself, perhaps Steinbeck's attitude toward science, is revealed in "The Snake."

## Identifying a Topic for Analysis

By now you should be quite familiar with the selection; consequently, you can begin to identify a topic for analysis that interests you. Here you should ask yourself if the topic you are considering is sufficiently interesting to be worth your effort. Once you are certain that it is worthwhile, you should choose a topic for analysis that grows out of the questions you asked about the literary selection. Some topics that might be considered for "The Snake" are as follows:

1. How the setting enhances and contributes to the tone.
2. How the woman challenges the doctor's philosophy.
3. The use of literary techniques to reveal the theme.

## Dividing the Topic

Now you are ready to develop your elements into a *working* thesis, a thesis sufficiently well thought out to begin writing but which might need some editing.

Once you have a working thesis, you can proceed promptly to the development of your outline. Beginning with your thesis, think about the paragraph division you want in your analysis. Then, when you have carefully considered what you want to cover, write out your potential topic sentences, in order, under your selected thesis.

Example: "The Snake"

1. The use of symbolism
2. The use of imagery
3. The use of metaphor to develop theme

## Possible Thesis Statements

Draft #1: Steinbeck employs symbolism, imagery, and metaphor to develop his theme.

Draft #2: The metaphoric connection between snake and woman is developed through the use of symbolism and imagery.

Still, for a short paper either one of these thesis sentences could go over 1,000 words; therefore, the thesis needs further narrowing.

Draft #3: Although he uses several literary devices in "The Snake," Steinbeck relies heavily upon imagery to create a metaphoric connection between the woman and the rattlesnake.

## The Outline

Once you have a working thesis, you can proceed promptly to the development of your outline. Beginning with your thesis think about the paragraph division you want in your analysis. Then, when you have carefully considered what you want to cover, write out your potential topic sentences, in order, under your selected thesis.

*Example:*

Thesis—Although he uses several literary devices in "The Snake," John Steinbeck relies heavily upon imagery to create a metaphoric connection between the woman and the rattlesnake.

Topic Sentence #1—Close examination of the story reveals that no metaphors actually compare the visiting woman with the snake she buys, but the imagery and the implied comparisons make this relationship impossible to overlook.

Topic Sentence #2—The movement of the snake and woman are also similar.

Topic Sentence #3—Situations that would probably cause some sort of reaction in most people do not even make her blink.

Topic Sentence #4—The woman's snake-like presence makes the doctor uneasy which further reveals her serpentine connection.

Topic Sentence #5—Even the snake seemed to recognize the connection.

## The Analysis

Now you should be ready to develop your full analysis. You have become familiar with the story's structure and after several readings you have discovered its many literary techniques. Moreover, you have asked yourself a whole list of questions about the story's situation and its structure. You have also developed a working thesis and carried it through several versions. The outline has been written; it is now time to write the first draft of the analysis. After revision, correcting for content and mechanical errors, and rewriting to correct any structural problems, you should be ready to write out your final copy.

The following student paper was written after having carried out these steps:

B. J. Henning
English 1B
Dr. Guches
October 14, 1975

THE SNAKE CHARMER

A FORMALISTIC CRITICAL ANALYSIS OF JOHN STEINBECK'S

THE SNAKE

John Steinbeck's short story "The Snake" has but two human
characters.  One is a solitary, studious scientist who lives and works
in an old, bleak laboratory building.  "Dr. Phillips climbed up the
wooden steps . . . and built a fire in the tin stove."  His bedroom,
". . . a book-lined cell, containing an army cot, a reading lamp, and
an uncomfortable chair" shows he has only the bare essentials.  The
words "cell" and "uncomfortable chair" infer that he is not especially
happy and that living there is rather tedious.  The second character
is a woman, a stranger, who comes to see the doctor about the purchase
of a male rattlesnake.  She buys one, feeds it a rat, then leaves never
to be seen again.  Although he uses several literary devices in "The
Snake," John Steinbeck relies heavily upon imagery to create a metaphoric connection between the woman and the rattlesnake.

A close examination of "The Snake" reveals that no metaphors
actually compare the visiting woman with the snake she purchases, but
the imagery and the implied comparisons make this relationship impossible to overlook.  The physical features of the woman and the snake
are remarkably similar.  The snake has ". . . dusty eyes that seemed
to look at nothing."  The woman's eyes are mentioned several times;
they ". . . glittered in the strong light . . ." much like a snake's
would when under a similar situation.  "Her eyes came out of their
dusty dream for a moment . . . her dusty eyes . . . her black eyes
were on him, but they did not seem to see him."  Dr. Phillips finds
himself avoiding ". . . the dark eyes that did not seem to look at anything."  A rattlesnake is slim in body.  It has a flat forehead, a
small chin, a blunt nose, and virtually no lips.  It is not a color-
ful reptile.  The woman had eyes with ". . . irises (that) were as
dark as the pupils, there was no color line between the two."  A snake

**90**

has no line between iris and pupil either.   ". . . The blunt dry
head . . . (and) with its blunt nose" describe physical characteristics of the snake that also pertain to the woman.  She is "a tall lean
woman . . . (with hair) growing low on her flat forehead."  Dr.
Phillips notices ". . . how short her chin was between lower lip and
point."  Sometimes ". . . the beginning of a smile formed on her thin
lips."

The movements of snake and woman are also similar.  A snake seems
to glide and move quietly and effortlessly.  Usually it moves along
unnoticed.  "The snake moved out smoothly, slowly.  The motion was so
gradual, so smooth that it did not seem to be motion at all."  The
woman, too, is quiet.  "The woman's motions could not be heard . . . .
He had not heard her get up from the chair; . . . (moreover), he
could not hear her walk away on the pavement."  Reptiles have low metabolic rates; they awaken and move slowly unless provoked.  Dr. Phillips,
in reference to the woman, thinks to himself that she has a "low metabolic rate, almost as low as a frog's."  "She seemed to awaken
slowly . . . .  The doctor wanted to shock her out of her inanition . . . .  She was completely at rest . . . .  The rest of her
was in a state of suspended animation . . . .  She had not moved, she
was still at rest."

What little movement the woman displayed suggests a further comparison.  "Her head raised . . . her head swung around . . . ."  When
a snake stalks its prey, its body stiffens for attack.  "He keeps the
striking curve ready."  As the snake prepares to strike, the woman
". . . crouched and stiffened . . ." at the same time.  The snake
weaved slowly back and forth.  ". . . And while the woman watched the
snake, she was weaving too."  When the snake strikes to kill, it hits
and then retreats quickly and quietly to watch.  "The snake backed
hurriedly into the corner from which it had come, and settled
down . . ." while "she relaxed, relaxed sleepily" after the snake
struck.  The woman uses her hands little and speaks without expression.
While her hands are at rest in her lap, she almost seems to be a slim
form lacking those appendages.  "Her hands rested side by side on her
lap.  Her hands remained side by side on her lap . . . .  Her two

quiet hands did not move."  The woman's voice is soft, much like one
would imagine a snake's hiss would be--without expression.  She spoke
in a ". . . soft throaty voice, . . . she said softly, . . . in her
low monotone . . . she said in her soft flat voice . . . ."

        Situations that would probably cause some sort of reaction in
most women do not even make her blink.  She has no qualms about putting her hand among the rattlesnakes to move one to another place.
When Dr. Phillips jerks her away from the snakes, her only response is,
"'You put him in the other cage then.'"  The woman exhibits none of the
characteristic curiosity over the doctor's experiment and microscope;
". . . a lack of interest in what he was doing irritated him."  Gore
and death do not faze her; "she looked without expression at the cat's
open throat."

        The woman's snake-like presence makes the doctor very uneasy,
further revealing her reptilian connection.  He talks more loudly than
usual, which shows his discomfort:  ". . . he said rather loudly;"
"he shivered . . ." when she stares unconcernedly at the cat's open
throat, as if evil were in his presence.  Dr. Phillips is "drawn back"
to the cage where the woman stands after he moves away to continue his
starfish experiment.  She makes him feel strange.  He has fed many
rats to many snakes, yet he feels it is sinful this time, and ". . . he
did not know why this desire (to watch the snake feed) sickened him."

        When the woman and snake first see each other, it is strange that
the snake's ". . . tongue slipped out and hung quivering for a long
moment" rather than flicking in and out rapidly.  Even the snake seemed
to recognize the connection which obviously pleased the woman.  The
woman shows a possessiveness towards the snake; rather than saying that
she wants to feed him, she says, "I want to feed my snake."  The only
time she shows any emotion or expression is when she knows her snake
is going to eat.  When she asks to see the snake eat and the doctor
says yes, ". . . a beginning of a smile formed on her thin lips."
When she knows the snake is going to eat the dead rat, ". . . the
corners of the woman's mouth turned up a trifle again."  Dr. Phillips
finally admits that he is in the presence of evil when the snake is
in the process of swallowing the rat.  He says to himself, "'If she's

opening her mouth, I'll be sick.  I'll be afraid.'"

To make the connection between the woman and the snake that is
the implied metaphor in the story, Steinbeck uses considerable imagery.
From the outset, the similarity of woman and snake is obvious.  Their
movements are similar; the woman's snake-like features make the doctor
very uneasy.  Even the snake is aware of some sort of kinship with the
woman.  Ultimately, it is the effective use of the imagery that establishes the woman's serpentine qualities and gives the story its tension.

## EXERCISE #2:

For each of the following selections list three topics that might be developed in a
formalistic analysis.

1. "To His Coy Mistress," page 164

_____

_____

_____

_____

_____

2. "To Build a Fire," page 205

_____

_____

_____

_____

3. "I Am a Cowboy in the Boat of Ra," page 171

_____

_____

_____

_____

# Analyzing the Performing Arts

"The purpose of playing [acting], whose end, both at the first and now, was and is, to hold, as 'twere, the mirror up to Nature."

HAMLET, Act III, Scene 2, *William Shakespeare* (1564-1616)

Drama is meant to be performed, to be seen and not merely read. It is through the immediacy of the theatrical experience that drama takes on an aura that radically separates it from other literary genres. Playwrights visualize their work as a presentation to a group; novelists, poets, even essayists view their work as it affects the individual. Herein lies part of the fascination of the stage performance over the book, for the book's imagery is abstract in the mind while a play's imagery is present and alive. A play's imagery is effective since the actors convince the members of the audience that the acting that is transpiring before their eyes is both real and significant. If the members of the audience are convinced, they are transported to a level of consciousness that makes drama, for many people, the most thrilling of literary experiences.

*Objectives:*

After completing this unit, you will be able to:

1. Identify the main element of drama.
2. Define catharsis.
3. Distinguish between classical and modern tragedy.
4. Analyze a short play for its dramatic characteristics.

5. Assess the value of those techniques unique to film.
6. Appraise a film's use of ten cinematic techniques.
7. Evaluate a film's and a play's literary elements.
8. Distinguish among the component parts of tragedy.
9. Express more critical judgment in evaluating what you choose to view.

*Pre-Assessment:*

_____ 1. The most important difference between plays and other literary forms is that (A) plays are never read (B) plays are a group experience (C) plays cannot use metaphor and imagery (D) plays are not considered literature (E) plays are an individual experience.

_____ 2. Which of the following is NOT a convention of drama?
(A) Characterization is through speech and action.
(B) Tone is part of meaning.
(C) The playwright is outside the action.
(D) Characters' thoughts may not be suggested.
(E) Moods may be suggested by lighting.

_____ 3. A film maker uses symbols to (A) lengthen the film's dramatic impact (B) amuse the intelligent members of the audience (C) divert overemphasis upon the plot (D) make it similar to literature (E) stimulate feelings or thoughtfulness.

_____ 4. According to the Greek philosopher, Aristotle, literature is (A) a lie, thus sinful (B) an imitation of reality (C) a fruitless waste of energy (D) a mere diversion for the wealthy (E) an escape into fantasy.

_____ 5. Which of the following is NOT part of tragedy?
(A) antecedent action
(B) suspense
(C) narration
(D) reversal
(E) catastrophe

MATCHING:

_____ 6. Explains events that occur prior to the play's beginning

_____ 7. The emotional tension that sustains interest

_____ 8. Hints about the outcome

_____ 9. Point at which catastrophe becomes inevitable

_____ 10. The unraveling or untangling of the plot action

A. suspense
B. reversal
C. antecedent action
D. foreshadowing
E. dramatic irony
F. climax
G. catastrophe
H. denouement
I. narration

96

# ANALYZING THE PERFORMING ARTS

*Learning Activity #1:*

## The Play

Although drama includes many of the same techniques other literary genres employ, there exist some profound differences. While writers of short stories and novels and plays have stories to tell, writers of plays have somewhat fewer technique options at their disposal. Playwrights cannot overtly tell audiences what characters look like, what they think, why they do what they do, or even what they are doing; all these must be shown. And they are shown through the interpretation of actors. Out of these limitations come the *central conventions of drama.*

1. The playwright is outside the action.
2. Characterization is through speech and action.
3. Tone is part of the meaning.
4. Characters' thoughts may be suggested by a line's content *and* its delivery.
5. Mood may be suggested by lighting.

Since even a three-act play will probably last less than two hours, a play's action must be compressed. Even what seems to be minor action must contribute to the meaning of the whole. As a result, the playwright's use of metaphor and symbol must not be too subtle and must be obviously attached to the play's meaning.

Unlike novels, which may be very subtle (and long), a play, to be convincing, should be unified in time and space. This means that a play's subject matter should commence as near to the *end* of an action as practical. In other words, since the audience wants to see the action at its climactic point, the action should start rather close to that point. *Hamlet*, for instance, begins with the sighting of the ghost of Hamlet's father, not with the elder Hamlet's death or even with the plot that led to his death. Rather, the action starts at the point where the ghost sets into motion the action that precipitates the climax. Consequently, playrights often limit their plays to a believable time span and as few setting changes as are absolutely necessary.

The most important difference between plays and other literary forms is that drama is a group experience. Poems, novels, and short stories unfold within the mind of each individual reader; they appeal to individual emotions, relatively unaffected by outside stimuli. Plays, however, derive much of their response from the fact that members of the audience are affected by one another. Humor, for example, may bring more response because the whole group is reacting to it, and each individual reacts to both the humor and to the group. Moreover, watching something happen, watching it along with others, makes it seem more realistic. Although the audience only watches, individual members participate in the action by identifying with the emotions being portrayed before them.

A play, then, is a very different kind of experience for viewers than other

**97**

forms of literature are for readers. However, although they are intended to be viewed, we do read plays. Consequently, play readers need to put themselves into a director's frame of mind. Through this process, readers can take a view that, while it is somewhat different from other reading, reading a play can be a richly rewarding experience. Furthermore, the rewards of reading drama are enhanced directly in proportion to readers' skills and experience in maintaining the director's point of view. Also, it should be remembered that a character's meaning is often indicated by the way a line is spoken: its tone. Therefore, the director's point of view requires readers to become alert to even very subtle shifts in tone, or the meaning can be either misinterpreted or lost.

Read *The Stronger* by August Strindberg, page 224.

EXERCISE #1:

In one paragraph tell how the tone of Mrs. X changes from the beginning of the play to the end.

_____

_____

_____

_____

_____

_____

_____

_____

_____

_____

_____

EXERCISE #2:

Identify the literary techniques that you studied earlier in this book that Strindberg has written into his short play.

_____

_____

_____

_____

_____

_____

_____

*Learning Activity #2:*

### *Tragedy*

Many people feel that the highest form of drama, and perhaps of all literature, is tragedy. From its earliest beginnings in ancient Greece down to today's tragic drama, tragedy seems to have universal appeal. Aristotle (384-322 B.C.), an ancient Greek philosopher, formulated a philosophic theory regarding tragedy's wide appeal. First, Aristotle believed that literature (all art for that matter), is an imitation of reality. As such, literature presents a heightened and harmonious exercising of individuals' feelings. This exercising of feelings results in their enlargement and in their refinement which leads to the ability to form a more perfect total person, thus reconciling and integrating both emotions and intelligent art. This, according to Aristotle, has an ethically desirable effect upon the total well being of people. Part of this positive effect entails the purgation of emotions which he called *catharsis* (katharsis).

Specifically, catharsis, Aristotle believed, purged the emotions of pity and fear. This purgation is accomplished in tragic drama, for example, by first exciting then tranquilizing emotions; it excites in order to tranquilize. The Greek view, as Aristotle expressed it, gave catharsis credit for the removal of disturbing, painful elements by purifying them in tragedy. This almost medicinal idea seems to fit well not only into Greek culture but into modern ideas of the arts as well. Part of the fascination of drama would seem to be that the audience identifies with the characters, fears for them as they proceed toward the inevitable, pities them as they plummet into the catastrophe.

**99**

**Tragedy's Three Components:**

Good tragedy has three basic components as it proceeds: 1. a beginning (introduction; antecedent action), 2. a middle (suspense; reversal; climax), and 3. an end (denouement; catastrophe).

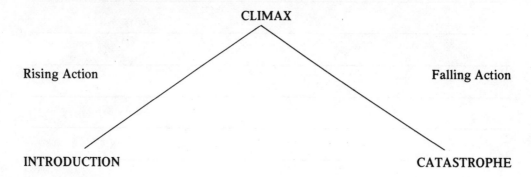

**Beginning**
1. *Introduction* (*How to Start*): Tragedy usually begins with one of five basic openings:
   a. a speech given by a major character
   b. small talk between minor characters
   c. a speech given by a chorus
   d. a recited prologue
   e. an exchange between major characters
   (*The Stronger* began with e above.)
2. *Antecedent Action:* In order to explain the present action of a play's characters, events that occur prior to the opening action must be explained. These events are the antecedent action. (In *The Stronger* we learn a great deal about the previous relationship of the two main characters and the relationship of each to Bob, the husband of Mrs. X.)

**Middle**
1. *Suspense:* As with any longer work of literature, something must be curious or sufficiently enthralling to maintain the self-discipline to read on or, as in the case with drama, to come back after the intermission. Without a doubt, one of the most effective methods of maintaining reader/viewer interest is through suspense. Suspense is more than simply curiosity, though. Suspense encompasses a tension, an emotional involvement that rivets spectators to their chairs or makes it nearly impossible to put down certain books. Suspense requires somewhat more than simply passive involvement with the literature; its cathartic effect fulfills our expectations and so intrigues us that we feel cleansed afterward.

   A playright may not only heighten suspense by making the members of the audience experience curiosity, and uncertainty or excitement because they do not know the outcome, but also through the technique of *foreshadowing*. Foreshadowing, you should remember, hints at what the outcome will be without actually giving away the plot. Sometimes foreshadowing is accomplished by dwelling on something that will be important later. For example, the letter opener that will later become the murder weapon in a mystery play will be examined and commented upon early in the action. In the popular movie *Jaws*, for another example, a picture of a shark destroying a small boat is shown relatively early in the film. This foreshadows the destruction of the boat by the giant shark at the film's conclusion. By letting an audience see hints that mirror later events, their curiosity is stimulated and suspense is enhanced.

Dramatic irony may also be used to stimulate suspense.

2. *Reversal:* The dramatic turning point (reversal) for the protagonist is that point at which it is discovered that the fate that was expected is not the fate that will transpire. Often during the beginning and the middle of a play, plans are made, character relationships established, and certain events are expected. Then suddenly, a dramatic reversal reveals that the main character's expectations will not occur as were anticipated. For example, Romeo, thinking that Juliet is dead, kills himself. Hamlet, seeking vengeance and the throne, is himself the object of vengeance which results in his death. Captain Ahab in *Moby Dick*, seeking to destroy the great white whale, is himself destroyed by the whale. The reversal is sometimes an odd twist of fate and at other times a logical outgrowth of a character's personality; in any case, the technique is dramatic and contributes to a play's cathartic value.

3. *Climax:* An often misunderstood term, the dramatic climax is not at the end of a play nor is it usually near the catastrophic events. Rather, the climax is that point at which the catastrophe becomes inevitable. Actually in many plays, such as in Shakespeare's tragedies, the climax comes during Act Three—directly in the middle of the play. For example, in *Hamlet's* rising action there are exposition, antecedent action, character introduction, and conflict. All these contribute to what Aristotle called "the complications" and results in mounting tension (suspense). The rising action peaks at the climax, after which the falling action begins. This falling action or turning point begins and the tragedy proceeds rapidly toward disaster again in *Hamlet*, when Hamlet mistakenly kills the King's chief counselor, the old fool Polonius.

**End**

*Catastrophe and Denouement:* Closely related in tragedy, the catastrophe and the denouement come at or near the end of a play. The catastrophe is that point at which the protagonist, and often those allies and loyal friends about him, are killed. Denouement is a general term which means unraveling or untangling. In it the plot action ends and any unanswered questions are explained. A denouement is necessary to the achievement of a satisfying drama so that members of the audience do not leave the theater puzzled about any part of the dramatic story.

Modern tragedy, while essentially the same as classic tragedy, has undergone a certain shift in emphasis. Contemporary emphasis has changed what the ancient Greeks called fate (the will of the gods) to a greater concern for the environment. In other words, the modern fates are the society or the system or whatever controls people's destiny. Moreover, the characters in classic tragedy really cared what happened to tragic protagonists because their deaths changed the fortunes of all people in a society. Modern protagonists, by contrast, do not have the fortunes of society resting upon their shoulders. In fact, their lives or deaths seem to have no significant impact upon the societies in which they live.

## Willing Suspension of Disbelief

The willing suspension of disbelief, while an awkward sounding expression, is of essential importance to the performing arts. Basically, it means that while you are in a theater watching a play or a movie you must, for that period of time, suspend disbelief—that is, pretend to believe that what you are seeing is actually taking place right before your eyes. If you are not able to do this, then the play or movie fails. It fails because you, the audience, remain unmoved and untouched by what you see. If you do not willingly suspend your disbelief, then you can never be frightened, thrilled, excited, or brought to tears because throughout it all you know the actors are only pretending. The performing arts presuppose the ability to suspend disbelief willingly because without it people would not attend plays nor would they go to movies. Drama and film grip, excite, and intrigue us precisely because we believe, for a time, that reality is occurring on the stage or screen, right before our eyes. We can, therefore, immerse ourselves in the performing arts and escape into another reality.

Read *Riders to the Sea* by John Millington Synge (see page 227).

EXERCISE #3:

Earlier in this chapter it was stated that we become acquainted with the characters in a play by how they look, what they do, what they say, how they speak, and what opinions others have of them. After listing some facts about either Cathleen or Nora, write a description of the one you choose.

EXERCISE #4:

A) In one paragraph describe Aristotle's view of what effect tragedy has upon those who view it.

_____

_____

_____

_____

_____

_____

_____

_____

B) In what ways does the play *Riders to the Sea* meet the requirements of tragedy?

_____

_____

_____

_____

_____

_____

C) In what ways does the play *Riders to the Sea* not meet the requirements of tragedy?

_____

_____

_____

_____

_____

_____

_____

**103**

*Learning Activity #3:*

### Film

While stage drama is greatly admired and quite popular, modern interest in performing arts centers upon the medium of film. Film, whether in a movie house or on the television screen, has the mass appeal and the financial rewards that can never be achieved by live actors upon a stage. Consequently, the movie, and its ability to stimulate emotional responses similar to those encouraged in stage productions, has become the dominant performing art of the twentieth century.

While there are certainly strong similarities between film and other kinds of literature, there are also significant differences. Analyzing a film, for example, is strikingly different from analyzing any other form of literature. It must be remembered that the film exists only on the celluloid and only in the theater; as a result, the film must be viewed. Whereas you may lay down a novel or short story and return to it at some later time, a film, like a play, is a continuous experience. Unless you attend another performance, you cannot simply pick up again from where you left off. Reading a film's script is a weak substitute to the multi-layered experience of viewing a movie because the script represents but a starting point, not a completed product. Consequently, writing an analysis of a film requires a good memory of what one saw in the film, but if one is sufficiently prepared by knowing what to look for, a critical analysis of a movie should not be particularly difficult.

*Steps in Analyzing a Film*

1. See the movie (more than once if possible).
2. Record your first impression.
3. Analyze your initial reaction.
4. Analyze the setting's significance.
5. Analyze the story's events.
6. Analyze the camera and editing techniques.
7. Analyze the film's characters (with some consideration of the actors' successes or failures to portray the characters effectively).
8. Analyze the film's symbols.
9. Examine the film's underlying idea (theme).
10. Write the analysis.

One must keep in mind that, as with all literature, popularity has little to do with art. This is especially true with film. It seldom happens that a film is both an effective work of art *and* a popular success with the general viewing public. In all probability it is a rare coincidence. The reason for this phenomenon should not be too difficult to understand, however. Most people go to the movies to be simply entertained. They want to laugh, to be thrilled, to be frightened, to live and enjoy in a way that they feel is absent from their own experiences. In other words, they do not go to the movies for the purpose of learning great truths. *However,* and this is an important "however," a good film—one that is both art and entertaining—employs the techniques of drama and other

**104**

literature to express truth—that is, to ask the universal questions and propose the tentative answers with which all great literature deals.

The theme of a film, not the plot, is often discernible by a repetition of visual symbols and the use of metaphors. As with metaphor in any literature, a cinematic metaphor is achieved through an implied comparison of similar things. In *The Planet of the Apes*, for example, the metaphoric comparison is between civilizations—apes and humans; in the barroom scene in *Star Wars* the comparison is between the technologically advanced civilization and the American old west. In *The Deer Hunter* the comparison is between hunting and war, and in *Easy Rider*, between motorcycles and horses.

A film uses symbols to stimulate feelings or thoughtfulness. Consider, for example, the monoliths of *2001: A Space Odyssey* or the Statue of Liberty at the end of *The Planet of the Apes*. Other film symbols have included the following: games of Russian roulette (*The Deer Hunter*), clocks (*High Noon*), a snow sled (*Citizen Kane*), and a pair of ball bearings (*The Caine Mutiny*).

Through an analysis of its metaphors and symbols, the theme of a film may be determined, and the relationship of the theme to the experiences of the viewers may be explored. Some ways to reveal a film's theme are to ask questions such as the following:

1. What is the *real* subject of the film?
2. Does the theme relate to the plot?
3. What are the metaphors and symbols?
4. Do the technical elements (sound, photography, setting) of the film promote or interfere with the development of the theme?

While such elements as theme, plot, and setting are useful in analyzing both movies and literature, some further elements are important to film. The total effect of a movie may involve some or all of the following; as a result, each should be considered as to its individual contribution and effect upon the whole film.

1. Theme
2. Plot
3. Script
4. Acting
5. Setting
6. Costumes and makeup
7. Sound
8. Photography
9. Direction
10. Editing

| *The Deer Hunter* | *The China Syndrome* |
|---|---|
| **THEME** | |
| —The effects of war upon the lives of those it touches. | —The consequences of individual action when it is contrary to the will of those in power. |

## PLOT

—The lives of a group of American steelworkers of Russian descent are radically altered by their experiences during the Vietnam War.

—A local television news crew stumbles upon serious defects in a nuclear power plant and elicits the assistance of a shift supervisor to make the truth public.

## SCRIPT

—The dialogue is lifelike and the continuity of the movie helps develop the plot. Moreover, the script makes the theme quite clear.

—The dialogue is realistic and the script clearly develops the theme.

## ACTING

—The acting is extraordinarily good as the actors capture the essence of blue-collar steelworkers caught up in the war. They give authenticity to their roles by living, as did actor Robert DeNiro, in a steel town with working men like those they would portray.

—Although the principals are well known, they successfully submersed their personalities into the characters they portrayed. Jane Fonda studied a local news team and went on assignment with it and Michael Douglas patterned his character after a well-known, independent photographer.

## SETTING

—Filmed on location in Pennsylvania, Washington State, and Thailand, the settings are visually stunning and realistic.

—Much of the action takes place inside a nuclear power plant and a television studio which lends realism to the action.

## COSTUMES AND MAKEUP

—The costuming and makeup is consistent with the kind of people and the kind of activity portrayed—blue-collar workers who are seen at work, at a wedding, on a hunting trip, and at a funeral.

—The costuming and makeup are appropriately inconsistent as are people who dress for the TV çamera but are actually on assignment where their dress is often inappropriate, e.g. prettily dressed, hair in place as if ready for an evening out but wearing a hardhat eight stories underground in the generating portion of a power plant.

## SOUND

—Stunningly effective sound (Dolby Stereo) inside the steel mill and especially at war—helicopters, explosions, and the thud of a pistol hammer hitting an empty chamber. However, some overdone musical background during hunting sequences is almost comic.

—Remarkably effective use of natural sound without musical background during much of the action.

## PHOTOGRAPHY

—Misty, ethereal lighting and use of filters give hunting sequences a spiritual quality. Emphasis is upon the faces of those in the center of the action.

—Camera angles place characters in context by framing them with appropriate backgrounds—the dome of the cooling tower or the dials in the instrument room. Also, effective use of TV monitor console to show simultaneous action through multiple images.

## DIRECTING

—Although the film's component parts fit well together, there are some scenes that do not seem necessary, especially since the movie is overlong. E.g. two scenes that could have been left out were the ones where Michael runs through the streets throwing off his clothes, and on the hunting trip when they stop by the side of the road and then repeatedly pretend to leave one of their party behind.

—The component parts of the film work well together and there seem to be no gratuitous scenes.

## EDITING

—The editing is brisk and generally adds to the illumination of the theme by sharply juxtaposing contrasting elements. One particularly effective bit of editing is the sudden jump from the end of the hunt to the heat of a Vietnam jungle battle.

—The picture flowed smoothly with no sharp jumps that were obtrusive or interfered with the chronological development of the story.

**EXERCISE #5:**

In the space provided, write a short evaluation for each of the categories listed above for a film that you have recently seen.

Name of film_____

Theme— _____

_____

_____

_____

Plot— _____

_____

_____

_____

Script— _____

_____

_____

Acting— _____

_____

_____

_____

Setting— _____

_____

_____

_____

**108**

Costumes and make-up— _____

_____

_____

_____

_____

Sound— _____

_____

_____

_____

Photography— _____

_____

_____

_____

Direction— _____

_____

_____

_____

Editing— _____

_____

_____

_____

_____

"The novel is concerned with *what has happened*. The theater asks
*what is about to happen*. The screen tells us *what is happening* . . . ."
*John Howard Lawson*

# Psychological and Archetypal Analysis

After Sigmund Freud began to probe the inner workings of the human mind through the psychoanalytic techniques he developed, literary critics and writers began to view literature in new and strikingly different ways. Critics looked at previous literature, all the way back to the ancient Greeks, for clues to the inner motivation of both writers and their characters. Writers, meanwhile, began to develop new types of characters, characters who could be understood fully only in light of Freud's theories. The psychoanalytic approach to literature is an outgrowth of the belief that, while Freud may have made certain psychic discoveries, what he discovered was not something new at all but may be likened to discovering gold in the American River in California in 1848. Both the human psyche and the gold were always there; it merely took Sigmund Freud and James Marshall, respectively, to make their discoveries. Consequently, if the inner psyche had always been there, then its evidence would surely exist in previous literature. While most literature prior to Freud's publishing his findings has been analyzed psychologically, the literature that was written with familiarity with Freud's theories was published in the nineteen twenties, thirties, and forties. Any serious student of literature today needs at least a rudimentary understanding of Freud's basic tenets to be perceptive about the literature of the twentieth century.

As innovative and astounding as Freud's work was, it has now become dated. As more and more research accumulates, it appears that Freud's theories only just tapped the hidden recesses of the psyche. Moreover, another psychologist—a student and later an adversary of Freud, Carl Jung—

went on to found his own school of psychology that has greatly influenced writers and critics of modern literature.

Many modern theorists and critics believe that the significance of a work of art may well lie in its universality—its appeal to all peoples regardless of time or culture. Certain images or situations create similar emotional responses in humans. Consequently, both visual or graphic artists and writers attempt to duplicate or imitate those experiences that create the most striking responses. Particularly in literature, this appeal to universal elements is both a joy and a critical puzzle for readers because emotional responses to literature are so universally satisfying, and because the origin of the responses is so bewildering. Critical readers should, however, be able to identify a selection's particular universal elements thereby enhancing their understanding of it. While it is rewarding for students of literature to interpret symbolism and structural techniques, the identification of archetypal elements can lead readers to the much deeper understanding necessary to realize fully a work's value.

Sometimes referred to as myth criticism, archetypal analysis is a method of criticism that enhances readers' critical abilities by requiring them to probe deeply into the mythic origins of the symbols, the imagery, and the situations that create emotional, universal reactions.

## Objectives:

After completing this unit, you will be able to:

1. Describe the archetypal or mythic approach to literary interpretation.
2. Define the literary terms that form the basic vocabulary of psychological and archetypal analysis.
3. Illustrate the relationship between the archetypal point of view and religion, anthropology, and mythology and the psychological point of view of the biological and experimental sciences.
4. Write an archetypal analysis of a literary selection.
5. Relate a story's psychological and archetypal elements.
6. Assess the contributions mythology has made upon contemporary life.
7. Appraise the value of the archetype of creation upon humans.
8. Evaluate how the shadow, anima, and persona affect your daily life.
9. Interpret a story's reliance upon the archetype of the hero.
10. Assess the effect of the unconscious mind upon literature.
11. Express greater confidence in your understanding of human nature in literature.

Place the letter of the correct answer in the space at the left of each question.

_____ 1. Archetypal analysis is based upon the work of (A) Sigmund Freud, (B) Carl Jung, (C) Charles Darwin, (D) C. P. Snow, (E) Rollo May.

_____ 2. Which of the following is NOT a characteristic of archetypes? (A) primordial, (B) universal, (C) recurrent, (D) personal, (E) part of the collective unconscious.

_____ 3. Groups of mythic situations that together make up a larger, universal story are referred to as archetypal (A) motifs, (B) images, (C) shadows, (D) animas, (E) initiations.

_____ 4. Which of the following is NOT an archetypal image of women? (A) earth mother, (B) the temptress, (C) the working woman, (D) soulmate, (E) mom.

_____ 5. The archetypal hero (A) usually achieves a victory over a king or a wild beast, (B) never becomes the king, (C) loses the beautiful princess, (D) has a happy childhood with his parents, (E) has the good graces of the gods throughout his life.

_____ 6. The part of the psyche called the shadow contains the (A) ego, (B) the psycho-motor responses, (C) initiation urge, (D) situations, (E) less pleasant aspects of the personality.

_____ 7. The anima represents the (A) bestial elements, (B) life force, (C) desire for idleness, (D) shadow, (E) male impulse.

_____ 8. The persona of a psychologically healthy, mature person must be (A) rigid, (B) satisfied, (C) rational, (D) arbitrary, (E) flexible.

_____ 9. Which of the following might lead to psychological problems? (A) a person who has a distorted view of his or her sexes' major attributes, (B) a conflict between the conscious and the unconscious, (C) a person who represses id drives, (D) all of the above.

_____ 10. Archetypes are found in the human psyche in the (A) personal unconscious, (B) subconscious, (C) collective unconscious, (D) spirit, (E) conscious.

_____ 11. The arbitrary zone of the human psyche is (A) id, (B) ego, (C) superego, (D) libido, (E) preconscious.

_____ 12. Freud asserted that dreams are the expressions of (A) the conscious mind, (B) the conscience, (C) the ego, (D) the unconscious mind, (E) the anima.

# PSYCHOLOGICAL AND ARCHETYPAL ANALYSIS

*Learning Activity #1:*

## *The Psychoanalysis of Sigmund Freud*

The implications of psychology have long been recognized as important to writers, who have perceived in human behavior certain forces, certain drives or needs that are significant motivators of human nature. Some of the world's most respected writers have supplied psychologists with such accurate case histories of mental functioning in their literature that their works have been cited as particularly significant in understanding human mental processes. Sophocles, Shakespeare, Dostoevsky, Melville, and Hawthorne among many others have contributed their insight about the human psyche through their literature. (Sigmund Freud wrote that it was "not I, but the poets [who] discovered the unconscious.") While psychologists have been busy searching through literature for authentication of their discoveries, writers and critics have been busy reading the works of such psychologists as Alfred Adler ("will to power" and "the inferiority complex"), Otto Rank ("the will and human personality"), Carl Jung ("introversion/extroversion" and "the collective unconscious"—see Learning Activity #4 of this chapter), and B. F. Skinner ("stimulus response" and "behavior modification through positive reinforcement"). The psychologist who has been the most influential in stimulating a psychoanalytical approach to literature, however, is Sigmund Freud (1856-1939).

Emphasizing individuals' conflicts, anxieties, and frustrations, psychoanalysis, as postulated by Freud, is primarily concerned with disturbed or abnormal people because it is a therapeutic science rather than a purely experimental discipline; it seeks to diagnose, treat, and cure. As a result, not all of Freud's theories are amenable to literary study, but those in the following list have been so influential as to alter the style of analytical thinking during this century.

Freud asserts that

1. the unconscious mind is pre-eminent,
2. the psyche is organized into three zones: id, ego, and superego,
3. dreams are manifestations of the unconscious mind,
4. infantile behavior is basically sexual,
5. neurosis is closely related to creativity.

### *1. The Unconscious Mind—*

*Most of the mental processes of human beings take place in the unconscious* is Freud's first major presupposition. Even the most conscious processes of the mind quickly become latent, although they may become conscious (active) later. Grouped in the "preconscious," he differentiates these processes from those that are found in the "unconscious," those that are brought to the conscious only with the greatest of difficulty or never at all.

Freud demonstrated through his carefully researched and recorded case studies that human actions are controlled by a psyche over which there exists only the most limited control. He likened the human mind to an iceberg: only

**114**

the smallest portion of the whole iceberg is above the water's surface as only the smallest portion of the human psyche is within the conscious. The great mass of an iceberg is out of sight, below the surface of the water, as most mental processes lie below the surface of consciousness.

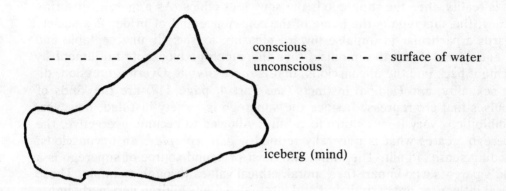

*2. The Psychic Zones: Id, Ego, Superego—*

Freud asserted that the mind's structural organization is in the form of psychic zones. These zones control certain of the mental functions out of which come human motivations.

A. *ID*—The id is totally submerged in the unconscious, and its function is to fulfill what is called the primordial life principle—or as Freud referred to it, the *pleasure principle*. Contained within the id is the *libido* from which comes the individual's psychic energy. Freud described this id as totally lacking in the laws of logic since mutually contradictory impulses may exist simultaneously without cancelling each other. Consequently, the id knows no ethics or values; it knows no good or evil; it encompasses no morality. Yet, the id is of source of human aggression and all desires. Since the id is both amoral and lawless, it demands gratification without regard for any religious or legal ethics, social conventions, or moral constraints. Concerned solely with instinctual, pleasurable gratification, the id would drive the individual to any lengths for this pleasure, even to self-destruction, for self-preservation is not an id impulse. Prior to Freud, these instincts toward excessive pleasure were attributed to outside, often supernatural, forces. In many ways, the old Puritan concept of the devil fits within the id psychic zone. Small children, not yet imbued with the restraints of society, operate on pure id impulses. They are egocentric, selfish, and solely interested in their own pleasure. Occasionally, one hears the old phrase that a child who is misbehaving is "full of the devil."

B. *EGO*—The ego is usually thought of as the conscious mind; however, a portion of it resides in the unconscious. Referred to as the *reality principle*, the ego's function is to govern the id and channel the id's drives into socially acceptable outlets. Since the id's pleasure demands are often not immediately obtainable, the ego postpones or even alters the demands into drives that are realistically obtainable. The ego's function is, then, to determine when,

**115**

where, and how the id's demands might best be gratified in ways that are acceptable for the well-being of the individual. In a normal, well-balanced person the ego and the id work harmoniously together; when the two are in conflict, repression and neurosis result.

C. *SUPEREGO*—If the id is the source of the drive for pleasure and the ego is reality, then the superego is the source of ethics. As a moral, censoring agency, the superego is the home of the conscience and of pride. If a society regards a particular id impulse toward pleasure as socially unacceptable and the ego cannot divert the impulse, then the superego blocks its fulfillment by forcing it back into the unconscious, that is *repressing* it. Overt aggression, direct sexuality, and Oedipal instincts (see Part 4, page 117) are the kinds of impulses that are repressed; since the superego is society-instilled, however, its inhibitions vary from culture to culture. Allowed to become overactive, the superego creates what is generally termed a *guilt complex*: an unconscious, brooding sense of guilt. The initial and most profound source of superego is a child's parents who impart their moral, ethical values through example. These ethical influences are assimilated and internalized by children very early in life (before school age); later, the outside influences of school, church, and peer group have some effect, but they are not nearly as influential as are the parents early in life.

## OVERVIEW

ID—Pleasure Principle
    —the source of energy
    —impulse toward satisfaction
    —no logic
    —no values
    —amoral
    —source of aggressions and desires
    —theologically similar to the Devil

EGO—Reality Principle
    —rationality
    —regulates id's drives
    —mediating agency of psyche

SUPEREGO—Morality Principle
    —protects society
    —censors or represses the id
    —source of conscience and pride

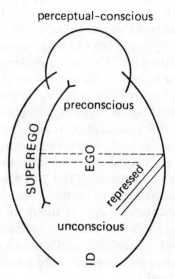

*3. Dreams—*

Since the unconscious is not observable by direct examination, the id may be revealed only through deep hypnosis, during unintentional expressions ("Freudian slips"), and during sleep through the analysis of dreams. Unfortunately, even during dreaming the inhibiting power of the superego is still

**116**

functioning; consequently, Freud viewed dreams themselves as only symbols of the unsatisfied and repressed desires of the id. If a dream's symbolic function comes too close to reality then the dreamer awakes and is often unable to recall the dream's content. Since dreams are expressions of the id, and the id is the source of sexual needs and desires, dreams are, Freud believed, best interpreted in terms of repressed sexuality. This theory has led many psychoanalytical critics to examine literature for images that are concave—calling them female or womb symbols (e.g. ponds, cups, rings, caves, wells), and for images that have greater length than diameter—calling them male or phallic symbols (e.g. swords, knives, towers, snakes, power poles, arrows, keys). Still other images are seen as sexual intercourse symbols (e.g. flying, walking on stairs, dancing, riding).

The greatest criticism of psychological analysis results from the overuse of sexual symbolism by psychoanalytic critics. These symbols, while they may help to suggest directions for further analysis are, in reality, far too simplistic for serious analytical work. Even Freud argued that dream images are too personal to use for general interpretation because they are not sufficiently universal. Many critics have employed dream symbol analysis to examine literature, however, and some continue to find insights into human and character motivation through its use.

## 4. Infantile Behavior—

While, at one time, the typical opinion held that children simply did not have sexual development until puberty, Freud asserted that childhood is, in fact, an intense period of erotic experience. (However, Freud's use of the term *sexual* is much broader in definition than the popular notion.) During the first years of children's lives, they pass through phases of sexual growth that are centered in *erogenous* zones, a portion of the human body where sexual pleasure is most intense. Freud identified three erogenous areas upon which children focus as they move toward maturation:

oral
anal
genital

These zones are connected with those id functions that demand gratification (and that are capable of giving pleasure since they are associated with such vital needs). The gratification and pleasure come through eating, eliminating, and sexuality. If children are unable to gratify a need, they may become *fixated* in that phase of development and this may result in an adult personality that is warped. For example, early weaning may result in oral fetishes such as cigarette smoking, fingernail biting, or compulsive pencil chewing. Excessively strict toilet training may lead to fastidiousness and obsessive orderliness. During the early genital phase, when children pass through an Oedipus complex (unconscious rivalry of a boy with his father over love for his mother) or an Electra complex (unconscious rivalry of a girl with her mother for love of her father), a frustrated rivalry with a parent may bring resentment toward parental authority and, as an adult, may manifest itself in an unreasonable hostility toward all authority.

**117**

## 5. Neurosis and Creativity

Sigmund Freud was interested in both psychology and literature. Indeed, Freud often expressed his indebtedness to literature as the best laboratory source to see his psychological observations in operation. Moreover, Freud's interest in psychology and literature led him to speculate about the nature of creativity. Freud asserted that writers, essentially introverted personality types, write as a sort of therapy that allows a kind of escape for repressed psychosexual desires. Consequently, the writer derives pleasure from the expressions of neuroses in ways that are socially acceptable.

Freud's ideas about the relationship between neurosis and creativity are used in three distinctly different ways by literary analysts. (1) The first way concentrates upon psychoanalyzing various writers by viewing their works essentially as expressions of neurotic tension produced by frustrated and repressed id drives. (2) The second way concentrates upon the psychological result of characters' infancy and childhood problems. While these problems are not themselves described in the literature, the problems' existence is clearly suggested by characters' actions. Emphasizing unconscious motivation for characters' actions, their style of criticism attempts to analyze characters' mental turmoil, fixations and repressions, and social or antisocial behavior. (3) The third, and most recent way, concentrates upon the repressions of puritanical, patriarchal society that writers are daring enough to reveal. The emphasis is here upon the unconscious of the majority in a society rather than upon the unconscious of writers or their characters.

Today, many critics and scholars are moving away from Freudian psychoanalysis. This disaffection for Freud may be attributed to two circumstances: first, the excesses of some psychoanalytic critics have resulted in their search through literature to find phallic and womb symbols and has generally attributed all literature to manifestations of repressed sexual fantasies. While sex certainly is a powerful source of human motivation, the zeal of Freudian critics to attribute *all* motivation to this human need, offends most casual readers and leads to a simplistic view of Freud's observations. Second, since Freud's death in 1939, research has continued and modern psychology has moved beyond Freud's findings. Besides, many people are put-off by Freud's diagnostic-treatment-cure approach which emphasizes the empirical sciences of biology and chemistry. Modern readers are less interested in therapy and more interested in literature as speculative, philosophic, and universal in its appeal; consequently, readers are more curious about literature's relationship to anthropology, religion, and mythology. It is this that has led to the current interest in the observations of one of Freud's students and early colleagues—Carl Jung (see Learning Activity #2).

EXERCISE #1:

Read "Young Goodman Brown" (p. 197) and list the psychological images and symbols that Hawthorne includes in his story. Consider the following:
1. What represents the unconscious?
2. What among the characters or setting represent psychic zone?
3. What are the dream symbols?
4. Of what psychological significance is it that Brown dreams the story?

_____

_____

_____

_____

_____

_____

_____

_____

_____

_____

_____

_____

_____

## Archetypes

The word *archetype* from Greek literally means *archo - tupos* or first type: the original pattern from which all other copies are made. The closest modern synonyms are prototype and model. From this definition you may begin to wonder how an analytical approach that emphasizes first patterns or models fits into a study of literature. Apparently even more confusing, archetypal analysis shares some of the basic concepts of other analytical approaches but completely rejects others. As with formalistic analysis, archetypal critics emphasize an intensively close, analytical reading of literature. Unlike the formalist, however, the archetypalist rejects the idea that nothing outside the printed page is of relevance. As one of the psychological critics, the archetypal critic searches the unconscious mind, but the interest is with the collective unconscious, those similarities in the unconscious shared by all humans, rather than with the unconscious of the personal or individual psyche. While all this may sound somewhat like Sigmund Freud, it is not. Archetypal analysis was developed by one of Freud's associates: Carl Jung (1875-1961), a Swiss psychologist. Archetypes, according to Jung, represent image or thematic patterns that are repeated so frequently in mythology, religion, and literature that they have taken on universal symbolic power.

Carl Jung, after working with Freud for several years, bitterly broke from the older man over differences in theory. While he agreed with Freud that all humans have, deep within their psyches, an unconscious which is unique to each individual, Jung further asserted that there exists one aspect of the unconscious mind that is the same for each individual in the human species. As each person's unconscious is the result of personal, environmental experience, Jung suggested that the *collective unconscious* is the mental record of all the experiences of those who have existed previously.

In his book, *Contributions to Analytical Psychology*, Jung states that there are three basic qualities that characterize archetypes. These archetypal qualities are *primordial, universal,* and *recurrent.*

### Primordial Characteristics

The most fundamental quality that characterizes archetypes is that they are *primordial:* they are within the preconscious, that area of the mind from which information can be recalled, even though it is not present in the conscious mind. As a result, these may sometimes be thought of as expressions of human's instinctual nature.

You must be very careful, however, about attributing instinctive motivations in humans. Very little agreement exists about the importance of human instincts or even about what they are. Most behavioral scientists agree that a human baby is born knowing how to suck and knowing a fear of falling. If you suggest most anything else as instinctual, however, you will find argument and controversy.

Although in the preconscious, the inborn behavior patterns that characterize most forms of lower animals—such as the migratory habits of whales, the nesting of birds, the ritual dances of bees, or the fear of hawks by chickens—is only partly related to what Jung is suggesting archetypes are in humans. What he has in mind is somewhat more subtle although it is based, as with animals, upon the same kinds of deep-rooted behavior that results from coded patterns. But, in humans, the experiences of the past that are so important for the species' survival, such as the fear of falling, are the result of untold numbers of experiences of the same kind, experiences that literally pre-exist consciousness. They are the *images* of an instinctual nature, the experiences of which were repeated so often that they formed deep impressions upon the human psyche. You might view this as having a cumulative effect much like what happens to photographic film passed through airport x-ray machines. One trip through an x-ray machine is probably not noticeable on the photographs, but if the film were to pass through the machines several times, as they would on a trip that required several flights, a haze would begin to appear. The more trips through the machine, the deeper the haze would become. The film "remembers" each x-ray and is affected by it; the human psyche remembers each experience and is cumulatively affected by it until it becomes codified into an archetype, buried deeply within the unconscious mind, and passed on by the species. These experiences represent those formed earliest in the development of the human species; therefore, they are primordial.

## Universal Characteristics

The second basic quality of archetypes is that they are *universal*; they are unaffected by time or situation, community or culture. They are now as they were in the past; they are as significant to the Tasaday tribe, so isolated in the jungles of the Philippines that they thought their twenty-four members were the only human beings in existence, as they are to NASA scientists, striving to solve the complex problems of space travel. The ancient Greeks battling over Helen at the walls of Troy were as affected by archetypes as are politicians today who are trying to calculate the interests and moods of the people so that successful election campaigns may be waged. Humans have changed little in the past 4,000 years of recorded history, an instant when compared with the backdrop of evolutionary time. The psychoneurological functions of the modern mind remain essentially unchanged from the minds of Neolithic peoples. As a result, we all share similar experiences, emotions, drives, needs, and archetypes with each other and with our ancient ancestors. Therefore, archetypes are truly universal.

## Recurrent Characteristics

The third basic quality of archetypes is that they are *recurrent*. Those who have conducted research in the fields of anthropology, comparative religion, and mythology have tended to confirm the similarities among peoples, while showing that what differences do exist are either inconsequential or local adaptation. It makes little difference, for example, where people are on the earth or when they exist; all people have been concerned with their creation and the meaning of their existence. These concerns are universal, therefore, archetypal. The most fascinating aspects of any comparison, however, comes with the realization that the explanations of human origin and worldly creation are strikingly similar.

For example, compare the following explanations of creation.

1. *Ancient Hewbrew*

King James
The First Book of Moses, Called
*GENESIS*

In the beginning God created the heaven and the earth.

And the earth was without form, and void; and darkness WAS upon the face of the deep. And the Spirit of God moved upon the face of the waters.

And God said, Let there be light: and there was light.

And God saw the light, that IT WAS good; and God divided the light from the darkness.

And God called the light Day, and the darkness he called Night. And the evening and the morning were the first day.

And God said, Let there be a firmament in the midst of the waters, and let it divide the waters from the waters.

And God made the firmament and divided the water which WERE under the firmament from the waters which WERE above the firmament; and it was so.

And God called the firmament Heaven. And the evening and the morning were the second day.

And God said, Let the waters under the heaven be gathered together unto one place, and let the dry LAND appear; and it was so.

And God called the dry LAND Earth; and the gathering together of the waters called he Seas: and God saw that IT WAS good.

(Later God [Yahueh (Jehovah) Elohin] took "the dust of the ground" to form the first man, Adam.)

2. *Ancient Greek*

In the beginning Earth, Sea, and Air were all mixed together in a formless, jumbled mass called Chaos

God and Nature, growing weary of the dead weight, at last put an end to the confusion by separating earth, sea, and heaven from one another

The brightest, lightest part of Chaos was formed into the sky; the air separated sky from earth, which because she was heaviest sank below buoyed by the water.

God and Nature then divided the earth by forming rivers, raising mountains, carving valleys, creating woods and fields and prairies.

The air, now cleared, let stars shine through; fishes ruled the sea, birds dominated the air and beasts prowled the land

But not all the gods were satisfied, a nobler animal was desired, so Prometheus, the creator, took some of the earth and carefully mixing it with water made man. He made man in the image of the gods so that among all the animals that must walk face downward, man walked upright, facing heavenward.

3. *Ancient Polynesian*

In the beginning everything was nothingness and void.

Slowly, ever so slowly Darkness began to emerge and

Darkness conceived something even greater—night

Night, after eons of time conceived thought which enlarged to Thought-Conception, then to Breath until it finally evolved to Thought in Immensity

After more eons passed Spirit and Breath of Life combined into the creator,
    Tangaloa, the Supreme
Tangaloa dwelt within the breathing space of Immensity.
The universe was in darkness, with water everywhere
There was no glimmer of dawn, no clearness, no light.
And he began by saying these words,
That he might cease remaining inactive.
"Darkness, become a light-possessing darkness."
And at once light appeared.
(Later Tangaloa—[or Ta'aroa as he was known in Tahiti and Kanaloa in Hawaii]
took clay and molded the first man, Tiki.)

While these explanations are remarkably similar, they serve also to
illustrate human concern with self-definition. All peoples want to understand
how the universe started and how humankind fits into the great plan of things.
Creation is, then, a fundamental recurrent archetype. Since creation involves
so much more than simply an image or single situation, all the stories together
form what is called a *motif*—in this instance, the archetypal motif of creation.
Of course, there are other motifs, but the creation motif is the most universal.

### Other Recurrent Archetypal Motifs

A. World Destruction by
    1. Flood
    2. Famine
    3. Plague
    4. Earthquake
B. Immortality
    1. Escape from time—beyond death, e.g. see stanza one of "To His
       Coy Mistress."
        a. Rewarded for "good" life—Valhalla; Elysian Fields; Heaven
        b. Punished for "bad" life—not permitted into the underworld;
                              condemned to the lowest region; Hell
    2. Submission into nature's eternal cycle, e.g. see stanza three of
       "To His Coy Mistress."
        a. Endless death and rebirth (e.g., the Phoenix bird)
        b. Loss of self into cyclical time
C. Hero (Savior or Deliverer) Tales
    1. The quest
    2. Initiation
        a. Separation
        b. Transformation
        c. Return
    3. Sacrificial scapegoat
D. Oedipus Legends
E. Slaying of Monsters
F. Sibling Rivalries
G. Incest Stories

EXERCISE #2:

Research another culture's creation motif—one not mentioned in this chapter—and relate it to the three previous stories of creation.

EXERCISE #3:

Write the answers to the following questions in the space provided.

1. Who is the originator of archetypal analysis? _____

2. Archetypes are located deep in a part of the mind referred to as what? _____

_____

3. Which of the following are generally agreed upon as instinctual behavior in human beings? (Circle the correct answer.)

yes   no   a. Sucking

yes   no   b. Fear of snakes

yes   no   c. Sex

yes   no   d. Fear of the dark

yes   no   e. Love of mother

yes   no   f. Fear of falling

yes   no   g. Taste for pablum

yes   no   h. Early dislike of school

yes   no   i. Fear of fire

yes   no   j. Eating three meals a day

4. What fields of research have tended to confirm the similarities of archetypes with all peoples?

a. _____

b. _____

c. _____

5. If an archetype involves a whole series of stories, it is referred to as an archetypal _____.

## Learning Activity #3:

### Images, Characters, and Situations

The possible number of potential archetypes is limited only by the number of recurrent human experiences. Deep within our collective unconsciousness may well lurk archetypes of which we are not even remotely aware, or perhaps we know of them only in our dreams, for dreams are thought to be fogged windows through which we can catch a fleeting view of the inner world of archetypes. Unfortunately, we know little about the human brain and how it functions. Some have called the study of the brain the next "new biology," more significant and important, perhaps, than the discovery of DNA, the code of life. In any case, the archetypes with which we are familiar seem to fall naturally into three groups: images or symbols, characters, and situations.

### Images or Symbols

Looked at in one way, we might say that archetypes are universal in their symbolism. In other words, certain images seem to have universal appeal to people. These images call from within us certain responses and associations, and they appeal to us in emotional ways quite apart from our intellect. Test

**124**

your own responses to the list of archetypal images below to see how closely you are in tune with the responses of others. Think about where you have read these images or seen them often repeated. (Here is a hint for No. 2 below. Think how old movie westerns always seem to end.)

EXERCISE #4:

In the line beside each image, write what you think it symbolizes and give an example for each. For example:

Ship—humankind's voyage through life

Example—The Pequod, the ship from *Moby Dick*, symbolizes the conflict between humans and nature.

or

Example—The ship in *Ship of Fools* symbolizes the inability of humans to make personal contact with one another as they sail through life.

1. rising sun— _____
   example— _____
2. setting sun— _____
   example— _____
3. colors—
   a. white— _____
      example— _____
   b. red— _____
      example— _____
   c. black— _____
      example— _____
   d. blue— _____
      example— _____
4. water (either sea or river)— _____
   example— _____
5. circle (ouroboros, mandala—page 134, yang-yin, egg)— _____
   example— _____
6. wind— _____
   example— _____
7. garden— _____
   example— _____
8. desert— _____
   example— _____
9. numbers (3, 4, & 7)— _____
   example— _____
10. snake— _____
    example— _____

Now check your responses with the responses of others. If you find similarities, to what do you attribute them?

There are lists of clichés that are very common, and also very archetypal. For example:

white as *snow*
good as *gold*
fast as the *wind*
*green* with envy
*black* as night

Archetypal images of women are especially interesting even though they are obviously male-dominated images. These view women only as they relate to men, not as individuals in their own right. As a result, few female characters achieve the character status that males have received. It can be expected that any culture, where women's status is equal to men's, will have major female characters. Women, according to these archetypal images, can be grouped into four basic categories. Any one female character may, however, have the characteristics of more than one category.

1. The *earth mother* is associated with birth, warmth, and protection. She is everyone's beloved "mom," representing growth, abundance, and fertility. This image has within it those good feelings of home, family, and heritage, one's roots.

2. The *temptress* is associated with danger, fear, and death. She is the evil witch or the siren, the wicked "step-" mother, the castrating, domineering wife.

3. The *soul-mate* is associated with inspiration and fulfillment, both physical and spiritual. She is the princess, the beauty, the damsel in distress, the all-submissive girl, lover, mistress.

4. The *platonic ideal* is associated with inspiration and the spiritual ideal on an intellectual level, not on the level of physical attraction.

Three of these archetypal women appear especially noticeable in the works of Ernest Hemingway. For example:

The Earth Mother—Pilar, *For Whom the Bell Tolls*
The Temptress—Lady Brett Ashley, *The Sun Also Rises*
The Soul-mate—Catherine, *Farewell to Arms*

EXERCISE #4:

Read "To His Coy Mistress" and indicate the archetypal images used by Marvell in each stanza. (See page 164.)

Stanza 1: _____

_____

_____

Stanza 2: _____

_____

_____

Stanza 3: _____

_____

_____

*Characters*

A number of recurrent, archetypal characters make up the cast of many works of literature, as well as mythology and religion. These characters share such remarkably similar experiences and behave in such a predetermined manner that their lives become almost rituals in their predictability. Probably the most common character is the hero.

The *hero's* life adventures are so familiar that you should be immediately able to identify several heroes' names as you read the following list of their lives' events.

a. A hero's conception is often unusual, and by tradition his mother is a virgin.
b. Usually there is a plot to kill him immediately after his birth.
c. Although little is known about his childhood, he grows to maturity in the home of foster parents after his narrow escape from death.
d. After he grows to manhood, he returns and achieves a victory over a king or a wild animal.
e. He marries the beautiful princess.
f. He becomes the king.
g. After a long and often uneventful rule and no longer in the good graces of the gods, he is driven from his kingdom where he mysteriously dies.
h. Although not buried, he typically has one or more holy graves.

While not all of these events occur in the life of each hero, the following heroes clearly embody these ritualistic events:

| | | | |
|---|---|---|---|
| King Arthur | Oedipus | Romulus | Hercules |
| Jesus Christ | Jason | Siegfried | Beowulf |
| Dionysus | Moses | Theseus | Gautama Buddha |
| Robin Hood | Perseus | Superman | |

The story of Oedipus seems to follow the pattern of the archetypal hero very well. Read his story and identify the predictable events of the hero's life.

### Oedipus

Shortly after the birth of their first child, Laius and Jocasta, King and Queen of Thebes, travel to Apollo's sanctuary, the Oracle at Delphi, to ask about their infant's destiny. The happy young parents are terror-struck when the oracle indicates that the child's fate is to murder his father and marry his mother. Feeling that they cannot allow the god's prediction to occur, the parents decide that their child must not be allowed to live. To avoid the wrath of the gods, however, they cannot actually kill him themselves. Rather, they order a servant shepherd of the palace to abandon the baby up on the mountainside; there he can die either from exposure or from wild animals, but the King and Queen can not be accused of murder.

In order to seal his fate absolutely, the child's feet are pinned together. This mutilation prevents the baby from crawling to safety, keeps him from coming back to haunt his parents after his death, and, they believe, makes him undesirable to save.

The shepherd who is ordered to abandon the child upon the mountain has no stomach for his assignment, however. He chances to meet a shepherd from the neighboring city of Corinth and persuades him to take the injured child. The shepherd happens to be employed by the King and Queen of Corinth, Polybus and Merope, who are childless; consequently, when the mutilated infant is presented to them, they are happy to doctor his wounds and adopt him as their own. He is the child for whom they have prayed to the gods for years.

Polybus and Merope name their new, adopted son Oedipus, which means swollen-foot, and pretend that he is their natural son, heir to the throne of Corinth.

As a young man he hears persistent rumors that he is adopted. Although his "parents" try to assure him that he is not, he journeys to the Oracle at Delphi to learn the truth from Apollo—the god of truth. The Oracle, in response to Oedipus' question about his parentage, states that he is destined to murder his father and marry his mother. Stunned, the young man immediately determines never to return to Corinth. Upon leaving Delphi he decides to travel toward Thebes.

At a narrow crossroads on the Corinth, Delphi, Thebes highway he meets a cantankerous old man on a chariot who will not let him pass. The old man is Laius, King of Thebes, on his way to the Oracle at Delphi to ask Apollo's assistance in ridding the City of Thebes of a terrible monster, the Sphinx.

(The Sphinx, who has the body of a lion, the wings of an eagle, and the head of a woman, stands outside the city gates and asks travellers to answer her riddle—what walks on four legs in the morning, two legs at noon, and three legs in the evening? Anyone who cannot correctly answer the riddle is devoured.)

Old Laius hits the young man with a stick and attempts to run Oedipus down in the crossroads, but Oedipus quickly jumps aside and strikes Laius a killing blow with his staff as the chariot charges by. Infuriated after killing the old man, Oedipus fights with and kills all but one of King Laius' guards and attendants. The one man escapes to return to Thebes to tell of a whole band of robbers who have ambushed the group and assassinated the King. The City, however, has greater worries because the Sphinx is still on the edge of town killing whosoever fails to answer her riddle.

After the slaughter at the crossroads, Oedipus proceeds toward Thebes. Upon arriving at the city's outskirts the Sphinx leaps out at him and demands that her riddle be correctly answered or she will eat him. She states her riddle and the wise Oedipus quickly and easily answers it—man crawls upon hands and feet in the morning of life, walks upright on two feet in the noon of life, and walks with the aid of a cane in the evening of life. Her riddle successfully answered, the Sphinx kills herself, and Oedipus is treated to a hero's welcome by the grateful citizens of Thebes. He is given wealth, made king, and given the queen, Jocasta, widow of the late King Laius, in marriage.

Oedipus rules uneventfully for many years, but as his oldest children approach adulthood, a great plague that kills young things strikes the city. Again it is necessary to take some action to save Thebes. Therefore, Creon, Jocasta's brother, is sent to the Oracle at Delphi to find the source of this calamity whereupon a solution might be found.

(*This is the point at which the ancient Greek play* Oedipus *by Sophocles begins. You may find a detailed account of this part of the story there.*)

After the truth is discovered, Jocasta hangs herself; Oedipus blinds himself and is sent into exile. After many years of wandering in the desert, led about by his youngest daughter, Antigone, the gods feel that he has suffered enough. Consequently, they decide to take him directly into the underworld, to the land ruled over by Hades, without having to pass through death. Thus, the earth opens up and Oedipus is taken directly down; he does not die but joins the dead without the unpleasantness of death.

You should have noted that the predictable patterns of a hero's life are all present in the story of Oedipus except one; there is nothing unusual about his conception. That is not at all unusual, however, for no one hero's life will contain every one of these events.

*Other Archetypal Characters* can be identified by what happens to them. Their experiences are not as long nor as varied as those of the heroes, but they are often represented in literature and mythology.

1. The *outcast* is a character who is condemned to wander for the rest of his life after he has committed some crime against his fellow countrymen. (e.g. Cain; The Ancient Mariner)

2. The *devil* character is as culturally defined the personification of evil. He often offers fortune, fame, or power in return for a soul. (e.g. Lucifer; Mephistopheles; Satan)

3. The *scapegoat* is a person whose death in a public ritual expiates the community's sins. (e.g. "The Lottery" by Shirley Jackson)

4. The *star-crossed lover's* relationship ends with the tragic death of one or both of them. (e.g. *Romeo and Juliet*)

5. The *intellectual* (mathematician, astronomer, scientist)
   a. Anti-social—wicked or mad scientist, Dr. Frankenstein
   b. Neutral—Dr. Strangelove
   c. Pro-social—Mr. Spock of *Star Trek*

Still other archetypal characters you may wish to investigate:

6. artist
7. shaman
8. old wise man or sage
9. trickster
10. fool
11. wise fool
12. warrior
13. the giant
14. king
15. the child or innocent
16. guru or disciple
17. the double
18. the father

EXERCISE #6:

Read the short story "Young Goodman Brown" by Nathaniel Hawthorne. When you have finished, list the dominate archetypal images. Following the images, indicate what archetypal characters Hawthorne uses in his story.

a. Images— _____

_____

_____

_____

_____

_____

_____

_____

_____

b. Characters— _____

_____

_____

_____

_____

_____

_____

_____

**130**

## Situation

Several recurrent *situations* have been identified in the world's literature through the use of archetypal analysis. These situations are what the images (p.124) suggest and what the characters (p.127) pursue. In one sense, the situation forms the basis for a plot in the literature of a mythic story. Some of the most common situations are the *initiations,* the *task*, the *quest*, the *fall*, and *death* and *rebirth.*

The initiation situation is usually concerned with the passage from childhood to maturity. The initiation becomes, then, a ritual introduction into adult life. The initiation usually symbolizes an increased awareness, a deeper perception, or an awakening of life, its meaning and its consequences. The initiation itself may be symbolic of those events in a culture that mark one's passage to maturity. In contemporary American society these symbolic acts involve such situations as acquiring a driver's license, receiving a first bra, having the first date, voting the first time, and drinking the first "legal" alcoholic beverage. (For examples in literature see *The Adventures of Huckleberry Finn, Catcher in the Rye,* and *Look Homeward, Angel.*)

Although the task and the quest are closely related, a difference does exist. In the *task*, a hero must perform some extraordinary, difficult thing in order to reassert his authority, marry the beautiful princess, or save the kingdom. (e.g. Odysseus strings the great bow after all others have failed, and Arthur pulls the great sword Excaliber from a stone.) The *quest*, on the other hand, involves a great search for someone or something that will bring about returned fertility to the land. The quest is really a large task—so large that often many of the participants cannot comprehend the end goal (e.g. the quest for the Holy Grail; the quest for the great white whale, Moby Dick; Jason's quest for the Golden Fleece).

The *fall* archetype describes a loss of power, status, or innocence. Accompanying the fall is, typically, a banishment from paradise, a state of pure happiness or bliss, to some less desirable locale. Resulting from moral misbehavior or disobedience, the punishment sometimes lasts for generations (e.g. Adam and Eve).

Perhaps the most popular archetypal situation with mythmakers and writers is *death and rebirth*. A close relationship exists between nature and life and their similar cycles. For example, death imagery suggests fall and winter because the natural environment's vegetation appears to die. Spring and summer, on the other hand, bring new life, a kind of rebirth; therefore, these seasons represent birth (or rebirth) and youth. Fertility rites, anthropologists suggest, are springtime activities because nature appears to support the ritual. Literature is filled with the close association of death with winter and birth with abundance. (e.g. Frost's "Stopping by Woods on a Snowy Evening" set in winter, suggests death; Cummings' "in Just—" set in spring, suggests rebirth.)

EXERCISE #7:

Look again at the short story "Young Goodman Brown." In the space provided identify which situations exist in the story and write two or three sentences summarizing each.

_____

_____

_____

_____

_____

_____

_____

_____

## Learning Activity #4:

### Shadow, Anima, and Persona

On a much deeper plane than images, characters, or situations, archetypal analysis is also concerned with the individual human psyche. Unlike Freud, however, Jung's approach is to probe the characters' psyches in a piece of literature in order to understand better the characters themselves, not to probe the psychological problems that may have confronted the author. As a result, you may find this approach somewhat more useful than Freud's psychological analysis.

Jung believed that, in addition to the collective unconscious, the mind has a personal subconscious. The darker half of this region he referred to as the *shadow*. In the shadow reside the less pleasant aspects of the personality. This dark half of the personality, often dangerous, belongs to the primitive, uncivilized, pre-evolutionary past of the species. Within the shadow reside emotions such as jealousy and repressed desires like avarice that most people would prefer not to recognize as part of their being. In literature, the shadow is represented by such characters as Iago in Shakespeare's *Othello*, Kurtz in Conrad's "Heart of Darkness," and the Lord of the Flies in Golding's novel of the same name. In the Hollywood western the shadow character is the villain.

While the shadow exists in everyone and is not a part of the personality we like to admit to, the *anima* is the element that sets humankind apart from other animals. The anima is the life force, the vital energy within everyone; it is the part of humans that is living and causes life. Jung asserts that without the anima humans would deteriorate into pathological idleness. The anima figures are central to much of literature because this is the most interesting part of the human personality.

**132**

One of the anima's functions is to mediate disputes within the personality, between consciousness and the unconscious. Moreover, the anima is a bisexual characteristic which mirrors in man a feminine image. In other words, within every man resides a female image that reveals herself in dreams or projections upon others in the environment. In women, this life force is referred to as the animus and is a masculine part of her psyche. For example, in the Hollywood western the anima is represented by the heroine. According to Jung, the anima is responsible for feelings of love because when a man finds a women who closely mirrors his anima, he will come to love her. The more closely she resembles his anima the more likely love will grow quickly. This, Jung believes, explains the phenomenon of love-at-first-sight. Working the same as the anima, a woman who finds a man who mirrors her inner animus will fall in love with him. The anima (animus) is the life force, the center of ambition and creativity.

The anima (animus), viewed culturally rather than universally, generally represents a background of the psyche close to the unconscious. Any person who dwells within his or her contrasexual self (male living in his female self or female living in her male self) lives in his or her psychic background and takes on some of the outward cultural characteristics of the opposite sex (e.g. an effeminate man or a masculine woman). However, society views as undesirable some of the traits that develop from living within one's contrasexual self. While women have a reputation for deep sensitivity and feelings, men who live in the anima are often characterized by undisciplined and irrational feelings. While men have a reputation for rational and independent thinking, women who live in the animus are (again only viewed culturally) often characterized as autocratic and aggressive. Each of these characteristics, in this view, is a distortion of each sex's major attributes. The conflict between the conscious and unconscious may represent the beginnings of neuroses, and it helps in the analysis of many literary characters (e.g. Willy Loman in *Death of a Salesman;* Piggy in *Lord of the Flies*).

*Some of the Characteristics Attributed to the Anima/Animus Life Force*

| ANIMA | ANIMUS |
|---|---|
| yin | yang |
| female principle | male principle |
| (dark, water, earth) | (light, fire, air) |
| 1. passive | 1. ego-centered |
| 2. affected by environment | 2. separated from environment |
| 3. non-aggressive | 3. aggressive |
| 4. peaceful | 4. prone to violence |
| 5. conservative | 5. creative |
| 6. irrational | 6. rational |
| 7. intuitive, emotional | 7. logical, analytical |
| 8. undisciplined, chaotic | 8. disciplined |
| 9. cooperative, communal | 9. independent, individualistic |
| 10. possessive | 10. autocratic, hierarchal |
| 11. democratic | 11. principled |
| 12. subjective | 12. objective |

**133**

The *persona* is a concept that is perhaps more often familiar. Simply put, the persona is the social personality or actor's mask that everyone puts on to face the world. Oftentimes, the persona is very different from one's true self. The chief function of the persona is to mediate between the ego and the larger world outside. A personality that is psychologically healthy and mature must possess a persona that is flexible. The healthy persona is represented by the hero in the Hollywood western. If, on the other hand, one's persona is too rigid, too inflexible, problems of personality and symptoms of neuroses may begin to develop, such as with the character, Dr. Phillips, in "The Snake." The persona is, then, the face we all put on to show the world (hero); the anima (animus) is the vital life force that gives us creativity and makes us human (heroine); the shadow is the darker side of the personality wherein reside the elements we often wish to suppress (villain).

Granted, many literary characters may be better understood by comparing their behavior with the principles of archetypal analysis, but in using the archetypal approach one must strive to remember that first and foremost, literature is art. It is much more than a clever medium for conveying mythic rituals and archetypes.

Read the following two papers for archetypal analysis in practice.

*Mandala*

Margaret Harbridge
English 1B
Dr. Guches
June 2, 1977

AN ARCHETYPAL ANALYSIS OF ALFRED, LORD TENNYSON'S "ULYSSES"

In his poem "Ulysses," Tennyson speculates, in a very subtle
manner, on the nature of human existence.  After preparing to set sail,
Ulysses is about to embark on his final sea voyage, from which he will
never return.  The mood of the poem is so stirring, the spirit of
Ulysses is so noble and admirable that the reader may easily overlook
the aspect of escapism in the poem.  Ulysses is actually a man well
past his prime who abandons his aged wife, his responsibilities, the
people under his rule, and leaves his son to "make mild a rugged
people, and through soft degrees/Subdue them to the useful and the
good."

Ulysses, king of Ithaca, is a legendary Greek hero.  He is a
major figure in Homer's Iliad, the hero of Homer's Odyssey, and a
minor figure in Dante's Divine Comedy.  After ten years at the siege
of Troy, Ulysses set sail for home.  Having incurred the wrath of the
god of the sea, however, he was subjected to many storms and diffi-
culties.  He was forced to wander for another ten years, having many
adventures and seeing most of the Mediterranean world before again
reaching Ithaca, his wife Penelope, and his son Telemachus.  But once
back home, he still wished to travel and "to follow virtue and knowledge like a sinking star."  As Tennyson presents him, Ulysses is a
combination of the archetypal hero and outcast figures.

Just as the traditional literary hero, Ulysses is the ruler of
a kingdom and renowned in battle.  At the same time, however, he may
be thought of as the outcast figure.  Although he has not committed a
crime against his countrymen (except, perhaps, one of neglect) and he
is not driven from his kingdom, Ulysses is condemned to wander by
the very nature of his being.  Despite his responsibilities and
duties as ruler of Ithaca, he speaks of himself as an "idle king"
and refers with contempt to the "common duties" which face him.
Ulysses' sense of alienation from his surroundings is not only a

**135**

common Tennysonian motif but is also present throughout much of
literature.

Tennyson's dramatic monologue may be divided into three parts.
Lines one through thirty-two are mainly concerned with Ulysses' past
exploits. Lines thirty-three through forty-four describe the uneventful present. Finally, in lines forty-five through seventy, Ulysses
resolves to set forth once again on his quest for a "newer world"
and an eternal rest. Together these make up the entire gamut or range
of every person's experience. The past, present, and future of a person's life represent the extent of his being--the cycle or wholeness
of his life.

In his description of Ulysses' experiences, Tennyson represents
him as a larger-than-life character. The poet gives to him an intensity and capacity to live greatly far beyond that of any ordinary man.
Ulysses says, "All times I have enjoyed/Greatly, have suffered
greatly." These qualities possessed by Ulysses are the very things
which make him a legendary character. He speaks in the same grandiose
terms as other literary egotists, such as Macbeth and Othello. "I am
become a name, . . . Much have I seen and known, . . . Myself not least,
but honored of them all, . . . I am a part of all that I have met."

Perhaps that which is most noble (or audacious) in Ulysses, and
distinguishes him from his countrymen, and even his mariners, is his
aspiration to be like the gods. He wishes to "follow knowledge like
a sinking star/Beyond the utmost bound of human thought," and to under-
take "some work of noble note . . . Not unbecoming men that strove
with Gods."

In this poem, it is interesting to note that the archetypal soul-
mate of Ulysses is not his wife, but rather his fellow mariners.
Ulysses feels no affinity with his aged wife, Penelope. His comrade-
ship with his mariners is the source of his spiritual inspiration and
fulfillment. He speaks lovingly of these mariners as "Souls that
have toiled, and wrought, and thought with me--/That ever with a
frolic welcome took/The thunder and the sunshine . . . ." In his old age
Ulysses abandons his wife and his homeland to be with his mariners.
"You and I are old/Old age hath yet his honor and his toil."

**136**

The symbolic significance of the poet having Ulysses, at last, sail westward can be explained in two ways.  This ancient hero wishes to set himself free from the limitations of his present life, and the reader at once envisions the unknown lands that await an adventurous spirit.  Also, in traditional literary motif, a journey westward suggests the conclusion or death of something which once existed.  Ulysses' ship and the water imagery present in the poem symbolize his voyage through life which is at last coming to an end.  With his nobility and greatness of character, it is especially fitting that Ulysses should exit with an assertion or challenge to "strive, to seek, to find, and not to yield."

Susan Saunders
English 1B
Dr. Guches
June 2, 1977

AN ARCHETYPAL ANALYSIS OF

JOHN STEINBECK'S "THE SNAKE"


Humans are intellectual as well as emotional creatures; the block-
age of one from the other causes insanity.  John Steinbeck's "The Snake"
is the story of a man, an intellectual, attacked and driven mad by his
emotional shadow.  The degeneration of the scientist is symbolized by
conflict on two planes:  the clash between the man and the woman and the
clash between the snake and the rat.  This conflict is specifically symbolized through Steinbeck's use of positive symbols of life and wholeness to
represent sanity, and symbols of death, darkness, and sleep for insanity.

From the very first sentence, it is clear the man is on the verge
of madness.  He is collecting specimens from a tide pool at dusk.  The
tide pool is an obvious archetype of life and, in this case, sanity.
Tide pools are round, full of water, and brimming with activity.  To
the aborigine and the scientist alike, water in any form is equated
with life.  From the zodiac to the mandala, circles and roundness
represent that which is complete, whole, and lifelike.  But the man is
not a participant of life.  He only studies life and collects specimens
in the "almost dark."  Deep within his consciousness, the scientist is
aware of his danger.  His bedroom, the abode of sleep and sanity, is
entered through a "side door" and is uncomfortable.  He is beset by
"many people" who wander in and ask questions.  Attacks upon the self
often come in plural form:  Jesus cast demons out of swine; Orestes
was pursued by Furies.  The man does not engage in inner dialogue.
"He had little routines of explanation for the commoner processes."

Still, the man is not yet mad.  Rooms and houses are frequently
symbols of the mind.  Dr. Phillips' mind stands "partly on piers over
the bay water and partly on the land."  He is yet aware of life.
Symbolically, he places his specimens of life in round watch glasses.
Sea water is tapped into the house; therefore, he has not surrendered
his sanity.  He kills a tabby cat.  Tabby cats are striped and varied

**138**

with black.  Cats are often familiars of witches, of evil, of madness.
Sanity struggles within the scientist.  The waves beat with "little
sighs against the piles under the floor" like a weak and pitiful dere-
lict knocking, begging entry.

Suddenly, in contrast to the feeble rappings of the waves, there
is a "strong knocking at the door."  "A tall lean woman," the shadow,
stands in the doorway.  She is "dressed in a severe dark suit; she has
straight black hair" and "eyes veiled with dust."  She is gaunt and
austere.  She is not like the others; she makes him uncomfortable.
The scientist seats her in "the uncomfortable chair from the bedroom."
She piques him.  "She makes him nervous."  He compares her to a frog,
a witch's favorite.  The waves under the building now beat "with little
shocks."  He wishes to change her, arouse her, shock her, frighten her.
She is unmoved.  She seems to "awaken slowly" and to "come up out of
some deep pool of consciousness."  She states her business; she wishes
to buy a male rattlesnake.

The burden of the action is now carried by the snake and rat
symbols.  Although snakes often are symbols of evil, snakes are also
symbols of wisdom.  Snakes entwined around a staff constitute the
emblem of doctors.  Rats, however, have always been symbols of evil
and darkness.  A "rat" leaves his bride at the church.  Rats desert
sinking ships.  Walter Brooks, the children's author, in his Freddy
the Pig series invariably employs "Simon the Rat" as his villain.
Steinbeck's rat is the woman.

The man is hesitant about selling the snake to the woman.  He
protests while she quietly insists.  The woman "wants him to be mine."
She flusters the man; she causes him to forget his experiment, his
study of life.  After he reluctantly sells her the reptile, she
demands a rat to feed her snake.  The thought disgusts him.  He is a
rational man, a man of science, a man of learning.  "He could kill a
thousand animals for knowledge, but not an insect for pleasure."  She
insists.  Again, he accedes to her demand.  Although he felt it was
"profoundly wrong" and "deeply sinful," he put the rat in the cage with
the snake.  Her desire sickened him.  The woman had won.  The man
thought he heard the water sigh among the piles.

The battle has begun, if at this point it is indeed a battle. The snake sways, tongue flicking, flows toward the rat. The woman sways, as though she is mesmerized in a demonic trance. The man is confused. He claims the snake is cautious, then cowardly. He compares the movements of the snake to those of a surgeon. "It's the most beautiful thing in the world." "It's the most terrible thing in the world." The snake strikes and the rat dies. The man turns on the woman and claims the snake, like a scientist who won't kill an insect for pleasure, didn't kill the rat "for thrill." The scenario is not yet finished. The woman wishes to see the snake eat the rat. The snake unhinges its jaws and begins to ingest the rat. Now the man is not only sick; he is afraid.

At last the snake consumes the rat; only a piece of the tail is left. Evil and darkness have been incorporated into wisdom. The man now is truly mad. He pours his watch glasses full of life into the sink. He drops his starfish "down into the water." The waves are "only a wet whisper," whimpering. It is a topsy-turvy world the woman has given him, devoid of life. The shadow defeated the man and so evil won. Wisdom killed the rat, but evil still won. In his madness he thinks the cat "crucified in the cradle." The woman leaves the man and promises to come again. Although he looks for her, she never returns. She has no need to return. "Remember," she admonishes, "He's mine."

"The Snake" is a chilling description of one man's descent into insanity. Dr. Phillips, the scientist, is a man who has banished normal emotions and feelings from his consciousness. Such an imbalance cannot exist within the self. The Yin-Yang symbol is an extension of the basic concept of wholeness. Half a Yin-Yang symbol does not exist, nor does half a self sanely exist. As repressed anger can grow in strength and defeat rationality, so can repressed emotions, even normal emotion. Exiled, Dr. Phillips' emotions joined forces with his shadow until, in strength, the woman attacked the man's totally intellectual self. Like a pendulum out of control, the woman swung him completely over to pure emotion: insanity.

The actual transformation was described on two levels: the clash

between the doctor and the woman, and the clash between the snake and
the rat.  The snake is unmistakably the man, while the rat is unmistakably the shadow.  Steinbeck employed lifelike symbols, water and
circles, to symbolize sanity.  Death, darkness, evil, and sleep were
symbols of madness.  One of the more interesting and salient features
was the time-honored use of witches, cats, and rats to represent evil
and insanity.  In Act I, Scene III, of <u>Macbeth</u>, the First Witch describes how she will persecute the sailor husband of a woman who denied
the witch chestnuts:  "But in a sieve I'll thither sail/And, like
a rat without a tail,/I'll do, I'll do, I'll do."  Shakespeare's witch
used a "rat without a tail" to torment her man; Steinbeck's witch used
a tail without a rat.

## EXERCISE #8:

Reread the short story "Young Goodman Brown." In the space below identify the elements of shadow, anima, and persona that Hawthorne has included in his story and in one or two sentences explain your selection of each.

A. Shadow: _____

_____

_____

_____

_____

_____

_____

B. Anima: _____

_____

_____

_____

_____

_____

_____

C. Persona: _____

_____

_____

_____

_____

_____

_____

**142**

For Further Reading:

Armans, *The Archetype of the Feminine in Literature.*

Brown, Norman, *Life versus Death.*

Bullfinch, *Mythology.*

Campbell, J., *Hero of 1,000 Faces, Myths to Live By,* and *The Masks of God: Primitive Mythology.*

Eliade, Mircea, *Cosmos and History; Myths, Dreams and Mysteries;* and *The Sacred and Profane.*

Fiedler, L. *Love and Death in the American Novel.*

Frazer, *The Golden Bough.*

Grear, Germaine, *The Female Eunuch* (especially good on the myth of romantic love and marriage).

Janeway, E., *Man's World, Woman's Place.*

Jaynes, J., *The Origin of Consciousness in the Breakdown of the Bicameral Mind.*

Jung, C. G., *Man and His Symbols, Complete Works,* Vol. IX (Part 1) "The Archetypes and the Collective Unconscious" and Vols. V, VIII, IX (Part 2), and XII.

Lewis, P., *The American Adam.*

Sebeok, T., *Myth: A Symposium.*

Slate, B., *Myth and Symbol.*

Smith, H., *Virgin Land.*

Suttie, Jan, *The Origins of Love and Hate.*

Vickery, J., *Myth and Literature.*

Watts, A., *Beat Zen, Square Zen and Zen; The Meaning of Happiness; Myth and Ritual in Christianity; The Spirit of Zen;* and others.

Weston, J., *From Romance to Ritual.*

# *Other Perspectives:*
## *1. Feminist Analysis*
## *2. Eclectic Analysis*

Many other analytical approaches have occupied positions of importance at different times. The ones discussed in the preceding chapters have been dominant. One that seems to be of rapidly increasing significance, and one that is relatively new, is feminist analysis. While it borrows heavily from other analytical points of view, its main concerns are somewhat different. Feminist critics are most concerned with challenging the traditional idea that all analytical perspectives are sexless. The fact is, they point out, a sexist point of view has far too long dominated the thinking of those who would closely examine the world's literatures. Claiming that most previous criticism has emphasized a male-dominated point of view, feminist analysis points toward the denunciation of a critical perspective that strives for universality while totally neglecting a feminine consciousness. An outgrowth of the women's liberation movement, the scope and influence of feminist analysis has grown rapidly during the 1970s.

Students often ask which, of all the different analytical approaches, is the best one. This desire is, of course, readily understandable; it would not take any great effort to look at all literature from the same point of view. The desire to take the easiest path does not consider the profound variety of literature: its multiple forms, drama, poetry, prose; its diversity of elements, plot, characters, setting; its assortment of figurative language, metaphor, symbol, hyperbole, irony; its various elements, imagery, connotation, allusion, tone; its significant themes, conflict, love and death; its quality, good or bad; its achievement, success or failure. The positive aspect of this vast assortment of literary forms and styles is the richness of the variety and its multiple appeal. The negative aspect of all this, for the beginning student of literature, is disquieting uncertainty about where to start. Once the choice of literary point of view is yours, however, eclecticism is the approach that will become most useful.

*Objectives:*

After completing this chapter, you will be able to:

1. Identify the main elements of feminist analysis.
2. Define eclecticism.
3. Distinguish between realistic and sexist literature from a feminist perspective.
4. Analyze a literary selection for its androgynist characteristics.
5. Analyze a literary selection eclectically.
6. Distinguish among analytical points of view to assess the ones with the most value to a literary selection.
7. Evaluate a literary selection's multiple appeal.
8. Express more critical judgment in evaluating what you choose to read and view.

*Pre-assessment:*

_____ 1. Feminists challenge the idea that previous analysis shows universality while ignoring (A) the images of women (B) feminine consciousness (C) women's political history (D) women's role as mothers (E) the feminine mystique.

_____ 2. Many feminist critics feel that the primary objective of feminist analysis should be (A) political and social (B) social and sexual (C) only descriptive (D) psychosexual (E) social Freudianism.

_____ 3. Previous analysis needs to be redone because (A) there is little new literature to analyze (B) it's good experience (C) previous analysis is male-dominated (D) few women can relate to male writers (E) it relies too little on Freud.

_____ 4. The ideal literature to feminists is (A) female dominated (B) when each sex is in its prescribed role (C) erotic (D) androgynous (E) romantic.

_____ 5. Feminists feel that the archetypal analysis of Jung (A) is most nearly perfect in its emphasis of the sexes (B) is most chauvinistic of all analytical perspectives (C) is without logical foundation (D) undervalues the roles of women (E) neglects the contributions of the housewife.

_____ 6. Eclectic analysis emphasizes the use of (A) psychology (B) history (C) a combination of approaches (D) feminism (E) sociology.

_____ 7. When critics use eclecticism they are (A) free to choose among different approaches (B) restricted to no more than two approaches (C) using the most structured approach (D) lazy critics (E) confined to its unique points.

8. Feminist analysis is, in part, an outgrowth of (A) the antiwar movement (B) women's liberation movement (C) increased rights for homosexuals (D) the movement to secure the right to vote for women (E) all of the above.

9. Feminist critics feel that formalists are (A) most sympathetic to feminism (B) most objective (C) least prejudicial (D) eclectic (E) not objective.

10. The best analytical approach is (A) formalistic (B) traditional (C) archetypal/psychological (D) eclectic (E) feminist.

## OTHER ANALYTICAL PERSPECTIVES

*Learning Activity #1:*

### Feminist Analysis

During the turbulent social upheavals of the 1960s and 1970s, several new analytical perspectives surfaced. The struggle for racial equality created new interest in black literature. The liberation movement for homosexuals stimulated an interest in the literature of homosexual writers and its criticism. Considering all the turmoil, the protests, the multiple demands for change, however, no social crusade has stimulated as much new literature, as much new printing of neglected writers from past years, nor such sustained new criticism as that attributed to the *women's liberation movement*. Consequently, although feminism is over 200 years old, in the space of one decade feminist criticism has achieved a position where it must receive serious consideration from modern readers.

As with any general protest movement, those interested in the liberation of women have the common opinion that the contemporary values of the society are inherently unfair. In particular, members of this movement feel that the patriarchal society is dehumanizing to over half, if not all the population. Feminists, whose ranks include both men and women, assert that society must be reoriented toward a system that eliminates the dominance of a *male*-oriented power structure. Out of this struggle for liberation and equality has developed the new feminist literary perspective which challenges the view that analysis is sexless. For example, how can any critical perspective profess universality yet exclude even the acknowledgement of the existence of a *feminine consciousness*?

Although feminist analysis may lack some of the unity of a traditional male criticism, three main points of emphasis among feminist critics are identifiable:

1. Feminist analysis should be principally social and political.
2. Literature that has been previously analyzed should be reanalyzed.
3. Literature and analysis should strive to achieve an androgynous perspective.

1. *Political and Social*—Often feminists challenge previous analytical critics over their claims to objectivity since they ignore literature's social environment. Consequently, feminists assert that the supposed objectivity of the formalists is specious, for they not only tend to neglect a primary explana-

**147**

tion for human motivation, but perpetuate oppression as well. Rather than objective, traditional analysis is often decidedly sexist. As a result, feminist analysis should acknowledge the social context of literature and strive for a political point of view by emphasizing the role of women within the historical era of both the literature and the writer.

To accomplish these political and social ends, feminist analysis must not be merely *descriptive*, describing reality, but be *prescriptive*, describing reality and suggesting an appropriate formula for change. The prescriptive view accepts the relevancy of a social context to analysis as well as promoting the politics of activism. It is through this prescriptive feminist analysis that the women's liberation movement may best be served, awareness increased, and attitudes changed. Making no claims to objectivity, feminists and feminist critics wish to be part of the politics of change—toward the realistic ideals of liberation and equality.

2. *Reanalyzing Literature*—Many feminists point out that previous analysis has been male dominated; therefore, literature needs to be reanalyzed with a feminist perspective. Feminists are particularly critical of the theories of Sigmund Freud and Carl Jung. Freud's ideas are attacked for their almost total disregard for the feminine psyche, not to mention their gross errors in feminine anatomy and sexuality. Moreover, they point out that Freud failed to understand the implications of the social environment's oppression of women and, as a result, failed to comprehend the real source of feminine neuroses. These misunderstandings led to wrongheaded and simplistic theories regarding women such as penis envy, vaginal orgasm, and inadequate parenthood. A great many feminists have concluded that the preference for Freud, among any number of practicing psychologists of his day, constitutes a further extension of political oppression against women— coming as it did at the very time when women were rising with the right to vote, the beginning of birth control, the first introduction of the Equal Rights Amendment (1923), and, for the first time, being granted custody of their children in divorce. Unfortunately, Freud's ideas have influenced literary analysis in ways that are detrimental to the interests of women.

The ideas of Carl Jung are attacked by feminists for their failure to understand and include a feminine consciousness which has led to mistaken literary analyses. Basically, archetypal analysis undervalues the roles of women, which even Jung admitted late in life. This underemphasis of women may be readily observed by comparing the many archetypal male characters with the few archetypal images of women. Granted, the traditional patriarchal value system emphasizes the male; however, when a society strives for equality, it must look beyond rigid, stereotypical views of people and strive to value all human beings—male and female—by emphasizing their equal importance. Many feminists use Jung's archetypal analysis of male characters in literature and adapt his theories to understand female characters. This involves emphasizing female characters in literature as archetypal characters, rather than merely images. Many feminist critics are concerned, consequently, with the image of women characters as they have emerged in the work of male writers who have a male or cultural bias, and concerned with the analysis of the work

**148**

of women writers whose work has previously been analyzed with the same cultural bias—or not reviewed at all.

3. *An Androgynous Perspective*—Many feminists emphasize that in both analysis and literature the ideal to be achieved is an androgynous perspective (from the Greek andros = man + gyne = woman), which stresses a unified male/female point of view. Moving beyond sexism, beyond even the sexes, this view emphasizes moving away from a male-oriented world toward a world where the aesthetics and feelings of both female and male are fused. The cultural enrichments possible through an androgynous point of view, feminists believe, will be the fruition of years of pain and anguish, oppression and struggle.

What an androgynous society, thus an androgynous literature, will be like is indicative of feminist idealism and feminist goals. In androgynous literature, characters do not have prescribed, stereotypical roles simply because of their sex. The most fundamental feminist belief, the right of each individual to have free, open, and unpredetermined choices, will be emphasized. The themes will have moved beyond the rigidity of sexism to deal with all characters' unique humanness without regard to a character's sex. For example, a farmer, a doctor, a lawyer, a mechanic, a truckdriver, a firefighter, a minister, a president, a nurse, a secretary, or a preschool teacher could be of either sex. Furthermore, the androgynous point of view emphasizes each person's bisexual nature as emphasized in Jung's theory about the anima/animus. Each individual has, in this view, the natural or cultural characteristics of each sex: creativity, logic, independence, tenderness, intuition, and emotions. As a movement and as an ideal, feminists believe that one of the best ways to illustrate that for which they have so long fought, is through realistic androgynous literature and androgynous analysis.

Read Charlotte Perkins Gilman's short story "The Yellow Wallpaper" (p. 187) then read the following analysis "The Pitfalls of Womanhood" by Dan Salter to see feminist analysis in practice.

Dan Salter
English 1B
Dr. Guches
April 17, 1979

### THE PITFALLS OF WOMANHOOD

Charlotte Perkins Gilman's short story, "The Yellow Wallpaper,"
is a story about the traps a society has for women.  It is a story
dealing with the attitudes held by society towards women and the
attitudes women have towards themselves.  The two main characters,
John and an unnamed woman who narrates the story, are both one dimen-
sional characters symbolizing different aspects of society.  These
characters are purposely never fully developed because to do so would
ruin their symbolic effect.  Gilman makes extensive use of symbolism
to show the different pitfalls that a woman must face in a society
dominated by men.

John, the husband of the woman who narrates the story, symbolizes
the stifling attitudes still held by many men.  In the story he con-
tinually forces demeaning roles on women.  He "absolutely forbids"
his wife to work at anything except entertaining and ordering.  He
is always saying that his wife is just being a silly girl and is not
really sick, but he allows her to be sick because "she'll be as sick
as she pleases."  He will not allow her to see her baby, a very
demoralizing and humiliating thing for a person to endure.  "It is
fortunate Mary is good with the baby.  Such a dear baby!  And yet I
cannot be with him, it makes me so nervous."  He also tells his wife
to have more self-control, implying that she cannot control herself.
". . . John says if I feel so, I shall neglect proper self-control,
so I take pains to control myself before him . . . ."  "He says . . .
that I must use my will and self-control and not let any silly fancies
run away with me."  He also forbids his wife to write, believing that
the writing would lead to "flights of fancy."  "There comes John, and
I must put this away--he hates to have me write a word."  This is the
most repressive thing he could have done because writing is his wife's
mental release.

John also epitomizes the repressive attitudes of science.  "He is
practical to the extreme.  He has no patience with faith, an intense

**150**

horror of superstition, and he scoffs openly at things that cannot be felt and seen and put down in figures." The scientific attitude is important because science is impersonal, and this can be seen in the way John treats his wife. He takes her out to the country and leaves her alone all day. "John is away all day, and even some nights when his cases are serious." He never listens to his wife's complaints, just hears them. He will not listen to her when she asks to leave, just tells her that she is better. "'You know the place is doing good.'" He also threatens to send her to another doctor, an act so impersonal that it frightens his wife.

The main character, John's wife, the person who tells the story, symbolizes the repressive roles some women accept for themselves. She does whatever her husband tells her to do, even if those things are against her will. She does not want to live in the old house but continues to do so because her husband wants her to. She wants to see her cousin but does not go because her husband says it would not be good for her. The only thing she does do that her husband did not give her permission to do is write. She does not tell her husband about the writing; he said she could not write, and she would be in trouble if she did. She also accepts the degrading roles her husband forces upon her. She doesn't work, and she allows herself to become separated from her baby. The acceptance of these roles causes her to go mad by the end of the story.

The room she stays in is a symbolic reference to the position of women in society. The location of the room is particularly symbolic. It is upstairs and away from the rest of the house, symbolizing the false pedestal upon which men put women. The room is isolated from the rest of the house, epitomizing the isolation many women feel. The windows in the room are barred, symbolically isolating the woman from society. The bed in the room is also symbolic. "I lie here on this great immovable bed." The steadfastness of the bed epitomizes the unchangeably repressive attitudes of John and many other men.

The major symbol in the story is the wallpaper. The wallpaper exemplifies the different attitudes and traps that society has for women. It acts as a cage for the main character, holding her in, not

letting her move.  She sees herself trapped by its perplexing pattern,
"a woman stooping down and creeping behind the pattern."  The wallpaper's intricate turns and somersaults mirror the unbreakable traps
society holds for women.  "You think you have mastered it, but just as
you get underway in following it turns a back somersault and there you
are.  It slaps you in the face, knocks you down, and tramples upon
you.  It is like a bad dream."  The wallpaper has a bad smell to it,
one from which the main character cannot escape.  "It creeps all over
the house.  It gets into my hair."  This smell exemplifies how the
traps cannot be escaped, for wherever she goes she finds the smell.
The fact that there are two patterns, one inside the other, is also
symbolic.  It shows that women must break two traps to be free:  the
pattern or trap men have set for them and the one they have set for
themselves.

     "The Yellow Wallpaper" is a story symbolizing a woman's desperate
need for freedom.  When denied this freedom she becomes insane.  Her
insanity is caused by the environment around her.  This environment
symbolizes the traps with which women must deal in their lives.  Her
husband John is symbolic of both the scientific and repressive attitudes that some men have towards women.  The woman is symbolic of the
women who accept the repressive roles given to them by men.  The upstairs room is symbolic of the falsely elevated pedestal upon which
some men place women.  The wallpaper represents the traps and the frustrations facing women in society and how these pitfalls cannot be
escaped.  These symbols are Gilman's way of identifying the stumbling
blocks a woman must overcome to achieve freedom.

EXERCISE #1:

Read Kate Chopin's short story "The Story of an Hour" (p. 175) and write a one-page feminist analysis of it.

EXERCISE #2:

List ideas in the poem "Equity" by Charlyne Nichols (p. 165) that would be emphasized in a feminist analysis.

_____

_____

_____

_____

_____

_____

_____

_____

_____

## Learning Activity #2:

### Eclectic Analysis

Many readers have become dissatisfied with the seemingly arbitrary restrictions that are imposed by the purists of each analytical approach. These restrictions have led modern analysts to the view that literary analysis should be eclectic; analysts should be free to select aspects from more than one approach. Eclectic analysts begin by reading (or viewing) a literary work and then deciding what *combination* of analytic points of view will contribute the most insight, the most understanding to the reader. The eclectic critic, then, analyzes by employing whatever approaches, or parts of approaches, seem to be demanded by the literature. Consequently, the boundaries between the author's life and the social conditions of the times, the literary techniques, psychology, archetypes, and feminism may be crossed to give added insight.

Neither a new nor an original idea, eclecticism is gaining in popularity and use. One reason for this new popularity is that the freedom to choose among approaches leads to a more thoughtful intermingling of ideas which, rather than complicating, actually tends to simplify and make analysis more understandable.

The main characteristic of eclecticism as an analytical approach is selectivity. In any one analysis, the critic is not obligated to include all analytical perspectives or even more than one. The chief virtue of eclecticism is in the *choice*; many literary works will seem almost to demand a particular

**153**

analytical view. Often choosing one predominant analytical point of view, and one or more insightful sections from others, gives a more perceptive analysis than would be possible by rigidly adhering to one arbitrary perspective. This kind of selectivity gives not only more freedom and responsibility to the analyst but far more understanding to the reader.

Because its insights are so much more rewarding, because the choices are yours to make, and because different literary selections require different points of view, eclecticism should combine the best of all analytical perspectives.

EXERCISE #3:

Read Sylvia Plath's poem "The Applicant" (p. 166) and list at least one analytical point from the poem for each of the following approaches.

1. traditional: _____

_____

2. formalistic: _____

_____

3. archetypal: _____

_____

4. feminist: _____

_____

EXERCISE #4:

On a poem of your choice, write one paragraph in which you combine several analytical approaches.

_____

_____

_____

_____

_____

_____

_____

_____

_____

# APPENDIX

*Literature for Analysis*
*Reference Sources*

## KUBLA KHAN
### A Vision in a Dream

In Xanadu did Kubla Khan
A stately pleasure-dome decree:
Where Alph, the sacred river, ran
Through caverns measureless to man
    Down to a sunless sea.
So twice five miles of fertile ground
With walls and towers were girdled round:
And here were gardens bright with sinuous rills,
Where blossomed many an incense-bearing tree;
And here were forests ancient as the hills,     10
Enfolding sunny spots of greenery.

But oh! that deep romantic chasm which slanted
Down the green hill athwart a cedarn cover!
A savage place! as holy and enchanted
As e'er beneath a waning moon was haunted
By woman wailing for her demon-lover!
And from this chasm, with ceaseless turmoil seething,
As if this earth in fast thick pants were breathing,
A mighty fountain momently was forced:
Amid whose swift half-intermitted burst     20
Huge fragments vaulted like rebounding hail,
Or chaffy grain beneath the thresher's flail:
And 'mid these dancing rocks at once and ever
It flung up momently the sacred river.
Five miles meandering with a mazy motion
Through wood and dale the sacred river ran,
Then reached the caverns measureless to man,
And sank in tumult to a lifeless ocean:
And 'mid this tumult Kubla heard from far
Ancestral voices prophesying war!     30
    The shadow of the dome of pleasure
    Floated midway on the waves;
    Where was heard the mingled measure
    From the fountain and the caves.
It was a miracle of rare device,
A sunny pleasure-dome with caves of ice!

    A damsel with a dulcimer
    In a vision once I saw:
    It was an Abyssinian maid,
    And on her dulcimer she played,     40
    Singing of Mount Abora.
    Could I revive within me,
    Her symphony and song,
    To such a deep delight 'twould win me,
That with music loud and long,
I would build that dome in air,
That sunny dome! those caves of ice!
And all who heard should see them there,
And all should cry, Beware! Beware!
His flashing eyes, his floating hair!     50
Weave a circle round him thrice,

And close your eyes with holy dread,
For he on honey-dew hath fed,
And drunk the milk of Paradise.

*Samuel Taylor Coleridge (1772-1834)*


  pity this busy monster, manunkind

pity this busy monster,manunkind,

not. Progress is a comfortable disease:
your victim(death and life safely beyond)

plays with the bigness of his littleness
—electrons deify one razorblade
into a mountainrange;lenses extend

unwish through curving wherewhen till unwish
returns on its unself.
                    A world of made
is not a world of born—pity poor flesh                    10

and trees,poor stars and stones,but never this
fine specimen of hypermagical

ultraomnipotence. We doctors know

a hopeless case if—listen:there's a hell
of a good universe next door;let's go
                    *—e. e. cummings (1894-1962)*


## MY LIFE HAD STOOD, A LOADED GUN
My life had stood, a loaded gun,
In corners, till a day
The owner passed, identified,
And carried me away.

And now we roam in sovereign woods,
And now we hunt the doe,
And every time I speak for him,
The mountains straight reply.

And do I smile, such cordial light
Upon the valley glow,                                     10
It is as a Vesuvian face
Had let its pleasure through.

And when at night, our good day done,
I guard my master's head,
'Tis better than the eider-duck's
Deep pillow, to have shared.

To foe of his I'm deadly foe:
None stir the second time
On whom I lay a yellow eye
Or an emphatic thumb.                                     20

Though I than he may longer live,
He longer must than I,
For I have but the power to kill,
Without the power to die.
                    *—Emily Dickinson (1830-1886)*

# THE LOVE SONG OF J. ALFRED PRUFROCK

*S'io credessi che mia risposta fosse*
*a persona che mai tornasse al mondo,*
*questa fiamma staria senza più scosse.*
*Ma per ciò che giammai di questo fondo*
*non tornò vivo alcun, s'i'odo il vero,*
*senza tema d'infamia ti rispondo.* *

Let us go then, you and I,
When the evening is spread out against the sky
Like a patient etherised upon a table;
Let us go, through certain half-deserted streets,
The muttering retreats
Of restless nights in one-night cheap hotels
And sawdust restaurants with oyster-shells:
Streets that follow like a tedious argument
Of insidious intent
To lead you to an overwhelming question . . .                          10
Oh, do not ask, "What is it?"
Let us go and make our visit.

In the room the women come and go
Talking of Michelangelo.

The yellow fog that rubs its back upon the window-panes,
The yellow smoke that rubs its muzzle on the window-panes,
Licked its tongue into the corners of the evening,
Lingered upon the pools that stand in drains,
Let fall upon its back the soot that falls from chimneys,
Slipped by the terrace, made a sudden leap,                             20
And seeing that it was a soft October night,
Curled once about the house, and fell asleep.

And indeed there will be time
For the yellow smoke that slides along the street
Rubbing its back upon the window-panes;
There will be time, there will be time
To prepare a face to meet the faces that you meet;
There will be time to murder and create,
And time for all the works and days of hands
That lift and drop a question on your plate;                           30
Time for you and time for me,
And time yet for a hundred indecisions,
And for a hundred visions and revisions,
Before the taking of a toast and tea.

In the room the women come and go
Talking of Michelangelo.

And indeed there will be time
To wonder, "Do I dare?" and, "Do I dare?"
Time to turn back and descend the stair,
With a bald spot in the middle of my hair—                             40
(They will say: "How his hair is growing thin!")
My morning coat, my collar mounting firmly to the chin,
My necktie rich and modest, but asserted by a simple pin—
(They will say: "But how his arms and legs are thin!")
Do I dare

**159**

Disturb the universe?
In a minute there is time
For decisions and revisions which a minute will reverse.

For I have known them all already, known them all—
Have known the evenings, mornings, afternoons,                50
I have measured out my life with coffee spoons;
I know the voices dying with a dying fall
Beneath the music from a farther room.
    So how should I presume?

And I have known the eyes already, known them all—
The eyes that fix you in a formulated phrase,
And when I am formulated, sprawling on a pin,
When I am pinned and wriggling on the wall,
Then how should I begin
To spit out all the butt-ends of my days and ways?           60
    And how should I presume?

And I have known the arms already, known them all—
Arms that are braceleted and white and bare
(But in the lamplight, downed with light brown hair!)
Is it perfume from a dress
That makes me so digress?
Arms that lie along a table, or wrap about a shawl.
    And should I then presume?
    And how should I begin?
        . . . . .

Shall I say, I have gone at dusk through narrow streets       70
And watched the smoke that rises from the pipes
Of lonely men in shirt-sleeves, leaning out of windows? . . .

I should have been a pair of ragged claws
Scuttling across the floors of silent seas.
        . . . . .
And the afternoon, the evening, sleeps so peacefully!
Smoothed by long fingers,
Asleep . . . tired . . . or it malingers,
Stretched on the floor, here beside you and me.
Should I, after tea and cakes and ices,
Have the strength to force the moment to its crisis?          80
But though I have wept and fasted, wept and prayed,
Though I have seen my head (grown slightly bald) brought in
        upon a platter,
I am no prophet—and here's no great matter;
I have seen the moment of my greatness flicker,
And I have seen the eternal Footman hold my coat, and snicker,
And in short, I was afraid.

And would it have been worth it, after all,
After the cups, the marmalade, the tea,
Among the porcelain, among some talk of you and me,
Would it have been worth while,                               90
To have bitten off the matter with a smile,
To have squeezed the universe into a ball
To roll it towards some overwhelming question,

**160**

To say: "I am Lazarus, come from the dead,
Come back to tell you all, I shall tell you all'—
If one, settling a pillow by her head,
　　Should say: 'That is not what I meant at all.
　　That is not it, at all.'

And would it have been worth it, after all,
Would it have been worth while,　　　　　　　　　　　　　100
After the sunsets and the dooryards and the sprinkled streets,
After the novels, after the teacups, after the skirts that trail along
　　the floor—
And this, and so much more?—
It is impossible to say just what I mean!
But as if a magic lantern threw the nerves in patterns on a
　　screen:
Would it have been worth while
If one, settling a pillow or throwing off a shawl,
And turning toward the window, should say:
　　"That is not it at all,
　　That is not what I meant, at all."　　　　　　　　　　110
　　. . . . .

No! I am not Prince Hamlet, nor was meant to be;
Am an attendant lord, one that will do
To swell a progress, start a scene or two,
Advise the prince; no doubt, an easy tool,
Deferential, glad to be of use,
Politic, cautious, and meticulous;
Full of high sentence, but a bit obtuse;
At times, indeed, almost ridiculous—
Almost, at times, the Fool.

I grow old . . . I grow old . . .　　　　　　　　　　　　120
I shall wear the bottoms of my trousers rolled.

Shall I part my hair behind? Do I dare to eat a peach?
I shall wear white flannel trousers, and walk upon the beach.
I have heard the mermaids singing, each to each.

I do not think that they will sing to me.

I have seen them riding seaward on the waves
Combing the white hair of the waves blown back
When the wind blows the water white and black.

We have lingered in the chambers of the sea
By sea-girls wreathed with seaweed red and brown　　　　130
'Till human voices wake us, and we drown.

　　　　　　　　　　—*T. S. Eliot* (1888-1965)


　　*"If I thought that my response would be addressed to one
　　who might go back alive, this flame would shake no more;
　　but since no one ever goes back alive out of these deeps (if
　　what I hear be true), without fear of infamy I answer you."
　　　　　　　　　　　　　　　　—*Dante's Inferno*

## STOPPING BY WOODS ON A SNOWY EVENING

Whose woods these are I think I know.
His house is in the village though;
He will not see me stopping here
To watch his woods fill up with snow.

My little horse must think it queer
To stop without a farmhouse near
Between the woods and frozen lake
The darkest evening of the year.

He gives his harness bells a shake
To ask if there is some mistake.                    10
The only other sound's the sweep
Of easy wind and downy flake.

The woods are lovely, dark and deep,
But I have promises to keep,
And miles to go before I sleep,
And miles to go before I sleep.

— *Robert Frost (1874-1963)*


## HE STANDS UPON HIS TOWER GAZING

He stands upon his tower gazing
          into the pool,
                    dreaming
                              of dancing and
                                        fire.
She sits absorbed
          by her ring,
                    fantasizing the high
                              flying serpent,
                                        beginning to
                                                  tire.                    10
Together they are apart,
          apart together; opposed in flesh,
                    combined in spirit.
Apart is dependence but no freedom;
          together fleshly — one,
                    but feeling
                              separate.
Union is tough,
          single is lonely and
                    rough.                    20
The id, super-ego battle is endless;
          ego,
                    caught between pleasure and
                              morality.
The only success is reality.

— *Richard C. Guches (1938-      )*

## "AN APPROVING GOD"

Life, what there was of it,
    had gone
    before I ever saw the wet
    bodies.

She struggled, wounded and confused,
    to deliver
    her first litter—
    alive.

Her foot, thorn swollen,
    made her groggy            10
    with stumbling
    pain.

Exhausted, lying beside two hairless lumps,
    I found her
    beyond help;
    numb.

More came, before the hour was out.
    I put all four
    into a bread
    sack.                      20

Abandoned, she sank into a corner,
    her great paw
    throbbing without
    mercy.

Despondent, she waited alone,
    for the peace of death
    to grant its
    release.
> —*Richard C. Guches (1938-    )*


## TO THE STONE-CUTTERS

Stone-cutters fighting time with marble, you foredefeated
Challengers of oblivion
Eat cynical earnings, knowing rock splits, records fall down,
The square limbed Roman letters
Scale in the thaws, wear in the rain. The poet as well
Builds his monument mockingly;
For man will be blotted out, the blithe earth die, the brave sun
Die blind and blacken to the heart.
Yet stones have stood for a thousand years, and pained
    thoughts found
The honey of peace in old poems.
> —*Robinson Jeffers (1887-1962)*

# TO HIS COY MISTRESS

Had we but world enough, and time,
This coyness*, lady, were no crime.   \*modesty, reluctance
We would sit down, and think which way
To walk, and pass our long love's day.
Thou by the Indian Ganges' side
Shouldst rubies find; I by the tide
Of Humber would complain*. I would  \*sing sad songs
Love you ten years before the Flood;
and you should, if you please, refuse
Till the conversion of the Jews.      10
My vegetable love should grow
Vaster than empires, and more slow.
A hundred years should go to praise
Thine eyes, and on thy forehead gaze;
Two hundred to adore each breast:
But thirty thousand to the rest;
An age at least to every part,
And the last age should show your heart.
For, lady, you deserve this state,
Nor would I love at lower rate.      20

  But at my back I always hear
Time's wingèd chariot hurrying near;
And yonder all before us lie
Deserts of vast eternity.
Thy beauty shall no more be found,
Nor in thy marble vault should sound
My echoing song; then worms shall try
That long preserved virginity,
And your quaint honor turn to dust,
And into ashes all my lust.       30
The grave's a fine and private place,
But none, I think, do there embrace.

  Now therefore, while the youthful hue
Sits on thy skin like morning dew*,   \*glow, warmth
And while thy willing soul transpires
At every pore with instant* fires,    \*urgent, eager
Now let us sport us while we may;
And now, like am'rous birds of prey,
Rather at once our time devour,
Than languish in his slow-chapped power.  40
Let us roll all our strength, and all
Our sweetness, up into one ball;
And tear our pleasure with rough strife
Thorough* the iron gate of life.    \*through
Thus, though we cannot make our sun
Stand still, yet we will make him run.

    *Andrew Marvell (1621-1678)*

## EQUITY

I (generic female of the species
  whose name is not even my own)

Did lawfully take that man
  (assertive, macho-proud)

To be my wedded husband,

To love, honor, and cherish . . .

  But later he insisted
    I'd promised to obey:
      "Clean the house,
      Do the laundry.             10
      Mow the lawn and
      Fix the faucet.
      Gas the car,
      Pay the bills
    And get this kid outa here, he's buggin' me.
        *

    And go get a job—
      You're in a rut and we need the money.
        *

    And by the way,              20
      bring me a beer, I'm
      right in the middle
      of a ballgame—jeez
      looka that sonofabitch Go!"
        *
        *
        *
        *

I do solemnly swear:

    "I'm tired, Judge,            30
      Just tell him, please,
      Marrying means sharing—
      It goes both ways."

The gavel sounded: Divorce Granted.
      —*Charlyne Nichols (1937-    )*

## BIRTHING A GREAT RIVER

  High
  Higher in the Rockies,
Water trickling over granite,
  cutting thin ribbons
  through fine moss, velvet
  clusters nurtured by the
  rills that slice them.
Summer verdure shelters
  this primal
  crib, half-hidden             10
  in fern fronds and wild strawberries
  and scant straying white daisies
  amid prayer-shaped
      pines.

Our breathing blends with pulsing
    quiet

    hush
broken only by
natal whispers of rippling water
        joining rippling waters.

            —*Charlyne Nichols (1937-      )*

    THE APPLICANT

First, are you our sort of person?
Do you wear
A glass eye, false teeth or a crutch,
A brace or a hook,
Rubber breasts or a rubber crotch,

Stitches to show something's missing? No, no? Then
How can we give you a thing?
Stop crying.
Open your hand.
Empty? Empty. Here is a hand                              10

To fill it and willing
To bring teacups and roll away headaches
And do whatever you tell it.
Will you marry it?
It is guaranteed

To thumb shut your eyes at the end
And dissolve of **sorrow**.
We make new stock from the salt.
I notice you are stark naked.
How about this suit—                                     20

Black and stiff, but not a bad fit.
Will you marry it?
It is waterproof, shatterproof, proof
Against fire and bombs through the roof.
Believe me, they'll bury you in it.

Now your head, excuse me, is empty.
I have the ticket for that.
Come here, sweetie, out of the closet.
Well, what do you think of *that*?
Naked as paper to start                                  30

But in twenty-five years she'll be silver,
In fifty, gold.
A living doll, everywhere you look.
It can sew, it can cook,
It can talk, talk, talk.

It works, there is nothing wrong with it.
You have a hole, it's a poultice.
You have an eye, it's an image.
My boy, it's your last resort.
Will you marry it, marry it, marry it.

            —*Sylvia Plath (1932-1963)*

## DADDY

You do not do, you do not do
Any more, black shoe
In which I have lived like a foot
For thirty years, poor and white,
Barely daring to breathe or Achoo.

Daddy, I have had to kill you.
You died before I had time—
Marble-heavy, a bag full of God,
Ghastly statue with one grey toe
Big as a Frisco seal                                          10

And a head in the freakish Atlantic
Where it pours bean green over blue
In the waters off beautiful Nauset.
I used to pray to recover you.
Ach, du.

In the German tongue, in the Polish town
Scraped flat by the roller
Of wars, wars, wars.
But the name of the town is common.
My Polack friend                                             20

Says there are a dozen or two.
So I never could tell where you
Put your foot, your root,
I never could talk to you.
The tongue stuck in my jaw.

It stuck in a barb wire snare.
Ich, ich, ich, ich,
I could hardly speak.
I thought every German was you.
And the language obscene                                     30

An engine, an engine
Chuffing me off like a Jew.
A Jew to Dachau, Auschwitz, Belsen.
I began to talk like a Jew.
I think I may well be a Jew.

The snows of the Tyrol, the clear beer of Vienna
Are not very pure or true.
With my gypsy ancestress and my weird luck
And my Taroc pack and my Taroc pack
I may be a bit of a Jew.                                      40

I have always been scared of you,
With your Luftwaffe, your gobbledygoo.
And your neat moustache
And your Aryan eye, bright blue.
Panzer-man, panzer-man, O You—

Not God but a swastika
So black no sky could squeak through.
Every woman adores a Fascist,
The boot in the face, the brute
Brute heart of a brute like you.

**167**

You stand at the blackboard, daddy,
In the picture I have of you,
A cleft in your chin instead of your foot
But no less a devil for that, no not
Any less the black man who

Bit my pretty red heart in two.
I was ten when they buried you.
At twenty I tried to die
And get back, back, back to you.
I thought even the bones would do.                    60

But they pulled me out of the sack,
And they stuck me together with glue.
And then I knew what to do.
I made a model of you,
A man in black with a Meinkampf look

And a love of the rack and the screw.
And I said I do, I do.
So daddy, I'm finally through.
The black telephone's off at the root,
The voices just can't worm through.                    70

If I've killed one man, I've killed two—
The vampire who said he was you
And drank my blood for a year,
Seven years, if you want to know.
Daddy, you can lie back now.

There's a stake in your fat black heart
And the villagers never liked you.
They are dancing and stamping on you.
They always *knew* it was you.
Daddy, daddy, you bastard, I'm through.                80

       *— Sylvia Plath (1932-1963)*


## LADY LAZARUS

I have done it again.
One year in every ten
I manage it—

A sort of walking miracle, my skin
Bright as a Nazi lampshade,
My right foot

A paperweight,
My face a featureless, fine
Jew linen.

Peel off the napkin                                    10
O my enemy.
Do I terrify?—

The nose, the eye pits, the full set of teeth?
The sour breath
Will vanish in a day.

Soon, soon the flesh
The grave cave ate will be
At home on me

And I a smiling woman.
I am only thirty.                                          20
And like the cat I have nine times to die.

This is Number Three.
What a trash
To annihilate each decade.

What a million filaments.
The peanut-crunching crowd
Shoves in to see

Them unwrap me hand and foot—
The big strip tease.
Gentlemen, ladies                                          30

These are my hands
My knees.
I may be skin and bone,

Nevertheless, I am the same, identical woman.
The first time it happened I was ten.
It was an accident.

The second time I meant
To last it out and not come back at all.
I rocked shut

As a seashell.                                             40
They had to call and call
And pick the worms off me like sticky pearls.

Dying
Is an art, like everything else.
I do it exceptionally well.

I do it so it feels like hell.
I do it so it feels real.
I guess you could say I've a call.

It's easy enough to do it in a cell.
It's easy enough to do it and stay put.                    50
It's the theatrical

Comeback in broad day
To the same place, the same face, the same brute
Amused shout:

"A miracle!"
That knocks me out.
There is a charge

For the eyeing of my scars, there is a charge
For the hearing of my heart—
It really goes.                                            60

And there is a charge, a very large charge
For a word or a touch
Or a bit of blood

Or a piece of my hair or my clothes.
So, so, Herr Doktor.
So, Herr Enemy.

I am your opus,
I am your valuable,
The pure gold baby

That melts to a shriek.                                          70
I turn and burn.
Do you think I underestimate your great concern.

    Ash, ash—
You poke and stir.
Flesh, bone, there is nothing there—

A cake of soap,
A wedding ring,
A gold filling.

Herr God, Herr Lucifer
Beware                                                           80
Beware.

Out of the ash
I rise with my red hair
And I eat men like air.

      —*Sylvia Plath (1932-1963)*


## MIRROR

I am silver and exact. I have no preconceptions.
Whatever I see I swallow immediately
Just as it is, unmisted by love or dislike.
I am not cruel, only truthful—
The eye of a little god, four-cornered.
Most of the time I meditate on the opposite wall.
It is pink, with speckles. I have looked at it so long
I think it is a part of my heart. But it flickers.
Faces and darkness separate us over and over.

Now I am a lake. A woman bends over me,                          10
Searching my reaches for what she really is.
Then she turns to those liars, the candles or the moon.
I see her back, and reflect it faithfully.
She rewards me with tears and an agitation of hands.
I am important to her. She comes and goes.
Each morning it is her face that replaces the darkness.
In me she has drowned a young girl, and in me an old woman
Rises toward her day after day, like a terrible fish.

      —*Sylvia Plath (1932-1963)*

# I AM A COWBOY IN THE BOAT OF RA

I am a cowboy in the boat of Ra,
sidewinders in the saloons of fools
bit my forehead     like     0
the untrustworthiness of Egyptologists
Who do not know their trips. Who was that
dog-faced man? they asked, the day I rode
from town.

School marms with halitosis cannot see
the Nefertiti fake chipped on the run by slick
germans, the hawk behind Sonny Rollins' head or                10
the ritual beard of his axe; a longhorn winding
its bells thru the Field of Reeds.

I am a cowboy in the boat of Ra. I bedded
down with Isis, Lady of the Boogaloo, dove
down deep in her horny, stuck up her Wells-Far-ago
in daring midday get away. "Start grabbing the
blue," i said from top of my double crown.

I am a cowboy in the boat of Ra. Ezzard Charles
of the Chisholm Trail. Took up the bass but they
blew off my thumb. Alchemist in ringmanship but a            20
sucker for the right cross.

I am a cowboy in the boat of Ra. Vamoosed from
the temple i bide my time. The price on the wanted
poster was a-going down, outlaw alias copped my stance
and moody greenhorns were making me dance; while my mouth's
shooting iron got its chambers jammed.

I am a cowboy in the boat of Ra. Boning-up in
the ol West i bide my time. You should see
me pick off these tin cans whippersnappers. I
write the motown longplays for the comeback of              30
Osiris. Make them up when stars stare at sleeping
steer out here near the campfire. Women arrive
on the backs of goats and throw themselves on
my Bowie.

I am a cowboy in the boat of Ra. Lord of the lash,
the Loup Garou Kid. Half breed son of Pisces and
Aquarius. I hold the souls of men in my pot. I do
the dirty boogie with scorpions. I make the bulls
keep still and was the first swinger to grape the taste

I am a cowboy in his boat. Pope Joan of the                 40
Ptah Ra. C/mere a minute willya doll?
Be a good girl and
Bring me my Buffalo Horn of black powder
Bring me my headdress of black feathers
Bring me my bones of Ju-Ju snake
Go get my eyelids of red paint.
Hand me my shadow
I'm going into town after Set

I am a cowboy in the boat of Ra
Look out Set     here i come Set
to get Set     to sunset Set
to unseat Set     to Set down Set
                    usurper of the Royal couch
                    imposter RAdio of Moses' bush
                    party pooper O hater of dance
                    vampire outlaw of the milky way

                    —*Ishmael Reed (1938-     )*


## ULYSSES

It little profits that an idle king,
By this still hearth, among these barren crags,
Matched with an agèd wife, I mete and dole
Unequal laws unto a savage race,
That hoard, and sleep, and feed, and know not me.
I cannot rest from travel; I will drink
Life to the lees. All times I have enjoyed
Greatly, have suffered greatly, both with those
That loved me, and alone; on shore, and when
Through scudding drifts the rainy Hyades                    10
Vext the dim sea. I am become a name;
For always roaming with a hungry heart
Much have I seen and known,—cities of men
And manners, climates, councils, governments,
Myself not least, but honored of them all;
And drunk delight of battle with my peers,
Far on the ringing plains of windy Troy.
I am a part of all that I have met;
Yet all experience is an arch wherethrough
Gleams that untraveled world, whose margin fades          20
For ever and for ever when I move.
How dull it is to pause, to make an end,
To rust unburnished, not to shine in use!
As though to breathe were life! Life piled on life
Were all too little, and of one to me
Little remains; but every hour is saved
From that eternal silence, something more,
A bringer of new things; and vile it were
For some three suns to store and hoard myself,
And this grey spirit yearning in desire                    30
To follow knowledge like a sinking star,
Beyond the utmost bound of human thought.

This is my son, mine own Telemachus,
To whom I leave the scepter and the isle—
Well-loved of me, discerning to fulfil
This labor, by slow prudence to make mild
A rugged people, and through soft degrees
Subdue them to the useful and the good.
Most blameless is he, centered in the sphere
Of common duties, decent not to fail                       40

In offices of tenderness, and pay
Meet adoration to my household gods,
When I am gone. He works his work, I mine.

There lies the port; the vessel puffs her sail:
There gloom the dark, broad seas. My mariners,
Souls that have toiled, and wrought, and thought with me—
That ever with a frolic welcome took
The thunder and the sunshine, and opposed
Free hearts, free foreheads—you and I are old;
Old age hath yet his honor and his toil.                              50
Death closes all; but something ere the end,
Some work of noble note, may yet be done,
Not unbecoming men that strove with Gods.
The lights begin to twinkle from the rocks;
The long day wanes; the slow moon climbs; the deep
Moans round with many voices. Come, my friends,
'Tis not too late to seek a newer world.
Push off, and sitting well in order smite
The sounding furrows; for my purpose holds
To sail beyond the sunset, and the baths                              60
Of all the western stars, until I die.
It may be that the gulfs will wash us down;
It may be we shall touch the Happy Isles,
And see the great Achilles, whom we knew.
Though much is taken, much abides; and though
We are not now that strength which in old days
Moved earth and heaven, that which we are, we are:
One equal temper of heroic hearts,
Made weak by time and fate, but strong in will
To strive, to seek, to find, and not to yield.                        70

      *Alfred, Lord Tennyson (1809-1892)*


## LEDA AND THE SWAN

A sudden blow: the great wings beating still
Above the staggering girl, her thighs caressed
By the dark webs, her nape caught in his bill,
He holds her helpless breast upon his breast.

How can those terrified fingers push
The feathered glory from her loosening thighs?
And how can body, laid in that white rush,
But feel the strange heart beating where it lies?

A shudder in the loins engenders there
The broken wall, the burning roof and tower
And Agamemnon dead.
            Being so caught up,
So mastered by the brute blood of the air,
Did she put on his knowledge with his power
Before the indifferent beak could let her drop?

      —*William Butler Yeats (1865-1939)*

**173**

# BIRTHDAY PARTY

They were a couple in their late thirties, and they looked unmistakably married. They sat on the banquette opposite us in a little narrow restaurant, having dinner. The man had a round, self-satisfied face, with glasses on it; the woman was fadingly pretty, in a big hat. There was nothing conspicuous about them, nothing particularly noticeable, until the end of their meal, when it suddenly became obvious that this was an Occasion—in fact, the husband's birthday, and the wife had planned a little surprise for him.

It arrived, in the form of a small but glossy birthday cake, with one pink candle burning in the center. The headwaiter brought it in and placed it before the husband, and meanwhile the violin-and-piano orchestra played "Happy Birthday to You" and the wife beamed with shy pride over her little surprise, and such few people as there were in the restaurant tried to help out with a pattering of applause. It became clear at once that help was needed, because the husband was not pleased. Instead he was hotly embarrassed, and indignant at his wife for embarrassing him.

You looked at him and you saw this and you thought, "Oh, now, don't be like that!" But he was like that, and as soon as the little cake had been deposited on the table, and the orchestra had finished the birthday piece, and the general attention had shifted from the man and woman, I saw him say something to her under his breath—some punishing thing, quick and curt and unkind. I couldn't bear to look at the woman then, so I stared at my plate and waited for quite a long time. Not long enough, though. She was still crying when I finally glanced over there again. Crying quietly and heartbrokenly and hopelessly, all to herself, under the gay big brim of her best hat.

—*Katharine Brush* (*1902-1952*)

# THE STORY OF AN HOUR

Knowing that Mrs. Mallard was afflicted with a heart trouble, great care was taken to break to her as gently as possible the news of her husband's death.

It was her sister Josephine who told her, in broken sentences; veiled hints that revealed in half concealing. Her husband's friend Richards was there, too, near her. It was he who had been in the newspaper office when intelligence of the railroad disaster was received, with Brently Mallard's name leading the list of "killed." He had only taken the time to assure himself of its truth by a second telegram, and had hastened to forestall any less careful, less tender friend in bearing the sad message.

She did not hear the story as many women have heard the same, with a paralyzed inability to accept its significance. She wept at once, with sudden, wild abandonment, in her sister's arms. When the storm of grief had spent itself she went away to her room alone. She would have no one follow her.

There stood, facing the open window, a comfortable, roomy armchair. Into this she sank, pressed down by a physical exhaustion that haunted her body and seemed to reach into her soul.

She could see in the open square before her house the tops of trees that were all aquiver with the new spring life. The delicious breath of rain was in the air. In the street below a peddler was crying his wares. The notes of a distant song which someone was singing reached her faintly, and countless sparrows were twittering in the eaves.

There were patches of blue sky showing here and there through the clouds that had met and piled one above the other in the west facing her window.

She sat with her head thrown back upon the cushion of the chair, quite motionless, except when a sob came up into her throat and shook her, as a child who has cried itself to sleep continues to sob in its dreams.

She was young, with a fair, calm face, whose lines bespoke repression and even a certain strength. But now there was a dull stare in her eyes, whose gaze was fixed away off yonder on one of those patches of blue sky. It was not a glance of reflection, but rather indicated a suspension of intelligent thought.

There was something coming to her and she was waiting for it, fearfully. What was it? She did not know; it was too subtle and elusive to name. But she felt it, creeping out of the sky, reaching toward her through the sounds, the scents, the color that filled the air.

Now her bosom rose and fell tumultuously. She was beginning to recognize this thing that was approaching to possess her, and she was striving to beat it back with her will—as powerless as her two white slender hands would have been.

When she abandoned herself a little whispered word escaped her slightly parted lips. She said it over and over under her breath: "free, free, free!" The vacant stare and the look of terror that had followed it went from her eyes. They stayed keen and bright. Her pulses beat fast, and the coursing blood warmed and relaxed every inch of her body.

She did not stop to ask if it were or were not a monstrous joy that held her. A clear and exalted perception enabled her to dismiss the suggestion as trivial.

She knew that she would weep again when she saw the kind, tender hands folded in death; the face that had never looked save with love upon her, fixed and gray and dead. But she saw beyond that bitter moment a long procession of years to come that would belong to her absolutely. And she opened and spread her arms out to them in welcome.

There would be no one to live for her during those coming years; she would live for herself. There would be no powerful will bending hers in that blind persistence with which men and women believe they have a right to impose a private will upon a fellow creature. A kind intention or a cruel intention made the act seem no less a crime as she looked upon it in that brief moment of illumination.

And yet she had loved him—sometimes. Often she had not. What did it matter! What could love, the unsolved mystery, count for in face of this possession of self-assertion which she suddenly recognized as the strongest impulse of her being!

"Free! Body and soul free!" she kept whispering.

Josephine was kneeling before the closed door with her lips to the keyhole, imploring for admission. "Louise, open the door! I beg; open the door—you will make yourself ill. What are you doing, Louise? For heaven's sake open the door."

"Go away. I am not making myself ill." No; she was drinking in a very elixir of life through that open window.

Her fancy was running riot along those days ahead of her. Spring days, summer days, and all sorts of days that would be her own. She breathed a quick prayer that life might be long. It was only yesterday she had thought with a shudder that life might be long.

She arose at length and opened the door to her sister's importunities. There was a feverish triumph in her eyes, and she carried herself unwittingly like a goddess of Victory. She clasped her sister's waist, and together they descended the stairs. Richards stood waiting for them at the bottom.

Someone was opening the front door with a latchkey. It was Brently Mallard who entered, a little travel-stained, composedly carrying his grip-sack and umbrella. He had been far from the scene of accident, and did not even know there had been one. He stood amazed at Josephine's piercing cry; at Richards's quick motion to screen him from the view of his wife.

But Richards was too late.

When the doctors came they said she had died of heart disease—of joy that kills.

—*Kate Chopin (1851-1904)*

176

# THE OLD PEOPLE

At first there was nothing. There was the faint, cold, steady rain, the gray and constant light of the late November dawn, with the voices of the hounds converging somewhere in it and toward them. Then Sam Fathers, standing just behind the boy as he had been standing when the boy shot his first running rabbit with his first gun and almost with the first load it ever carried, touched his shoulder and he began to shake, not with any cold. Then the buck was there. He did not come into sight; he was just there, looking not like a ghost but as if all of light were condensed in him and he were the source of it, not only moving in it but disseminating it, already running, seen first as you always see the deer, in that split second after he has already seen you, already slanting away in that first soaring bound, the antlers even in that dim light looking like a small rocking-chair balanced on his head.

"Now," Sam Fathers said, "shoot quick, and slow."

The boy did not remember that shot at all. He would live to be eighty, as his father and his father's twin brother and their father in his turn had lived to be, but he would never hear that shot nor remember even the shock of the gun-butt. He didn't even remember what he did with the gun afterward. He was running. Then he was standing over the buck where it lay on the wet earth still in the attitude of speed and not looking at all dead, standing over it shaking and jerking, with Sam Fathers beside him again, extending the knife. "Dont walk up to him in front," Sam said. "If he aint dead, he will cut you all to pieces with his feet. Walk up to him from behind and take him by the horn first, so you can hold his head down until you can jump away. Then slip your other hand down and hook your fingers in his nostrils."

The boy did that—drew the head back and the throat taut and drew Sam Fathers' knife across the throat and Sam stooped and dipped his hands in the hot smoking blood and wiped them back and forth across the boy's face. Then Sam's horn rang in the wet gray woods and again and again; there was a boiling wave of dogs about them, with Tennie's Jim and Boon Hogganbeck whipping them back after each had had a taste of the blood, then the men, the true hunters—Walter Ewell whose rifle never missed, and Major de Spain and old General Compson and the boy's cousin, McCaslin Edmonds, grandson of his father's sister, sixteen years his senior and, since both he and McCaslin were only children and the boy's father had been nearing seventy when he was born, more his brother than his cousin and more his father than either—sitting their horses and looking down at them: at the old man of seventy who had been a negro for two generations now but whose face and bearing were still those of the Chickasaw chief who had been his father; and the white boy of twelve with the prints of the bloody hands on his face, who had nothing to do now but stand straight and not let the trembling show.

"Did he do all right, Sam?" his cousin McCaslin said.

"He done all right," Sam Fathers said.

They were the white boy, marked forever, and the old dark man sired on both sides by savage kings, who had marked him, whose bloody hands had merely formally consecrated him to that which, under the man's tutelage, he had already accepted, humbly and joyfully, with abnegation and with pride too; the hands, the touch, the first worthy blood which he had been found at last worthy to draw, joining him and the man forever, so that the man would continue to live past the boy's seventy years and then eighty years, long after the man himself had entered the earth as chiefs and kings entered it;—the child, not yet a man, whose grandfather had lived in the same country and in almost the same manner as the boy himself would grow up to live, leaving his descendants in the land in his turn as his grandfather had done, and the old man past seventy whose grandfathers had owned the land long before the white men ever saw it and who had vanished from it now with all their kind, what of blood they left behind them running now in another race and for a while even in bondage

**177**

and now drawing toward the end of its alien and irrevocable course, barren, since Sam Fathers had no children.

His father was Ikkemotubbe himself, who had named himself Doom. Sam told the boy about that—how Ikkemotubbe, old Issetibbcha's sister's son, had run away to New Orleans in his youth and returned seven years later with a French companion calling himself the Chevalier Soeur-Blonde de Vitry, who must have been the Ikkemotubbe of his family too and who was already addressing Ikkemotubbe as *Du Homme*;—returned, came home again, with his foreign Aramis and the quadroon slave woman who was to be Sam's mother, and a gold-laced hat and coat and a wicker wine-hamper containing a litter of month-old puppies and a gold snuff-box filled with a white powder resembling fine sugar. And how he was met at the River landing by three or four companions of his bachelor youth, and while the light of a smoking torch gleamed on the glittering braid of the hat and coat Doom squatted in the mud of the land and took one of the puppies from the hamper and put a pinch of the white powder on its tongue and the puppy died before the one who was holding it could cast it away. And how they returned to the Plantation where Issetibbeha, dead now, had been succeeded by his son, Doom's fat cousin Moketubbe, and the next day Moketubbe's eight-year-old son died suddenly and that afternoon, in the presence of Moketubbe and most of the others (the People, Sam Fathers called them) Doom produced another puppy from the wine-hamper and put a pinch of the white powder on its tongue and Moketubbe abdicated and Doom became in fact The Man which his French friend already called him. And how on the day after that, during the ceremony of accession, Doom pronounced a marriage between the pregnant quadroon and one of the slave men which he had just inherited (that was how Sam Fathers got his name, which in Chickasaw had been Had-Two-Fathers) and two years later sold the man and woman and the child who was his own son to his white neighbor, Carothers McCaslin.

That was seventy years ago. The Sam Fathers whom the boy knew was already sixty—a man not tall, squat rather, almost sedentary, flabby-looking though he actually was not, with hair like a horse's mane which even at seventy showed no trace of white and a face which showed no age until he smiled, whose only visible trace of negro blood was a slight dullness of the hair and the fingernails, and something else which you did notice about the eyes, which you noticed because it was not always there, only in repose and not always then—something not in their shape nor pigment but in their expression, and the boy's cousin McCaslin told him what that was: not the heritage of Ham, not the mark of servitude but of bondage; the knowledge that for a while that part of his blood had been the blood of slaves. "Like an old lion or a bear in a cage," McCaslin said. "He was born in the cage and has been in it all his life; he knows nothing else. Then he smells something. It might be anything, any breeze blowing past anything and then into his nostrils. But there for a second was the hot sand or the cane-brake that he never even saw himself, might not even know if he did see it and probably does know he couldn't hold his own with it if he got back to it. But that's not what he smells then. It was the cage he smelled. He hadn't smelled the cage until that minute. Then the hot sand or the brake blew into his nostrils and blew away, and all he could smell was the cage. That's what makes his eyes look like that."

"Then let him go!" the boy cried. "Let him go!"

His cousin laughed shortly. Then he stopped laughing, making the sound that is. It had never been laughing. "His cage aint McCaslins," he said. "He was a wild man. When he was born, all his blood on both sides, except the little white part, knew things that had been tamed out of our blood so long ago that we have not only forgotten them, we have to live together in herds to protect ourselves from our own sources. He was the direct son not only of a warrior but of a chief. Then he grew up and began to learn things, and all of a sudden one day he found out that he had been betrayed, the blood of the warriors and chiefs had been betrayed. Not by his father," he added quickly. "He probably never held it against old Doom for selling him and his mother into slavery, because he probably believed the damage was already done before then and it was the same warriors' and chiefs' blood in him and Doom both that was betrayed through the black blood which his mother gave him. Not betrayed by the black blood and not wilfully betrayed by his mother, but betrayed by her all the same, who had bequeathed him not only the blood of slaves but even a little of the very blood which had enslaved it; himself his own battleground, the scene of his own vanquishment and the mausoleum of his defeat. His cage aint us," McCaslin said. "Did you ever know anybody yet, even your father and Uncle Buddy, that ever told him to do or not do anything that he ever paid any attention to?"

That was true. The boy first remembered him as sitting in the door of the plantation blacksmith-shop, where he sharpened plow-points and mended tools and even did rough carpenter-work when he was not in the woods. And sometimes, even when the woods had not drawn him, even with the shop cluttered with work which the farm waited on, Sam would sit there, doing nothing at all for half a day or a whole one, and no man, neither the boy's father and twin uncle in their day nor his cousin McCaslin after he became practical though not yet titular master, ever to say to him, "I want this finished by sundown" or "why wasn't this done yesterday?" And once each year, in the late fall, in November, the boy would watch the wagon, the hooped canvas top erected now, being loaded—the food, hams and sausage from the smokehouse, coffee and flour and molasses from the commissary, a whole beef killed just last night for the dogs until there would be meat in camp, the crate containing the dogs themselves, then the bedding, the guns, the horns and lanterns and axes, and his cousin McCaslin and Sam Fathers in their hunting clothes would mount to the seat and with Tennie's Jim sitting on the dog-crate they would drive away to Jefferson, to join Major de Spain and General Compson and Boon Hogganbeck and Walter Ewell and go on into the big bottom of the Tallahatchie where the deer and bear were, to be gone two weeks. But before the wagon was even loaded the boy would find that he could watch no longer. He would go away, running almost, to stand behind the corner where he could not see the wagon and nobody could see him, not crying, holding himself rigid except for the trembling, whispering to himself: "Soon now. Soon now. Just three more years" (or two more or one more) "and I will be ten. Then Cass said I can go."

White man's work, when Sam did work. Because he did nothing else: farmed no allotted acres of his own, as the other ex-slaves of old Carothers McCaslin did, performed no field-work for daily wages as the younger and newer negroes did—and the boy never knew just how that had been settled between Sam and old Carothers, or perhaps with old Carothers' twin sons after him. For, although Sam lived among the negroes, in a cabin among the other cabins in the quarters, and consorted with negroes (what of consorting with anyone Sam did after the boy got big enough to walk alone from the house to the blacksmith-shop and then to carry a gun) and dressed like them and talked like them and even went with them to the negro church now and then, he was still the son of that Chickasaw chief and the negroes knew it. And, it seemed to the boy, not only negroes. Boon Hogganbeck's grandmother had been a Chickasaw woman too, and although the blood had run white since and Boon was a white man, it was not chief's blood. To the boy at least, the difference was apparent immediately you saw Boon and Sam together, and even Boon seemed to know it was there—even Boon, to whom in his tradition it had never occurred that anyone might be better born than himself. A man might be smarter, he admitted that, or richer (luckier, he called it) but not better born. Boon was a mastiff, absolutely faithful, dividing his fidelity equally between Major de Spain and the boy's cousin McCaslin, absolutely dependent for his very bread and dividing that impartially too between Major de Spain and McCaslin, hardy, generous, courageous enough, a slave to all the appetites and almost unratiocinative. In the boy's eyes at least it was Sam Fathers, the negro, who bore himself not only toward his cousin McCaslin and Major de Spain but toward all white men, with gravity and dignity and without servility or recourse to that impenetrable wall of ready and easy mirth which negroes sustain between themselves and white men, bearing himself toward his cousin McCaslin not only as one man to another but as an older man to a younger.

He taught the boy the woods, to hunt, when to shoot and when not to shoot, when to kill and when not to kill, and better, what to do with it afterward. Then he would talk to the boy, the two of them sitting beneath the close fierce stars on a summer hilltop while they waited for the hounds to bring the fox back within hearing, or beside a fire in the November or December woods while the dogs worked out a coon's trail along the creek, or fireless in the pitch dark and heavy dew of April mornings while they squatted beneath a turkey-roost. The boy would never question him; Sam did not react to questions. The boy would just wait and then listen and Sam would begin, talking about the old days and the People whom he had not had time ever to know and so could not remember (he did not remember ever having seen his father's face), and in place of whom the other race into which his blood had run supplied him with no substitute.

And as he talked about those old times and those dead and vanished men of another race from either that the boy knew, gradually to the boy those old times would cease to be old times and would become a part of the boy's present, not only as if they had happened yesterday but as if they were still happening, the men who walked through them actually walking in breath and air and casting an actual shadow on the earth they had not quitted. And more: as if some of them had not happened yet but would occur tomorrow, until at last it would seem to the boy that he himself had not come into existence yet, that none of his race nor the other subject race which his people had brought with them into the land had come here yet; that although it had been his grandfather's and then his father's and uncle's and was now his cousin's and someday would be his own land which he and Sam hunted over, their hold upon it actually was as trivial and without reality as the now faded and archaic script in the chancery book in Jefferson which allocated it to them and that it was he, the boy, who was the guest here and Sam Father's voice was the mouthpiece of the host.

Until three years ago there had been two of them, the other a full-blood Chickasaw, in a sense even more incredibly lost than Sam Fathers. He called himself Jobaker, as if it were one word. Nobody knew his history at all. He was a hermit, living in a foul little shack at the forks of the creek five miles from the plantation and about that far from any other habitation. He was a market hunter and fisherman and he consorted with nobody, black or white; no negro would even cross his path and no man dared approach his hut except Sam. And perhaps once a month the boy would find them in Sam's shop—two old men squatting on their heels on the dirt floor, talking in a mixture of negroid English and flat hill dialect and now and then a phrase of that old tongue which as time went on and the boy squatted there too listening, he began to learn. Then Jobaker died. That is, nobody had seen him in some time. Then one morning Sam was missing, nobody, not even the boy, knew when nor where, until that night when some negroes hunting in the creek bottom saw the sudden burst of flame and approached. It was Jobaker's hut, but before they got anywhere near it, someone shot at them from the shadows beyond it. It was Sam who fired, but nobody ever found Jobaker's grave.

The next morning, sitting at breakfast with his cousin, the boy saw Sam pass the dining-room window and he remembered then that never in his life before had he seen Sam nearer the house than the blacksmith-shop. He stopped eating even; he sat there and he and his cousin both heard the voices from beyond the pantry door, then the door opened and Sam entered, carrying his hat in his hand but without knocking as anyone else on the place except a house servant would have done, entered just far enough for the door to close behind him and stood looking at neither of them—the

Indian face above the nigger clothes, looking at something over their heads or at something not even in the room.

"I want to go," he said. "I want to go to the Big Bottom to live."

"To live?" the boy's cousin said.

"At Major de Spain's and your camp, where you go to hunt," Sam said. "I could take care of it for you all while you aint there. I will build me a little house in the woods, if you rather I didn't stay in the big one."

"What about Isaac here?" his cousin said. "How will you get away from him? Are you going to take him with you?" But still Sam looked at neither of them, standing just inside the room with that face which showed nothing, which showed that he was an old man only when it smiled.

"I want to go," he said. "Let me go."

"Yes," the cousin said quietly. "Of course. I'll fix it with Major de Spain. You want to go soon?"

"I'm going now," Sam said. He went out. And that was all. The boy was nine then; it seemed perfectly natural that nobody, not even his cousin McCaslin, should argue with Sam. Also, since he was nine now, he could understand that Sam could leave him and their days and nights in the woods together without any wrench. He believed that he and Sam both knew that this was not only temporary but that the exigencies of his maturing, of that for which Sam had been training him all his life some day to dedicate himself, required it. They had settled that one night last summer while they listened to the hounds bringing a fox back up the creek valley; now the boy discerned in that very talk under the high, fierce August stars a presage, a warning, of this moment today. "I done taught you all there is of this settled country," Sam said. "You can hunt it good as I can now. You are ready for the Big Bottom now, for bear and deer. Hunter's meat," he said. "Next year you will be ten. You will write your age in two numbers and you will be ready to become a man. Your pa" (Sam always referred to the boy's cousin as his father, establishing even before the boy's orphanhood did that relation between them not of the ward to his guardian and kinsman and chief and head of his blood, but of the child to the man who sired his flesh and his thinking too.) "promised you can go with us then." So the boy could understand Sam's going. But he couldn't understand why now, in March, six months before the moon for hunting.

"If Jobaker's dead like they say," he said, "and Sam hasn't got anybody but us at all kin to him, why does he want to go to the Big Bottom now, when it will be six months before we get there?"

"Maybe that's what he wants," McCaslin said. "Maybe he wants to get away from you a little while."

But that was all right. McCaslin and other grown people often said things like that and he paid no attention to them, just as he paid no attention to Sam saying he wanted to go to the Big Bottom to live. After all, he would have to live there for six months, because there would be no use in going at all if he was going to turn right around and come back. And, as Sam himself had told him, he already knew all about hunting in this settled country that Sam or anybody else could teach him. So it would be all right. Summer, then the bright days after the first frost, then the cold and himself on the wagon with McCaslin this time and the moment would come and he would draw the blood, the big blood which would make him a man, a hunter, and Sam would come back home with them and he too would have outgrown the child's pursuit of rabbits and possums. Then he too would make one before the winter fire, talking of the old hunts and the hunts to come as hunters talked.

So Sam departed. He owned so little that he could carry it. He walked. He would neither let McCaslin send him in the wagon, nor take a mule to ride. No one saw him go even. He was just gone one morning, the cabin which had never had very much in it, vacant and empty, the shop in which there never had been very much done, standing idle. Then November came at last, and now the boy made one—himself and his cousin McCaslin and Tennie's Jim, and Major de Spain and General Compson and Walter Ewell and Boon and old Uncle Ash to do the cooking, waiting for them in Jefferson with the other wagon, and the surrey in which he and McCaslin and General Compson and Major de Spain would ride.

Sam was waiting at the camp to meet them. If he was glad to see them, he did not show it. And if, when they broke camp two weeks later to return home, he was sorry to see them go, he did not show that either. Because he did not come back with them. It was only the boy who returned, returning solitary and alone to the settled familiar land, to follow for eleven months the childish business of rabbits and such while he waited to go back, having brought with him, even from his brief first sojourn, an unforgettable sense of the big woods—not a quality dangerous or particularly inimical, but profound, sentient, gigantic and brooding amid which he had been permitted to go to and fro at will, unscathed, why he knew not, but dwarfed and, until he had drawn honorably blood worthy of being drawn, alien.

Then November, and they would come back. Each morning Sam would take the boy out to the stand allotted him. It would be one of the poorer stands of course, since he was only ten and eleven and twelve and he had never even seen a deer running yet. But they would stand there, Sam a little behind him and without a gun himself, as he had been standing when the boy shot the running rabbit when he was eight years old. They would stand there in the November dawns, and after a while they would hear the dogs. Sometimes the chase would sweep up and past quite close, belling and invisible; once they heard the two heavy reports of Boon Hogganbeck's old gun with which he had never killed anything larger than a squirrel and that sitting, and twice they heard the flat unreverberant clap of Walter Ewell's rifle, following which you did not even wait to hear his horn.

"I'll never get a shot," the boy said. "I'll never kill one."

"Yes you will," Sam said. "You wait. You'll be a hunter. You'll be a man."

But Sam wouldn't come out. They would leave him there. He would come as far as the road where the surrey waited, to take the riding horses back, and that was all. The men would ride the horses and Uncle Ash and Tennie's Jim and the boy would follow in the wagon with Sam, with the camp equipment and the trophies, the meat, the heads, the antlers, the good ones, the wagon winding on among the tremendous gums and cypresses and oaks where no axe save that of the hunter had ever sounded, between the impenetrable walls of cane and brier—the two changing yet constant walls just beyond which the wilderness whose mark he had brought away forever on his spirit even from that first two weeks seemed to lean, stooping a little, watching them and listening, not quite inimical because they were too small, even those such as Walter and Major de Spain and old General Compson who had killed many deer and bear, their sojourn too brief and too harmless to excite to that, but just brooding, secret, tremendous, almost inattentive.

Then they would emerge, they would be out of it, the line as sharp as the demarcation of a doored wall. Suddenly skeleton cotton- and corn-fields would flow away on either hand, gaunt and motionless beneath the gray rain; there would be a house, barns, fences, where the hand of man had clawed for an instant, holding, the wall of the wilderness behind them now, tremendous and still and seemingly impenetrable in the gray and fading light, the very tiny orifice through which they had emerged apparently swallowed up. The surrey would be waiting, his cousin McCaslin and Major de Spain and General Compson and Walter and Boon dismounted beside it. Then Sam would get down from the wagon and mount one of the horses and, with the others on a rope behind him, he would turn back. The boy would watch him for a while against that tall and secret wall, growing smaller and smaller against it, never looking back. Then he would enter it, returning to what the boy believed, and thought that his cousin McCaslin believed, was his loneliness and solitude.

**182**

So the instant came. He pulled the trigger and Sam Fathers marked his face with the hot blood which he had spilled and he ceased to be a child and became a hunter and a man. It was the last day. They broke camp that afternoon and went out, his cousin and Major de Spain and General Compson and Boon on the horses, Walter Ewell and the negroes in the wagon with him and Sam and his hide and antlers. There could have been (and were) other trophies in the wagon. But for him they did not exist, just as for all practical purposes he and Sam Fathers were still alone together as they had been that morning. The wagon wound and jolted between the slow and shifting yet constant walls from beyond and above which the wilderness watched them pass, less than inimical now and never to be inimical again since the buck still and forever leaped, the shaking gun-barrels coming constantly and forever steady at last, crashing, and still out of his instant of immortality the buck sprang, forever immortal; —the wagon jolting and bouncing on, the moment of the buck, the shot, Sam Fathers and himself and the blood with which Sam had marked him forever one with the wilderness which had accepted him since Sam said that he had done all right, when suddenly Sam reined back and stopped the wagon and they all heard the unmistakable and unforgettable sound of a deer breaking cover.

Then Boon shouted from beyond the bend of the trail and while they sat motionless in the halted wagon, Walter and the boy already reaching for their guns, Boon came galloping back, flogging his mule with his hat, his face wild and amazed as he shouted down at them. Then the other riders came around the bend, also spurring.

"Get the dogs!" Boon cried. "Get the dogs! If he had a nub on his head, he had fourteen points! Laying right there by the road in the pawpaw thicket! If I'd a knowed he was there, I could have cut his throat with my pocket knife!"

"Maybe that's why he run," Walter said. "He saw you never had your gun." He was already out of the wagon with his rifle. Then the boy was out too with his gun, and the other riders came up and Boon got off his mule somehow and was scrabbling and clawing among the duffel in the wagon, still shouting, "Get the dogs! Get the dogs!" And it seemed to the boy too that it would take them forever to decide what to do—the old men in whom the blood ran cold and slow, in whom during the intervening years between them and himself the blood had become a different and colder substance from that which ran in him and even in Boon and Walter.

"What about it, Sam?" Major de Spain said. "Could the dogs bring him back?"

"We wont need the dogs," Sam said. "If he dont hear the dogs behind him, he will circle back in here about sundown to bed."

"All right," Major de Spain said. "You boys take the horses. We'll go out to the road in the wagon and wait there." He and General Compson and McCaslin got into the wagon and Boon and Walter and Sam and the boy mounted the horses and turned back and out of the trail. Sam led them for an hour through the gray and unmarked afternoon whose light was little different from what it had been at dawn and which would become darkness without any graduation between. Then Sam stopped them.

"This is far enough," he said. "He'll be coming upwind, and he dont want to smell the mules." They tied the mounts in a thicket. Sam led them on foot now, unpathed through the markless afternoon, the boy pressing close behind him, the two others, or so it seemed to the boy, on his heels. But they were not. Twice Sam turned his head slightly and spoke back to him across his shoulder, still walking: "You got time. We'll get there fore he does."

So he tried to go slower. He tried deliberately to decelerate the dizzy rushing of time in which the buck which he had not even seen was moving, which it seemed to him must be carrying the buck farther and farther and more and more irretrievably away from them even though there were no dogs behind him now to make him run, even though, according to Sam, he must have completed his circle now and was heading back toward them. They went on; it could have been another hour or twice that or less than half, the boy could not have said. Then they were on a ridge. He had never been in here before and he could not see that it was a ridge. He just knew that the earth had risen slightly because the underbrush had thinned a little, the ground sloping invisibly away toward a dense wall of cane. Sam stopped. "This is it," he said. He spoke to Walter and Boon: "Follow this ridge and you will come to two crossings. You will see the tracks. If he crosses, it will be at one of these three."

Walter looked about for a moment. "I know it," he said. "I've even seen your deer. I was in here last Monday. He aint nothing but a yearling."

"A yearling?" Boon said. He was panting from the walking. His face still looked a little wild. "If the one I saw was any yearling, I'm still in kindergarten."

"Then I must have seen a rabbit," Walter said. "I always heard you quit school altogether two years before the first grade."

Boon glared at Walter. "If you dont want to shoot him, get out of the way," he said. "Set down somewhere. By God, I—"

"Aint nobody going to shoot him standing here," Sam said quietly.

"Sam's right," Walter said. He moved, slanting the worn, silver-colored barrel of his rifle downward to walk with it again. "A little more moving and a little more quiet too. Five miles is still Hogganbeck range, even if we wasn't downwind." They went on. The boy could still hear Boon talking, though presently that ceased too. Then once more he and and Sam stood motionless together against a tremendous pin oak in a little thicket, and again there was nothing. There was only the soaring and sombre solitude in the dim light, there was the thin murmur of the faint cold rain which had not ceased all day. Then, as if it had waited for them to find their positions and become still, the wilderness breathed again. It seemed to lean inward above them, above himself and Sam and Walter and Boon in their separate lurking-places, tremendous, attentive, impartial and omniscient, the buck moving in it somewhere, not running yet since he had not been pursued, not frightened yet and never fearsome but just alert also as they were alert, perhaps already circling back, perhaps quite near, perhaps conscious also of the eye of the ancient immortal Umpire. Because he was just twelve then, and that morning something had happened to him: in less than a second he had ceased forever to be the child he was yesterday. Or perhaps that made no difference, perhaps even a city-bred man, let alone a child, could not have understood it; perhaps only a country-bred one could comprehend loving the life he spills. He began to shake again.

"I'm glad it's started now," he whispered. He did not move to speak; only his lips shaped the expiring words: "Then it will be gone when I raise the gun—"

Nor did Sam. "Hush," he said.

"Is he that near?" the boy whispered. "Do you think—"

"Hush," Sam said. So he hushed. But he could not stop the shaking. He did not try, because he knew it would go away when he needed the steadiness—had not Sam Fathers already consecrated and absolved him from weakness and regret too?—not from love and pity for all which lived and ran and then ceased to live in a second in the very midst of splendor and speed, but from weakness and regret. So they stood motionless, breathing deep and quiet and steady. If there had been any sun, it would be near to setting now; there was a condensing, a densifying, of what he had thought was the gray and unchanging light until he realized suddenly that it was his own breathing, his heart, his blood—something, all things, and that Sam Fathers had marked him indeed, not as a mere hunter, but with something Sam had had in his turn of his vanished and forgotten people. He stopped breathing then; there was only his heart, his blood, and in the following silence the wilderness ceased to breathe also, leaning, stooping overhead with its breath held, tremendous and impartial and waiting. Then the shaking stopped too, as he had known it would, and he drew back the two heavy hammers of the gun.

**184**

Then it had passed. It was over. The solitude did not breathe again yet; it had merely stopped watching him and was looking somewhere else, even turning its back on him, looking on away up the ridge at another point, and the boy knew as well as if he had seen him that the buck had come to the edge of the cane and had either seen or scented them and faded back into it. But the solitude did not breathe again. It should have suspired again then but it did not. It was still facing, watching, what it had been watching and it was not here, not where he and Sam stood; rigid, not breathing himself, he thought, cried *No! No!*, knowing already that it was too late, thinking with the old despair of two and three years ago: *I'll never get a shot.* Then he heard it—the flat single clap of Walter Ewell's rifle which never missed. Then the mellow sound of the horn came down the ridge and something went out of him and he knew then he had never expected to get the shot at all.

"I reckon that's it," he said. "Walter got him." He had raised the gun slightly without knowing it. He lowered it again and had lowered one of the hammers and was already moving out of the thicket when Sam spoke.

"Wait."

"Wait?" the boy cried. And he would remember that—how he turned upon Sam in the truculence of a boy's grief over the missed opportunity, the missed luck. "What for? Dont you hear that horn?"

And he would remember how Sam was standing. Sam had not moved. He was not tall, squat rather and broad, and the boy had been growing fast for the past year or so and there was not much difference between them in height, yet Sam was looking over the boy's head and up the ridge toward the sound of the horn and the boy knew that Sam did not even see him; that Sam knew he was still there beside him but he did not see the boy. Then the boy saw the buck. It was coming down the ridge, as if it were walking out of the very sound of the horn which related its death. It was not running, it was walking, tremendous, unhurried, slanting and tilting its head to pass the antlers through the undergrowth, and the boy standing with Sam beside him now instead of behind him as Sam always stood, and the gun still partly aimed and one of the hammers still cocked.

Then it saw them. And still it did not begin to run. It just stopped for an instant, taller than any man, looking at them; then its muscles suppled, gathered. It did not even alter its course, not fleeing, not even running, just moving with that winged and effortless ease with which deer move, passing within twenty feet of them, its head high and the eye not proud and not haughty but just full and wild and unafraid, and Sam standing beside the boy now, his right arm raised at full length, palm-outward, speaking in that tongue which the boy had learned from listening to him and Joe Baker in the blacksmith shop, while up the ridge Walter Ewell's horn was still blowing them in to a dead buck.

"Oleh, Chief," Sam said. "Grandfather."

When they reached Walter, he was standing with his back toward them, quite still, bemused almost, looking down at his feet. He didn't look up at all.

"Come here, Sam," he said quietly. When they reached him he still did not look up, standing above a little spike buck which had still been a fawn last spring. "He was so little I pretty near let him go," Walter said. "But just look at the track he was making. It's pretty near big as a cow's. If there were any more tracks here besides the ones he is laying in, I would swear there was another buck here that I never even saw."

3.

It was dark when they reached the road where the surrey waited. It was turning cold, the rain had stopped, and the sky was beginning to blow clear. His cousin and

Major de Spain and General Compson had a fire going. "Did you get him?" Major de Spain said.

"Got a good-sized swamp-rabbit with spike horns," Walter said. He slid the little buck down from his mule. The boy's cousin McCaslin looked at it.

"Nobody saw the big one?" he said.

"I dont even believe Boon saw it," Walter said. "He probably jumped somebody's straw cow in that thicket." Boon started cursing, swearing at Walter and at Sam for not getting the dogs in the first place and at the buck and all.

"Never mind," Major de Spain said. "He'll be here for us next fall. Let's get started home."

It was after midnight when they let Walter out at his gate two miles from Jefferson and later still when they took General Compson to his house and then returned to Major de Spain's, where he and McCaslin would spend the rest of the night, since it was still seventeen miles home. It was cold, the sky was clear now; there would be a heavy frost by sunup and the ground was already frozen beneath the horses' feet and the wheels and beneath their own feet as they crossed Major de Spain's yard and entered the house, the warm dark house, feeling their way up the dark stairs until Major de Spain found a candle and lit it, and into the strange room and the big deep bed, the still cold sheets until they began to warm to their bodies and at last the shaking stopped and suddenly he was telling McCaslin about it while McCaslin listened, quietly until he had finished. "You dont believe it," the boy said. "I know you dont—"

"Why not?" McCaslin said. "Think of all that has happened here, on this earth. All the blood hot and strong for living, pleasuring, that has soaked back into it. For grieving and suffering too, of course, but still getting something out of it for all that, getting a lot out of it, because after all you dont have to continue to bear what you believe is suffering; you can always choose to stop that, put an end to that. And even suffering and grieving is better than nothing; there is only one thing worse than not being alive, and that's shame. But you cant be alive forever, and you always wear out life long before you have exhausted the possibilities of living. And all that must be somewhere; all that could not have been invented and created just to be thrown away. And the earth is shallow; there is not a great deal of it before you come to the rock. And the earth dont want to just keep things, hoard them; it wants to use them again. Look at the seed, the acorns, at what happens even to carrion when you try to bury it: it refuses too, seethes and struggles too until it reaches light and air again, hunting the sun still. And they—" the boy saw his hand in silhouette for a moment against the window beyond which, accustomed to the darkness now, he could see sky where the scoured and icy stars glittered "—they dont want it, need it. Besides, what would it want, itself, knocking around out there, when it never had enough time about the earth as it was, when there is plenty of room about the earth, plenty of places still unchanged from what they were when the blood used and pleasured in them while it was still blood?"

"But we want them," the boy said. "We want them too. There is plenty of room for us and them too."

"That's right," McCaslin said. "Suppose they dont have substance, cant cast a shadow—"

"But I saw it!" the boy cried. "I saw him!"

"Steady," McCaslin said. For an instant his hand touched the boy's flank beneath the covers. "Steady. I know you did. So did I. Sam took me in there once after I killed my first deer."

—William Faulkner (1897-1962)

186

# THE YELLOW WALLPAPER

It is very seldom that mere ordinary people like John and myself secure ancestral halls for the summer.

A colonial mansion, a hereditary estate, I would say a haunted house, and reach the height of much of fate!

Still I will proudly declare that there is something queer about it.

Else, why should it be let so cheaply? And why have stood so long untenanted?

John laughs at me, of course, but one expects that in marriage.

John is practical in the extreme. He has no patience with faith, an intense horror of superstition, and he scoffs openly at any talk of things not to be felt and seen and put down in figures.

John is a physician, and *perhaps*—(I would not say it to a living soul, of course, but this is dead paper and a great relief to my mind)—*perhaps* that is one reason I do not get well faster.

You see he does not believe I am sick!

And what can one do?

If a physician of high standing, and one's own husband, assures friends and relatives that there is really nothing the matter with one but temporary nervous depression—a slight hysterical tendency—what is one to do?

My brother is also a physician, and also of high standing, and he says the same thing.

So I take phosphates or phosphites—whichever it is, and tonics, and journeys, and air, and exercise, and am absolutely forbidden to "work" until I am well again.

Personally, I disagree with their ideas.

Personally, I believe that congenial work, with excitement and change, would do me good.

But what is one to do?

I did write for a while in spite of them; but it does exhaust me a good deal—having to be so sly about it, or else meet with heavy opposition.

I sometimes fancy that in my condition if I had less opposition and more society and stimulus—but John says the very worst thing I can do is to think about my condition, And I confess it always makes me feel bad.

So I will let it alone and talk about the house.

The most beautiful place! It is quite alone, standing well back from the road, quite three miles from the village. It makes me think of English places that you read about, for there are hedges and walls and gates that lock, and lots of separate little houses for the gardeners and people.

There is a *delicious* garden! I never saw such a garden—large and shady, full of box-bordered paths, and lined with long grape-covered arbors with seats under them.

There were greenhouses, too, but they are all broken now.

There was some legal trouble, I believe, something about the heirs and coheirs; anyhow, the place has been empty for years.

That spoils my ghostliness, I am afraid, but I don't care—there is something strange about the house—I can feel it.

I even said so to John one moonlight evening, but he said what I felt was a *draught*, and shut the window.

I get unreasonably angry with John sometimes. I'm sure I never used to be so sensitive. I think it is due to this nervous condition.

But John says if I feel so, I shall neglect proper self-control; so I take pains to control myself—before him, at least, and that makes me very tired.

I don't like our room a bit. I wanted one downstairs that opened on the piazza and had roses all over the window, and such pretty old-fashioned chintz hangings! but John would not hear of it.

He said there was only one window and not room for two beds, and no near room for him if he took another.

He is very careful and loving, and hardly lets me stir without special direction.

I have a schedule prescription for each hour in the day; he takes all care from me, and so I feel basely ungrateful not to value it more.

He said we came here solely on my account, that I was to have perfect rest and all the air I could get. "Your exercise depends on your strength, my dear," said he, "and your food somewhat on your appetite; but air you can absorb all the time." So we took the nursery at the top of the house.

It is a big, airy room, the whole floor nearly, with windows that look all ways, and air and sunshine galore. It was nursery first and then playroom and gymnasium, I should judge; for the windows are barred for little children, and there are rings and things in the walls.

The paint and paper look as if a boys' school had used it. It is stripped off—the paper—in great patches all around the head of my bed, about as far as I can reach, and in a great place on the other side of the room low down. I never saw a worse paper in my life.

One of those sprawling flamboyant patterns committing every artistic sin.

It is dull enough to confuse the eye in following, pronounced enough to constantly irritate and provoke study, and when you follow the lame uncertain curves for a little distance they suddenly commit suicide—plunge off at our outrageous angles, destroy themselves in unheard of contradictions.

The color is repellent, almost revolting; a smouldering unclean yellow, strangely faded by the slow-turning sunlight.

It is a dull yet lurid orange in some places, a sickly sulphur tint in others.

No wonder the children hated it! I should hate it myself if I had to live in this room long.

There comes John, and I must put this away,—he hates to have me write a word.

We have been here two weeks, and I haven't felt like writing before, since that first day.

I am sitting by the window now, up in this atrocious nursery, and there is nothing to hinder my writing as much as I please, save lack of strength.

John is away all day, and even some nights when his cases are serious.

I am glad my case is not serious!

But these nervous troubles are dreadfully depressing.

John does not know how much I really suffer. He knows there is no *reason* to suffer, and that satisfies him.

Of course it is only nervousness. It does weigh on me so not to do my duty in any way!

I meant to be such a help to John, such a real rest and comfort, and here I am a comparative burden already!

Nobody would believe what an effort it is to do what little I am able,—to dress and entertain, and order things.

It is fortunate Mary is so good with the baby. Such a dear baby!

And yet I *cannot* be with him, it makes me so nervous.

I suppose John never was nervous in his life. He laughs at me so about this wallpaper!

At first he meant to repaper the room, but afterwards he said that I was letting it get the better of me, and that nothing was worse for a nervous patient than to give way to such fancies.

He said that after the wallpaper was changed it would be the heavy bedstead, and then the barred windows, and then that gate at the head of the stairs, and so on.

**188**

"You know the place is doing you good," he said, "and really, dear, I don't care to renovate the house just for a three-months' rental."

"Then do let us go downstairs," I said, "there are such pretty rooms there."

Then he took me in his arms and called me a blessed little goose, and said he would go down to the cellar, if I wished, and have it whitewashed into the bargain.

But he is right enough about the beds and windows and things.

It is an airy and comfortable room as any one need wish, and, of course, I would not be so silly as to make him uncomfortable just for a whim.

I'm really getting quite fond of the big room, all but that horrid paper.

Out of one window I can see the garden, those mysterious deepshaded arbors, the riotous old-fashioned flowers, and bushes and gnarly trees.

Out of another I get a lovely view of the bay and a little private wharf belonging to the estate. There is a beautiful shaded lane that runs down there from the house. I always fancy I see people walking in these numerous paths and arbors, but John has cautioned me not to give way to fancy in the least. He says that with my imaginative power and habit of story-making, a nervous weakness like mine is sure to lead to all manner of excited fancies, and that I ought to use my will and good sense to check the tendency. So I try.

I think sometimes that if I were only well enough to write a little it would relieve the press of ideas and rest me.

But I find I get pretty tired when I try.

It is so discouraging not to have any advice and companionship about my work. When I get really well, John says we will ask Cousin Henry and Julia down for a long visit; but he says he would as soon put fireworks in my pillow-case as to let me have those stimulating people about now.

I wish I could get well faster.

But I must not think about that. This paper looks to me as if it *knew* what a vicious influence it had!

There is a recurrent spot where the pattern lolls like a broken neck and two bulbous eyes stare at you upside down.

I get positively angry with the impertinence of it and the everlastingness. Up and down and sideways they crawl, and those absurd, unblinking eyes are everywhere. There is one place where two breadths didn't match, and the eyes go all up and down the line, one a little higher than the other.

I never saw so much expression in an inanimate thing before, and we all know how much expression they have! I used to lie awake as a child and get more entertainment and terror out of blank walls and plain furniture than most children could find in a toy-store.

I remember what a kindly wink the knobs of our big, old bureau used to have, and there was one chair that always seemed like a strong friend.

I used to feel that if any of the other things looked too fierce I could always hop into that chair and be safe.

The furniture in this room is no worse than inharmonious, however, for we had to bring it all from downstairs. I suppose when this was used as a playroom they had to take the nursery things out, and no wonder! I never saw such ravages as the children have made here.

The wallpaper, as I said before, is torn off in spots, and it sticketh closer than a brother—they must have had perseverance as well as hatred.

Then the floor is scratched and gouged and splintered, the plaster itself is dug out here and there, and this great heavy bed which is all we found in the room, looks as if it had been through the wars.

But I don't mind it a bit—only the paper.

There comes John's sister. Such a dear girl as she is, and so careful of me! I must not let her find me writing.

**189**

She is a perfect and enthusiastic housekeeper, and hopes for no better professions. I verily believe she thinks it is the writing which made me sick!

But I can write when she is out, and see her a long way off from these windows.

There is one that commands the road, a lovely shaded winding road, and one that just looks off over the country. A lovely country, too, full of great elms and velvet meadows.

This wallpaper has a kind of subpattern in a different shade, a particularly irritating one, for you can only see it in certain lights, and not clearly then.

But in the places where it isn't faded and where the sun is just so—I can see a strange, provoking, formless sort of figure, that seems to skulk about behind that silly and conspicuous front design.

There's sister on the stairs!


Well, the Fourth of July is over! The people are all gone and I am tired out. John thought it might do me good to see a little company, so we just had mother and Nellie and the children down for a week.

Of course I didn't do a thing. Jennie sees to everything now.

But it tired me all the same.

John says if I don't pick up faster he shall send me to Weir Mitchell in the fall.

But I don't want to go there at all. I had a friend who was in his hands once, and she says he is just like John and my brother, only more so!

Besides, it is such an undertaking to go so far.

I don't feel as if it was worthwhile to turn my hand over for anything, and I'm getting dreadfully fretful and querulous.

I cry at nothing, and cry most of the time.

Of course I don't when John is here, or anybody else, but when I am alone.

And I am alone a good deal just now. John is kept in town very often by serious cases, and Jennie is good and lets me alone when I want her to.

So I walk a little in the garden or down that lovely lane, sit on the porch under the roses, and lie down up here a good deal.

I'm getting really fond of the room in spite of the wallpaper. Perhaps *because* of the wallpaper.

It dwells in my mind so!

I lie here on this great immovable bed—it is nailed down, I believe—and follow that pattern about by the hour. It is as good as gymnastics, I assure you. I start, we'll say, at the bottom, down in the corner over there where it has not been touched, and I determine for the thousandth time that I *will* follow that pointless pattern to some sort of a conclusion.

I know a little of the principle of design, and I know this thing was not arranged on any laws of radiation, or alternation, or repetition, or symmetry, or anything else that I ever heard of.

It is repeated, of course, by the breadths, but not otherwise.

Looked at in one way each breadth stands alone, the bloated curves and flourishes—a kind of "debased Romanesque" with *delirium tremens*—go waddling up and down in isolated columns of fatuity.

But, on the other hand, they connect diagonally, and the sprawling outlines run off in great slanting waves of optic horror, like a lot of wallowing seaweeds in full chase.

The whole thing goes horizontally, too, at least it seems so, and I exhaust myself in trying to distinguish the order of its going in that direction.

They have used a horizontal breadth for a frieze, and that adds wonderfully to the confusion.

There is one end of the room where it is almost intact, and there, when the cross-lights fade and the low sun shines directly upon it, I can almost fancy radiation after all,—the interminable grotesques seem to form around a common center and rush off in headlong plunges of equal distraction.

It makes me tired to follow it. I will take a nap I guess.

I don't know why I should write this.

I don't want to.

I don't feel able.

And I know John would think it absurd. But I *must* say what I feel and think in some way—it is such a relief!

But the effort is getting to be greater than the relief.

Half the time now I am awfully lazy, and lie down ever so much.

John says I mustn't lose my strength, and has me take cod liver oil and lots of tonics and things, to say nothing of ale and wine and rare meat.

Dear John! He loves me very dearly, and hates to have me sick. I tried to have a real earnest reasonable talk with him the other day, and tell him how I wish he would let me go and make a visit to Cousin Henry and Julia.

But he said I wasn't able to go, nor able to stand it after I got there; and I did not make out a very good case for myself, for I was crying before I had finished.

It is getting to be a great effort for me to think straight. Just this nervous weakness I suppose.

And dear John gathered me up in his arms, and just carried me upstairs and laid me on the bed, and sat by me and read to me till it tired my head.

He said I was his darling and his comfort and all he had, and that I must take care of myself for his sake, and keep well.

He says no one but myself can help me out of it, that I must use my will and self-control and not let any silly fancies run away with me.

There's one comfort, the baby is well and happy, and does not have to occupy this nursery with the horrid wallpaper.

If we had not used it, that blessed child would have! What a fortunate escape! Why, I wouldn't have a child of mine, an impressionable little thing, live in such a room for worlds.

I never thought of it before, but it is lucky that John kept me here after all, I can stand it so much easier than a baby, you see.

Of course I never mention it to them any more—I am too wise,—but I keep watch of it all the same.

There are things in that paper that nobody knows but me, or ever will.

Behind that outside pattern the dim shapes get clearer every day.

It is always the same shape, only very numerous.

And it is like a woman stooping down and creeping about behind that pattern. I don't like it a bit. I wonder—I begin to think—I wish John would take me away from here!

It is so hard to talk with John about my case, because he is so wise, and because he loves me so.

But I tried it last night.

It was moonlight. The moon shines in all around just as the sun does.

I hate to see it sometimes, it creeps so slowly, and always comes in by one window or another.

John was asleep and I hated to waken him, so I kept still and watched the moonlight on that undulating wallpaper till I felt creepy.

The faint figure behind seemed to shake the pattern, just as if she wanted to get out.

I got up softly and went to feel and see if the paper *did* move, and when I came back John was awake.

**191**

"What is it, little girl?" he said. "Don't go walking about like that—you'll get cold."

I thought it was a good time to talk, so I told him that I really was not gaining here, and that I wished he would take me away.

"Why darling!" said he, "our lease will be up in three weeks, and I can't see how to leave before.

"The repairs are not done at home, and I cannot possibly leave town just now. Of course if you were in any danger, I could and would, but you really are better, dear, whether you can see it or not. I am a doctor, dear, and I know. You are gaining flesh and color, your appetite is better, I feel really much easier about you."

"I don't weigh a bit more," said I, "nor as much; and my appetite may be better in the evening when you are here, but it is worse in the morning when you are away!"

"Bless her little heart!" said he with a big hug, "she shall be as sick as she pleases! But now let's improve the shining hours by going to sleep, and talk about it in the morning!"

"And you won't go away?" I asked gloomily.

"Why, how can I, dear? It is only three weeks more and then we'll take a nice little trip of a few days while Jennie is getting the house ready. Really, dear, you are better!"

"Better in body perhaps—" I began, and stopped short, for he sat up straight and looked at me with such a stern, reproachful look that I could not say another word.

"My darling," said he, "I beg of you, for my sake and for our child's sake, as well as for your own, that you will never for one instant let that idea enter your mind! There is nothing so dangerous, so fascinating, to a temperament like yours. It is a false and foolish fancy. Can you not trust me as a physician when I tell you so?"

So of course I said no more on that score, and we went to sleep before long. He thought I was asleep first, but I wasn't, and lay there for hours trying to decide whether that front pattern and the back pattern really did move together or separately.

On a pattern like this, by daylight, there is a lack of sequence, a defiance of law, that is a constant irritant to a normal mind.

The color is hideous enough, and unreliable enough, and infuriating enough, but the pattern is torturing.

You think you have mastered it, but just as you get well underway in following, it turns a back somersault and there you are. It slaps you in the face, knocks you down, and tramples upon you. It is like a bad dream.

The outside pattern is a florid arabesque, reminding one of a fungus. If you can imagine a toadstool in joints, an interminable string of toadstools, budding and sprouting in endless convolutions—why, that is something like it.

That is, sometimes!

There is one marked peculiarity about this paper, a thing nobody seems to notice but myself, and that is that it changes as the light changes.

When the sun shoots in through the east window—I always watch for that first long, straight ray—it changes so quickly that I never can quite believe it.

That is why I watch it always.

By moonlight—the moon shines in all night when there is a moon—I wouldn't know it was the same paper.

At night in any kind of light, in twilight, candlelight, lamplight, and worst of all by moonlight, it becomes bars! The outside pattern I mean, and the woman behind it is as plain as can be.

I didn't realize for a long time what the thing was that showed behind, that dim subpattern, but now I am quite sure it is a woman.

**192**

By daylight she is subdued, quiet. I fancy it is the pattern that keeps her so still. It is so puzzling. It keeps me quiet by the hour.

I lie down ever so much now. John says it is good for me, and to sleep all I can.

Indeed he started the habit by making me lie down for an hour after each meal.

It is a very bad habit I am convinced, for you see I don't sleep.

And that cultivates deceit, for I don't tell them I'm awake—Oh no!

The fact is I am getting a little afraid of John.

He seems very queer sometimes, and even Jennie has an inexplicable look.

It strikes me occasionally, just as a scientific hypothesis,—that perhaps it is the paper!

I have watched John when he did not know I was looking, and come into the room suddenly on the most innocent excuses, and I've caught him several times *looking at the paper*! And Jennie, too. I caught Jennie with her hand on it once.

She didn't know I was in the room, and when I asked her in a quiet, a very quiet voice, with the most restrained manner possible, what she was doing with the paper—she turned around as if she had been caught stealing, and looked quite angry—asked me why I should frighten her so!

Then she said that the paper stained everything it touched, that she had found yellow smooches on all my clothes and John's, and she wished we would be more careful!

Did not that sound innocent? But I know she was studying that pattern, and I am determined that nobody shall find it out but myself!

Life is very much more exciting now than it used to be. You see I have something more to expect, to look forward to, to watch. I really do eat better, and am more quiet than I was.

John is so pleased to see me improve! He laughed a little the other day, and said I seemed to be flourishing in spite of my wallpaper.

I turned it off with a laugh. I had no intention of telling him it was *because* of the wallpaper—he would make fun of me. He might even want to take me away.

I don't want to leave now until I have found it out. There is a week more, and I think that will be enough.

I'm feeling ever so much better! I don't sleep much at night, for it is so interesting to watch developments; but I sleep a good deal in the daytime.

In the daytime it is tiresome and perplexing.

There are always new shoots on the fungus, and new shades of yellow all over it. I cannot keep count of them, though I have tried conscientiously.

It is the strangest yellow, that wallpaper! It makes me think of all the yellow things I ever saw—not beautiful ones like buttercups, but old foul, bad yellow things.

But there is something else about that paper—the smell! I noticed it the moment we came into the room, but with so much air and sun it was not bad. Now we have had a week of fog and rain, and whether the windows are open or not, the smell is here.

It creeps all over the house.

I find it hovering in the dining room, skulking in the parlor, hiding in the hall, lying in wait for me on the stairs.

It gets into my hair.

Even when I go to ride, if I turn my head suddenly and surprise it—there is that smell!

Such a peculiar odor, too! I have spent hours in trying to analyze it, to find what it smelled like.

It is not bad—at first, and very gentle, but quite the subtlest, most enduring odor I ever met.

In this damp weather it is awful, I wake up in the night and find it hanging over me.

**193**

It used to disturb me at first. I thought seriously of burning the house—to reach the smell.

But now I am used to it. The only thing I can think of that it is like is the *color* of the paper! A yellow smell.

There is a very funny mark on this wall, low down, near the mopboard. A streak that runs round the room. It goes behind every piece of furniture, except the bed, a long, straight, even *smooch*, as if it had been rubbed over and over.

I wonder how it was done and who did it, and what they did it for. Round and round and round—round and round and round—it makes me dizzy!

I really have discovered something at last.

Through watching so much at night, when it changes so, I have finally found out.

The front pattern *does* move—and no wonder! The woman behind shakes it!

Sometimes I think there are a great many women behind, and sometimes only one, and she crawls around fast, and her crawling shakes it all over.

Then in the very bright spots she keeps still, and in the very shady spots she just takes hold of the bars and shakes them hard.

And she is all the time trying to climb through. But nobody could climb through that pattern—it strangles so; I think that is why it has so many heads.

They get through, and then the pattern strangles them off and turns them upside down, and makes their eyes white!

If those heads were covered or taken off it would not be half so bad.

I think the woman gets out in the daytime!

And I'll tell you why—privately—I've seen her!

I can see her out of every one of my windows!

It is the same woman, I know, for she is always creeping, and most women do not creep by daylight.

I see her on that long road under the trees, creeping along, and when a carriage comes she hides under the blackberry vines.

I don't blame her a bit. It must be very humiliating to be caught creeping by daylight!

I always lock the door when I creep by daylight. I can't do it at night, for I know John would suspect something at once.

And John is so queer now, that I don't want to irritate him. I wish he would take another room! Besides, I don't want anybody to get that woman out at night but myself.

I often wonder if I could see her out of all the windows at once.

But, turn as fast as I can, I can only see out of one at one time.

And though I always see her, she *may* be able to creep faster than I can turn!

I have watched her sometimes away off in the open country, creeping as fast as a cloud shadow in a high wind.

If only that top pattern could be gotten off from the under one! I mean to try it, little by little.

I have found out another funny thing, but I shan't tell it this time! It does not do to trust people too much.

There are only two more days to get this paper off, and I believe John is beginning to notice. I don't like the look in his eyes.

And I heard him ask Jennie a lot of professional questions about me. She had a very good report to give.

She said I slept a good deal in the daytime.

John knows I don't sleep very well at night, for all I'm so quiet!

He asked me all sorts of questions, too, and pretended to be very loving and kind.

As if I couldn't see through him!

**194**

Still, I don't wonder he acts so, sleeping under this paper for three months.

It only interests me, but I feel sure John and Jennie are secretly affected by it.


Hurrah! This is the last day, but it is enough. John to stay in town overnight, and won't be out until this evening.

Jennie wanted to sleep with me—the sly thing! but I told her I should undoubtedly rest better for a night all alone.

That was clever, for really I wasn't alone a bit! As soon as it was moonlight and that poor thing began to crawl and shake the pattern, I got up and ran to help her.

I pulled and she shook, I shook and she pulled, and before morning we had peeled off yards of that paper.

A strip about as high as my head and half around the room.

And then when the sun came and that awful pattern began to laugh at me, I declared I would finish it today!

We go away tomorrow, and they are moving all my furniture down again to leave things as they were before.

Jennie looked at the wall in amazement, but I told her merrily that I did it out of pure spite at the vicious thing.

She laughed and said she wouldn't mind doing it herself, but I must not get tired.

How she betrayed herself that time!

But I am here, and no person touches this paper but me,—not *alive*!

She tried to get me out of the room—it was too patent! But I said it was so quiet and empty and clean now that I believed I would lie down again and sleep all I could; and not to wake me even for dinner—I would call when I woke.

So now she is gone, and the servants are gone, and the things are gone, and there is nothing left but that great bedstead nailed down, with the canvas mattress we found on it.

We shall sleep downstairs tonight, and take the boat home tomorrow.

I quite enjoy the room, now it is bare again.

How those children did tear about here!

This bedstead is fairly gnawed!

But I must get to work.

I have locked the door and thrown the key down into the front path.

I don't want to go out, and I don't want to have anybody come in, 'til John comes.

I want to astonish him.

I've got a rope up here that even Jennie did not find. If that woman does get out, and tries to get away, I can tie her!

But I forgot I could not reach far without anything to stand on!

This bed will *not* move!

I tried to lift and push it until I was lame, and then I got so angry I bit off a little piece at one corner—but it hurt my teeth.

Then I peeled off all the paper I could reach standing on the floor. It sticks horribly and the pattern just enjoys it! All those strangled heads and bulbous eyes and waddling fungus growths just shriek with derision!

I am getting angry enough to do something desperate. To jump out of the window would be admirable exercise, but the bars are too strong even to try.

Besides I wouldn't do it. Of course not. I know well enough that a step like that is improper and might be misconstrued.

I don't like to look out of the windows even—there are so many of those creeping women, and they creep so fast.

I wonder if they all come out of that wallpaper as I did?

But I am securely fastened now by my well hidden rope—you don't get *me* out in the road there!

I suppose I shall have to get back behind the pattern when it comes at night, and that is hard!

It is so pleasant to be out in this great room and creep around as I please!

I don't want to go outside. I won't, even if Jennie asks me to.

For outside you have to creep on the ground, and everything is green instead of yellow.

But here I can creep smoothly on the floor, and my shoulder just fits in that long smooch around the wall, so I cannot lose my way.

Why there's John at the door!

It is no use, young man, you can't open it!

How he does call and pound!

Now he's crying for an axe.

It would be a shame to break down that beautiful door!

"John dear!" said I in the gentlest voice, "the key is down by the front steps, under a plantain leaf!"

That silenced him for a few moments.

Then he said—very quietly indeed, "Open the door, my darling!"

"I can't," said I. "The key is down by the front door under a plantain leaf!"

And then I said it again, several times, very gently and slowly, and said it so often that he had to go and see, and he got it of course, and came in. He stopped short by the door.

"What is the matter?" he cried. "For God's sake, what are you doing!"

I kept on creeping just the same, but I looked at him over my shoulder.

"I've got out at last," said I, "in spite of you and Jane. And I've pulled off most of the paper, so you can't put me back!"

Now why should that man have fainted? But he did, and right across my path by the wall, so that I had to creep over him every time!

—*Charlotte Perkins Gilman* (1860-1935)

# YOUNG GOODMAN BROWN

Young Goodman Brown came forth at sunset into the street of Salem village; but put his head back, after crossing the threshold, to exchange a parting kiss with his young wife. And Faith, as the wife was aptly named, thrust her own pretty head into the street, letting the wind play with the pink ribbons of her cap while she called to Goodman Brown.

"Dearest heart," whispered she, softly and rather sadly, when her lips were close to his ear, "prithee put off your journey until sunrise and sleep in your own bed tonight. A lone woman is troubled with such dreams and such thoughts that she's afeared of herself sometimes. Pray tarry with me this night, dear husband, of all nights in the year."

"My love and my Faith," replied young Goodman Brown, "of all nights in the year, this one night must I tarry away from thee. My journey, as thou callest it, forth and back again, must needs be done 'twixt now and sunrise. What, my sweet, pretty wife, dost thou doubt me already, and we but three months married?"

"Then God bless you!" said Faith, with the pink ribbons; "and may you find all well when you come back."

"Amen!" cried Goodman Brown. "Say thy prayers, dear Faith, and go to bed at dusk, and no harm will come to thee."

So they parted; and the young man pursued his way until, being about to turn the corner by the meeting house, he looked back and saw the head of Faith still peeping after him with a melancholy air, in spite of her pink ribbons.

"Poor little Faith!" thought he, for his heart smote him. "What a wretch am I to leave her on such an errand! She talks of dreams, too. Methought as she spoke there was trouble in her face, as if a dream had warned her what work is to be done tonight. But no, no; 'twould kill her to think it. Well, she's a blessed angel on earth; and after this one night I'll cling to her skirts and follow her to heaven."

With this excellent resolve for the future, Goodman Brown felt himself justified in making more haste on his present evil purpose. He had taken a dreary road, darkened by all the gloomiest trees of the forest, which barely stood aside to let the narrow path creep through, and closed immediately behind. It was all as lonely as could be; and there is this peculiarity in such solitude, that the traveller knows not who may be concealed by the innumerable trunks and thick boughs overhead; so that with lonely footsteps he may yet be passing through an unseen multitude.

"There may be a devilish Indian behind every tree," said Goodman Brown to himself; and he glanced fearfully behind him as he added, "What if the devil himself should be at my very elbow!"

His head being turned back, he passed a crook of the road, and, looking forward again, beheld the figure of a man, in grave and decent attire, seated at the foot of an old tree. He arose at Goodman Brown's approach and walked onward side by side with him.

"You are late, Goodman Brown," said he. "The clock of the Old South was striking as I came through Boston; and that is full fifteen minutes agone."

"Faith kept me back a while," replied the young man, with a tremor in his voice, caused by the sudden appearance of his companion, though not wholly unexpected.

It was now deep dusk in the forest, and deepest in that part of it where these two were journeying. As nearly as could be discerned, the second traveller was about fifty years old, apparently in the same rank of life as Goodman Brown, and bearing a considerable resemblance to him, though perhaps more in expression than features. Still they might have been taken for father and son. And yet, though the elder person was as simply clad as the younger and as simple in manner too, he had an indescribable air of one who knew the world, and who would not have felt abashed at the governor's dinner table or in King William's court, were it possible that his affairs

**197**

should call him thither. But the only thing about him that could be fixed upon as remarkable was his staff, which bore the likeness of a great black snake, so curiously wrought that it might almost be seen to twist and wriggle itself like a living serpent. This, of course, must have been an ocular deception, assisted by the uncertain light.

"Come, Goodman Brown," cried his fellow-traveller, "this is a dull pace for the beginning of a journey. Take my staff, if you are so soon weary."

"Friend," said the other, exchanging his slow pace for a full stop, "having kept covenant by meeting thee here, it is my purpose now to return whence I came. I have scruples touching the matter thou wot'st of."

"Sayest thou so?" replied he of the serpent, smiling apart. "Let us walk on, nevertheless, reasoning as we go; and if I convince thee not thou shalt turn back. We are but a little way in the forest yet."

"Too far! too far!" exclaimed the goodman, unconsciously resuming his walk. "My father never went into the woods on such an errand; nor his father before him. We have been a race of honest men and good Christians since the days of the martyrs; and shall I be the first of the name of Brown that ever took this path and kept—"

"Such company, thou wouldst say," observed the elder person, interpreting his pause. "Well said, Goodman Brown! I have been well acquainted with your family as with ever a one among the Puritans; and that's no trifle to say. I helped your grandfather, the constable, when he lashed the Quaker woman so smartly through the streets of Salem; and it was I that brought your father a pitch-pine knot, kindled at my own hearth, to set fire to an Indian village, in King Philip's war. They were my good friends, both; and many a pleasant walk have we had along this path, and returned merrily after midnight. I would fain be friends with you for their sake."

"If it be as thou sayest," replied Goodman Brown, "I marvel they never spoke of these matters; or, verily, I marvel not, seeing that the least rumor of the sort would have driven them from New England. We are a people of prayer, and good works to boot, and abide no such wickedness."

"Wickedness or not," said the traveller with the twisted staff, "I have a very general acquaintance here in New England. The deacons of many a church have drunk the communion wine with me; the selectmen of divers towns make me their chairman; and a majority of the Great and General Court are firm supporters of my interest. The governor and I, too—But these are state secrets."

"Can this be so?" cried Goodman Brown, with a stare of amazement at his undisturbed companion. "Howbeit, I have nothing to do with the governor and council; they have their own ways, and are no rule for a simple husbandman like me. But, were I to go on with thee, how should I meet the eye of that good old man, our minister, at Salem village: O, his voice would make me tremble both Sabbath day and lecture day."

Thus far the elder traveller had listened with due gravity; but now burst into a fit of irrepressible mirth, shaking himself so violently that his snakelike staff actually seemed to wriggle in sympathy.

"Ha! ha! ha!" shouted he again and again; then composing himself. "Well, go on, Goodman Brown, go on; but, prithee, don't kill me with laughing."

"Well, then, to end the matter at once," said Goodman Brown, considerably nettled, "there is my wife, Faith. It would break her dear little heart; and I'd rather break my own."

"Nay, if that be the case," answered the other, "e'en go thy ways, Goodman Brown. I would not for twenty old women like the one hobbling before us that Faith should come to any harm."

As he spoke, he pointed his staff at a female figure on the path, in whom Goodman Brown recognized a very pious and exemplary dame, who had taught him

**198**

his catechism in youth, and was still his moral and spiritual adviser, jointly with the minister and Deacon Gookin.

"A marvel, truly, that Goody Cloyse should be so far in the wilderness at nightfall," said he. "But, with your leave, friend, I shall take a cut through the woods until we have left this Christian woman behind. Being a stranger to you, she might ask whom I was consorting with and whither I was going."

"Be it so," said his fellow-traveller. "Betake you to the woods, and let me keep the path."

Accordingly the young man turned aside, but took care to watch his companion, who advanced softly along the road until he had come within a staff's length of the old dame. She, meanwhile, was making the best of her way, with singular speed for so aged a woman, and mumbling some indistinct words—a prayer, doubtless—as she went. The traveller put forth his staff and touched her withered neck with what seemed the serpent's tail.

"The devil!" screamed the pious old lady.

"Then Goody Cloyse knows her old friend?" observed the traveller, confronting her and leaning on his writhing stick.

"Ah, forsooth, and is it your worship indeed?" cried the good dame. "Yea, truly is it, and in the very image of my old gossip, Goodman Brown, the grandfather of the silly fellow that now is. But—would your worship believe it?—my broomstick hath strangely disappeared, stolen, as I suspect, by that unhanged witch, Goody Cory, and that, too, when I was all anointed with the juice of smallage, and cinquefoil, and wolf's bane—"

"Mingled with fine wheat and the fat of a new-born babe," said the shape of old Goodman Brown.

"Ah, your worship knows the recipe," cried the old lady, cackling aloud. "So, as I was saying, being all ready for the meeting and no horse to ride on, I made up my mind to foot it; for they tell me there is a nice young man to be taken into communion tonight. But now your good worship will lend me your arm, and we shall be there in a twinkling."

"That can hardly be," answered her friend. "I may not spare you my arm, Goody Cloyse; but here is my staff, if you will."

So saying, he threw it down at her feet, where, perhaps, it assumed life, being one of the rods which its owner had formerly let to the Egyptian magi. Of this fact, however, Goodman Brown could not take cognizance. He had cast up his eyes in astonishment, and, looking down again, beheld neither Goody Cloyse nor the serpentine staff, but his fellow-traveller alone, who waited for him as calmly as if nothing had happened.

"That old woman taught me my catechism," said the young man; and there was a world of meaning in this simple comment.

They continued to walk onward, while the elder traveller exhorted his companion to make good speed and persevere in the path, discoursing so aptly that his arguments seemed rather to spring up in the bosom of his auditor than to be suggested by himself. As they went, he plucked a branch of maple to serve for a walking stick, and began to strip it of the twigs and little boughs, which were wet with evening dew. The moment his fingers touched them they became strangely withered and dried up as with a week's sunshine. Thus the pair proceeded, at a good free pace, until suddenly, in a gloomy hollow of the road, Goodman Brown sat himself down on the stump of a tree and refused to go any farther.

"Friend," said he, stubbornly, "my mind is made up. Not another step will I budge on this errand. What if a wretched old woman do choose to go to the devil when I thought she was going to heaven: is that any reason why I should quit my dear Faith and go after her?"

"You will think better of this by and by," said his acquaintance, composedly.

"Sit here and rest yourself a while; and when you feel like moving again, there is my staff to help you along."

Without more words, he threw his companion the maple stick, and was as speedily out of sight as if he had vanished into the deepening gloom. The young man sat a few moments by the roadside, applauding himself greatly, and thinking with how clear a conscience he should meet the minister in his morning walk, nor shrink from the eye of good old Deacon Gookin. And what calm sleep would be his that very night, which was to have been spent so wickedly, but so purely and sweetly now, in the arms of Faith! Amidst these pleasant and praiseworthy meditations, Goodman Brown heard the tramp of horses along the road, and deemed it advisable to conceal himself within the verge of the forest, conscious of the guilty purpose that had brought him thither, though now so happily turned from it.

On came the hoof tramps and the voices of the riders, two grave old voices, conversing soberly as they drew near. These mingled sounds appeared to pass along the road, within a few yards of the young man's hiding place; but, owing doubtless to the depth of the gloom at that particular spot, neither the travellers nor their steeds were visible. Though their figures brushed the small boughs by the wayside, it could not be seen that they intercepted, even for a moment, the faint gleam from the strip of bright sky athwart which they must have passed. Goodman Brown alternately crouched and stood on tiptoe, pulling aside the branches and thrusting forth his head as far as he durst without discerning so much as a shadow. It vexed him the more, because he could have sworn, were such a thing possible, that he recognized the voices of the minister and Deacon Gookin, jogging along quietly, as they were wont to do, when bound to some ordination or ecclesiastical council. While yet within hearing, one of the riders stopped to pluck a switch.

"Of the two, reverend sir," said the voice like the deacon's, "I had rather miss an ordination dinner than tonight's meeting. They tell me that some of our community are to be here from Falmouth and beyond, and others from Connecticut and Rhode Island, besides several of the Indian powwows, who, after their fashion, know almost as much deviltry as the best of us. Moreover, there is a goodly young woman to be taken into communion."

"Mighty well, Deacon Gookin!" replied the solemn old tones of the minister. "Spur up, or we shall be late. Nothing can be done, you know, until I get on the ground."

The hoofs clattered again; and the voices, talking so strangely in the empty air, passed on through the forest, where no church had ever been gathered or solitary Christian prayed. Whither, then, could these holy men be journeying so deep into the heathen wilderness? Young Goodman Brown caught hold of a tree for support, being ready to sink down on the ground, faint and overburdened with the heavy sickness of his heart. He looked up to the sky, doubting whether there really was a heaven above him. Yet there was the blue arch, and the stars brightening in it.

"With heaven above and Faith below, I will yet stand firm against the devil!" cried Goodman Brown.

While he still gazed upward into the deep arch of the firmament and had lifted his hands to pray, a cloud, though no wind was stirring, hurried across the zenith and hid the brightening stars. The blue sky was still visible except directly overhead, where this black mass of cloud was sweeping swiftly northward. Aloft in the air, as if from the depths of the cloud, came a confused and doubtful sound of voices. Once the listener fancied that he could distinguish the accents of townspeople of his own, men and women, both pious and ungodly, many of whom he had met at the communion table, and had seen others rioting at the tavern. The next moment, so indistinct were the sounds, he doubted whether he had heard aught but the murmur of the old forest, whispering without a wind. Then came a stronger swell of those familiar tones, heard daily in the sunshine at Salem village, but never until now from a cloud of night.

**200**

There was one voice, of a young woman, uttering lamentations, yet with an uncertain sorrow, and entreating for some favor, which, perhaps, it would grieve her to obtain; and all the unseen multitude, both saints and sinners, seemed to encourage her onward.

"Faith!" shouted Goodman Brown, in a voice of agony and desperation; and the echoes of the forest mocked him, crying, "Faith! Faith!" as if bewildered wretches were seeking her all through the wilderness.

The cry of grief, rage, and terror was yet piercing the night, when the unhappy husband held his breath for a response. There was a scream, drowned immediately in a louder murmur of voices, fading into far-off laughter, as the dark cloud swept away, leaving the clear and silent sky above Goodman Brown. But something fluttered lightly down through the air and caught on the branch of a tree. The young man seized it, and beheld a pink ribbon.

"My Faith is gone!" cried he, after one stupefied moment. "There is no good on earth; and sin is but a name. Come, devil; for to thee is this world given."

And, maddened with despair, so that he laughed loud and long, did Goodman Brown grasp his staff and set forth again, at such a rate that he seemed to fly along the forest path rather than to walk or run. The road grew wilder and drearier and more faintly traced, and vanished at length, leaving him in the heart of the dark wilderness, still rushing onward with the instinct that guides mortal man to evil. The whole forest was peopled with frightful sounds—the creaking of the trees, the howling of wild beasts, and the yell of Indians; while sometimes the wind tolled like a distant bell, and sometimes gave a broad roar around the traveller, as if all Nature were laughing him to scorn. But he was himself the chief horror of the scene, and shrank not from its other horrors.

"Ha! ha! ha!" roared Goodman Brown when the wind laughed at him. "Let us hear which will laugh loudest. Think not to frighten me with your deviltry. Come witch, come wizard, come Indian powwow, come devil himself, and here comes Goodman Brown. You may as well fear him as he fears you."

In truth, all through the haunted forest there could be nothing more frightful than the figure of Goodman Brown. On he flew among the black pines, brandishing his staff with frenzied gestures, now giving vent to an inspiration of horrid blasphemy, and now shouting forth such laughter as set all the echoes of the forest laughing like demons around him. The fiend in his own shape is less hideous than when he rages in the breast of man. Thus sped the demoniac on his course, until, quivering among the trees, he saw a red light before him, as when the felled trunks and branches of a clearing have been set on fire, and throw up their lurid blaze against the sky, at the hour of midnight. He paused, in a lull of the tempest that had driven him onward, and heard the swell of what seemed a hymn, rolling solemnly from a distance with the weight of many voices. He knew the tune; it was a familiar one in the choir of the village meeting house. The verse died heavily away, and was lengthened by a chorus, not of human voices, but of all the sounds of the benighted wilderness pealing in awful harmony together. Goodman Brown cried out; and his cry was lost to his own ear by its unison with the cry of the desert.

In the interval of silence he stole forward until the light glared full upon his eyes. At one extremity of an open space, hemmed in by the dark wall of the forest, arose a rock, bearing some rude, natural resemblance either to an altar or a pulpit, and surrounded by four blazing pines, their tops aflame, their stems untouched, like candles at an evening meeting. The mass of foliage that had overgrown the summit of the rock was all on fire, blazing high into the night and fitfully illuminating the whole field. Each pendent twig and leafy festoon was in a blaze. As the red light arose and fell, a numerous congregation alternately shone forth, then disappeared in shadow, and again grew, as it were, out of the darkness, peopling the heart of the solitary woods at once.

"A grave and dark-clad company," quoth Goodman Brown.

In truth they were such. Among them, quivering to and fro between gloom and splendor, appeared faces that would be seen next day at the council board of the province, and others which, Sabbath after Sabbath, looked devoutly heavenward, and benignantly over the crowded pews, from the holiest pulpits in the land. Some affirm that the lady of the governor was there. At least there were high dames well known to her, and wives of honored husbands, and widows, a great multitude, and ancient maidens, all of excellent repute, and fair young girls, who trembled lest their mothers should espy them. Either the sudden gleams of light flashing over the obscure field bedazzled Goodman Brown, or he recognized a score of the church members of Salem village famous for their especial sanctity. Good old Deacon Gookin had arrived, and waited at the skirts of that venerable saint, his reverend pastor. But, irreverently consorting with these grave, reputable, and pious people, these elders of the church, these chaste dames and dewy virgins, there were men of dissolute lives and women of spotted fame, wretches given over to all mean and filthy vice, and suspected even of horrid crimes. It was strange to see that the good shrank not from the wicked, nor were the sinners abashed by the saints. Scattered also among their palefaced enemies were the Indian priests, or powwows, who had often scared their native forest with more hideous incantations than any known to English witchcraft.

"But where is Faith?" thought Goodman Brown, and, as hope came into his heart, he trembled.

Another verse of the hymn arose, a slow and mournful strain, such as the pious love, but joined to words which expressed all that our nature can conceive of sin, and darkly hinted at far more. Unfathomable to mere mortals is the lore of fiends. Verse after verse was sung; and still the chorus of the desert swelled between like the deepest tone of a mighty organ; and with the final peal of that dreadful anthem there came a sound, as if the roaring wind, the rushing streams, the howling beasts, and every other voice of the unconverted wilderness were mingling and according with the voice of guilty man in homage to the prince of all. The four blazing pines threw up a loftier flame, and obscurely discovered shapes and visages of horror on the smoke wreaths above the impious assembly. At the same moment the fire on the rock shot redly forth and formed a glowing arch above its base, where now appeared a figure. With reverence be it spoken, the figure bore no slight similitude, both in garb and manner, to some grave divine of the New England churches.

"Bring forth the converts!" cried a voice that echoed through the field and rolled into the forest.

At the word, Goodman Brown stepped forth from the shadow of the trees and approached the congregation, with whom he felt a loathful brotherhood by the sympathy of all that was wicked in his heart. He could have well nigh sworn that the shape of his own dead father beckoned him to advance, looking downward from a smoke wreath, while a woman, with dim features of despair, threw her hand to warn him back. Was it his mother? But he had no power to retreat one step, nor to resist, even in thought, when the minister and good old Deacon Gookin seized his arms and led him to the blazing rock. Thither came also the slender form of a veiled female, led between Goody Cloyse, that pious teacher of the catechism, and Martha Carrier, who had received the devil's promise to be queen of hell. A rampant hag was she. And there stood the proselytes beneath the canopy of fire.

"Welcome, my children," said the dark figure, "to the communion of your race. Ye have found thus young your nature and your destiny. My children, look behind you!"

They turned; and flashing forth, as it were, in a sheet of flame, the fiend worshippers were seen; the smile of welcome gleamed darkly on every visage.

"There," resumed the sable form, "are all whom ye have reverenced from youth. Ye deemed them holier than yourselves, and shrank from your own sin, con-

**202**

trasting it with their lives of righteousness and prayerful aspirations heavenward. Yet here are they all my worshipping assembly. This night it shall be granted you to know their secret deeds; how hoarybearded elders of the church have whispered wanton words to the young maids of their households; how many a woman, eager for widows' weeds, has given her husband a drink at bedtime and let him sleep his last sleep in her bosom; how beardless youths have made haste to inherit their fathers' wealth; and how fair damsels—blush not, sweet ones—have dug little graves in the garden, and bidden me, the sole guest, to an infant's funeral. By the sympathy of your human hearts for sin ye shall scent out all the places—whether in church, bed chamber, street, field, or forest—where crime has been committed, and shall exult to behold the whole earth one stain of guilt, one mighty blood spot. Far more than this. It shall be yours to penetrate, in every bosom, the deep mystery of sin, the fountain of all wicked arts, and which inexhaustibly supplies more evil impulses than human power—than my power at its utmost—can make manifest in deeds. And now, my children, look upon each other."

They did so; and, by the blaze of the hell-kindled torches, the wretched man beheld his Faith, and the wife her husband, trembling before that unhallowed altar.

"Lo, there ye stand, my children," said the figure, in a deep and solemn tone, almost sad with its despairing awfulness, as if his once angelic nature could yet mourn for our miserable race. "Depending upon one another's hearts, yet had still hoped that virtue were not all a dream. Now are ye undeceived. Evil is the nature of mankind. Evil must be your only happiness. Welcome again, my children, to the communion of your race."

"Welcome," repeated the fiend worshippers, in one cry of despair and triumph.

And there they stood, the only pair, as it seemed, who were yet hesitating on the verge of wickedness in this dark world. A basin was hollowed, naturally, in the rock. Did it contain water, reddened by the lurid light? or was it blood? or, perchance, a liquid flame? Herein did the shape of evil dip his hand and prepare to lay the mark of baptism upon their foreheads, that they might be partakers of the mystery of sin, more conscious of the secret guilt of others, both in deed and thought, than they could now be of their own. The husband cast one look at his pale wife, and Faith at him. What polluted wretches would the next glance show them to each other, shuddering alike at what they disclosed and what they saw!

"Faith! Faith!" cried the husband, "look up to heaven, and resist the wicked one."

Whether Faith obeyed, he knew not. Hardly had he spoken when he found himself amid calm night and solitude, listening to a roar of the wind which died heavily away through the forest. He staggered against the rock, and felt it chill and damp; while a hanging twig, that had been all on fire, besprinkled his cheek with the coldest dew.

The next morning young Goodman Brown came slowly into the street of Salem village, staring around him like a bewildered man. The good old minister was taking a walk along the graveyard to get an appetite for breakfast and meditate his sermon, and bestowed a blessing, as he passed, on Goodman Brown. He shrank from the venerable saint as if to avoid an anathema. Old Deacon Gookin was at domestic worship, and the holy words of his prayer were heard through the open window. "What God doth the wizard pray to?" quoth Goodman Brown. Goody Cloyse, that excellent old Christian, stood in the early sunshine at her own lattice, catechizing a little girl who had brought her a pint of morning's milk. Goodman Brown snatched away the child as from the grasp of the fiend himself. Turning the corner by the meeting house, he spied the head of Faith, with the pink ribbons, gazing anxiously forth, and bursting into such joy at the sight of him that she skipped along the street and almost kissed her husband before the whole village. But Goodman Brown looked sternly and sadly into her face, and passed on without a greeting.

Had Goodman Brown fallen asleep in the forest and only dreamed a wild dream of a witch meeting?

Be it so, if you will; but, alas; it was a dream of evil omen for young Goodman Brown. A stern, a sad, a darkly meditative, a distrustful, if not a desperate, man did he become from the night of that fearful dream. On the Sabbath day, when the congregation were singing a holy psalm, he could not listen, because an anthem of sin rushed loudly upon his ear and drowned all the blessed strain. When the minister spoke from the pulpit, with power and fervid eloquence and with his hand on the open Bible, of the sacred truths of our religion, and of saintlike lives and triumphant deaths, and of future bliss or misery unutterable, then did Goodman Brown turn pale, dreading lest the roof should thunder down upon the gray blasphemer and his hearers. Often, awaking suddenly at midnight, he shrank from the bosom of Faith; and at morning or eventide, when the family knelt down at prayer, he scowled, and muttered to himself, and gazed sternly at his wife, and turned away. And when he had lived long, and was borne to his grave, a hoary corpse, followed by Faith, an aged woman, and children and grandchildren, a goodly procession, besides neighbors not a few, they carved no hopeful verse upon his tombstone; for his dying hour was gloom.

—*Nathaniel Hawthorne (1804-1864)*

# TO BUILD A FIRE

Day had broken cold and gray, exceedingly cold and gray, when the man turned aside from the main Yukon trail and climbed the high earth-bank, where a dim and little-traveled trail led eastward through the fat spruce timberland. It was a steep bank, and he paused for breath at the top, excusing the act to himself by looking at his watch. It was nine o'clock. There was no sun nor hint of sun, though there was not a cloud in the sky. It was a clear day, and yet there seemed an intangible pall over the face of things, a subtle gloom that made the day dark, and that was due to the absence of sun. This fact did not worry the man. He was used to the lack of sun. It had been days since he had seen the sun, and he knew that a few more days must pass before that cheerful orb, due south, would just peep above the sky-line and dip immediately from view.

The man flung a look back along the way he had come. The Yukon lay a mile wide and hidden under three feet of ice. On top of this ice were as many feet of snow. It was all pure white, rolling in gentle undulations where the ice-jams of the freeze-up had formed. North and south, as far as his eye could see, it was unbroken white, save for a dark hairline that curved and twisted from around the spruce-covered island to the south, and that curved and twisted away into the north, where it disappeared behind another spruce-covered island. This dark hair-line was the trail—the main trail—that led south five hundred miles to the Chilcoot Pass, Dyea, and salt water; and that led north seventy miles to Dawson, and still on to the north a thousand miles to Nulato, and finally to St. Michael on Bering Sea, a thousand miles and half a thousand more.

But all this—the mysterious, far-reaching hair-line trail, the absence of sun from the sky, the tremendous cold, and the strangeness and weirdness of it all—made no impression on the man. It was not because he was long used to it. He was a newcomer in the land, a *chechaquo*, and this was his first winter. The trouble with him was that he was without imagination. He was quick and alert in the things of life, but only in the things, and not in the significances. Fifty degrees below zero meant eighty-odd degrees of frost. Such fact impressed him as being cold and uncomfortable, and that was all. It did not lead him to meditate upon his frailty as a creature of temperature, and upon man's frailty in general, able only to live within certain narrow limits of heat and cold; and from there on it did not lead him to the conjectural field of immortality and man's place in the universe. Fifty degrees below zero stood for a bite of frost that hurt and that must be guarded against by the use of mittens, ear-flaps, warm moccasins, and thick socks. Fifty degrees below zero was to him just precisely fifty degrees below zero. That there should be anything more to it than that was a thought that never entered his head.

As he turned to go on, he spat speculatively. There was a sharp, explosive crackle that startled him. He spat again. And again, in the air, before it could fall to the snow, the spittle crackled. He knew that at fifty below spittle crackled on the snow, but this spittle had crackled in the air. Undoubtedly it was colder than fifty below—how much colder he did not know. But the temperature did not matter. He was bound for the old claim on the left fork of Henderson Creek, where the boys were already. They had come over across the divide from the Indian Creek country, while he had come the roundabout way to take a look at the possibilities of getting out logs in the spring from the islands in the Yukon. He would be in to camp by six o'clock; a bit after dark, it was true, but the boys would be there, a fire would be going, and a hot supper would be ready. As for lunch, he pressed his hand against the protruding bundle under his jacket. It was also under his shirt, wrapped up in a handkerchief and lying against the naked skin. It was the only way to keep the biscuits from freezing. He smiled agreeably to himself as he thought of those biscuits, each cut open and sopped in bacon grease, and each enclosing a generous slice of fried bacon.

He plunged in among the big spruce trees. The trail was faint. A foot of snow had fallen since the last sled had passed over, and he was glad he was without a sled, traveling light. In fact, he carried nothing but the lunch wrapped in the handkerchief. He was surprised, however, at the cold. It certainly was cold, he concluded, as he rubbed his numb nose and cheek-bones with his mittened hand. He was a warm-whiskered man, but the hair on his face did not protect the high cheek-bones and the eager nose that thrust itself agressively into the frosty air.

At the man's heels trotted a dog, a big native husky, the proper wolfdog, gray-coated and without any visible or temperamental difference from its brother, the wild wolf. The animal was depressed by the tremendous cold. It knew that it was no time for traveling. Its instinct told it a truer tale than was told to the man by the man's judgment. In reality, it was not merely colder than fifty below zero; it was colder than sixty below, than seventy below. It was seventy-five below zero. Since the freezing point is thirty-two above zero, it meant that one hundred and seven degrees of frost obtained. The dog did not know anything about thermometers. Possibly in its brain there was no sharp consciousness of a condition of very cold such as was in the man's brain. But the brute had its instinct. It experienced a vague but menacing apprehension that subdued it and made it slink along at the man's heels, and that made it question eagerly every unwonted movement of the man as if expecting him to go into camp or to seek shelter somewhere and build a fire. The dog had learned fire, and it wanted fire, or else to burrow under the snow and cuddle its warmth away from the air.

The frozen moisture of its breathing had settled on its fur in a fine powder of frost, and especially were its jowls, muzzle, and eyelashes whitened by its crystalled breath. The man's red beard and mustache were likewise frosted, but more solidly, the deposit taking the form of ice and increasing with every warm, moist breath he exhaled. Also, the man was chewing tobacco, and the muzzle of ice held his lips so rigidly that he was unable to clear his chin when he expelled the juice. The result was that a crystal beard of the color and solidity of amber was increasing its length on his chin. If he fell down it would shatter itself, like glass, into brittle fragments. But he did not mind the appendage. It was the penalty all tobacco chewers paid in that country, and he had been out before in two cold snaps. They had not been so cold as this, he knew, but by the spirit thermometer at Sixty Mile he knew they had been registered at fifty below and at fifty-five.

He held on through the level stretch of woods for several miles, crossed a wide flat of nigger-heads, and dropped down a bank to the frozen bed of a small stream. This was Henderson Creek, and he knew he was ten miles from the forks. He looked at his watch. It was ten o'clock. He was making four miles an hour, and he calculated that he would arrive at the forks at half-past twelve. He decided to celebrate that event by eating his lunch there.

The dog dropped in again at his heels, with a tail drooping discouragement, as the man swung along the creek-bed. The furrow of the old sled-trail was plainly visible, but a dozen inches of snow covered the marks of the last runners. In a month no man had come up or down that silent creek. The man held steadily on. He was not much given to thinking, and just then particularly he had nothing to think about save that he would eat lunch at the forks and that at six o'clock he would be in camp with the boys. There was nobody to talk to; and, had there been, speech would have been impossible because of the ice-muzzle on his mouth. So he continued monotonously to chew tobacco and to increase the length of his amber beard.

Once in a while the thought reiterated itself that it was very cold and that he had never experienced such cold. As he walked along he rubbed his cheek-bones and nose with the back of his mittened hand. He did this automatically, now and again changing hands. But rub as he would, the instant he stopped his cheek-bones went numb, and the following instant the end of his nose went numb. He was sure to frost

**206**

his cheeks; he knew that, and experienced a pang of regret that he had not devised a nose-strap of the sort Bud wore in cold snaps. Such a strap passed across the cheeks, as well, and saved them. But it didn't matter much, after all. What were frosted cheeks? A bit painful, that was all; they were never serious.

Empty as the man's mind was of thoughts, he was keenly observant and he noticed the changes in the creek, the curves and bends and timber-jams, and always he sharply noted where he placed his feet. Once, coming around a bend, he shied abruptly, like a startled horse, curved away from the place where he had been walking, and retreated several paces back along the trail. The creek he knew was frozen clear to the bottom,—no creek could contain water in that arctic winter,—but he knew also that there were springs that bubbled out from the hillsides and ran along under the snow and on top of the ice of the creek. He knew that the coldest snaps never froze these springs, and he knew likewise their danger. They were traps. They hid pools of water under the snow that might be three inches deep, or three feet. Sometimes a skin of ice half an inch thick covered them, and in turn was covered by the snow. Sometimes there were alternate layers of water and ice-skins, so that when one broke through he kept on breaking through for a while, sometimes wetting himself to the waist.

That was why he had shied in such panic. He had felt the give under his feet and heard the crackle of a snow-hidden ice-skin. And to get his feet wet in such a temperature meant trouble and danger. At the very least it meant delay, for he would be forced to stop and build a fire, and under its protection to bare his feet while he dried his socks and moccasins. He stood and studied the creek-bed and its banks, and decided that the flow of water came from the right. He reflected a while, rubbing his nose and cheeks, then skirted to the left, stepping gingerly and testing the footing for each step. Once clear of the danger, he took a fresh chew of tobacco and swung along at his four-mile gait.

In the course of the next two hours he came upon several similar traps. Usually the snow above the hidden pools had a sunken, candied appearance that advertised the danger. Once again, however, he had a close call; and once, suspecting danger, he compelled the dog to go on in front. The dog did not want to go. It hung back until the man shoved it forward, and then it went quickly across the white, unbroken surface. Suddenly it broke through, floundered to one side, and got away to firmer footing. It had wet its forefeet and legs, and almost immediately the water that clung to it turned to ice. It made quick efforts to lick the ice off its legs, then dropped down in the snow and began to bite out the ice that had formed between the toes. This was a matter of instinct. To permit the ice to remain would mean sore feet. It did not know this. It merely obeyed the mysterious prompting that arose from the deep crypts of its being. But the man knew, having achieved a judgment on the subject, and he removed the mitten from his right hand and helped tear out the ice-particles. He did not expose his fingers more than a minute, and was astonished at the swift numbness that smote them. It certainly was cold. He pulled on the mitten hastily, and beat the hand savagely across his chest.

At twelve o'clock the day was at its brightest. Yet the sun was too far south on its winter journey to clear the horizon. The bulge of the earth intervened between it and Henderson Creek, where the man walked under a clear sky at noon and cast no shadow. At half-past twelve, to the minute, he arrived at the forks of the creek. He was pleased at the speed he had made. If he kept it up, he would certainly be with the boys by six. He unbuttoned his jacket and shirt and drew forth his lunch. The action consumed no more than a quarter of a minute, yet in that brief moment the numbness laid hold of the exposed fingers. He did not put the mitten on, but, instead, struck the fingers a dozen sharp smashes against his leg. Then he sat down on a snow-covered log to eat. The sting that followed upon the striking of his fingers against his leg ceased so quickly that he was startled. He had had no chance to take a bite of biscuit.

**207**

He struck the fingers repeatedly and returned them to the mitten, baring the other hand for the purpose of eating. He tried to take a mouthful, but the ice-muzzle prevented. He had forgotten to build a fire and thaw out. He chuckled at his foolishness, and as he chuckled he noted the numbness creeping into the exposed fingers. Also, he noted that the stinging which had first come to his toes when he sat down was already passing away. He wondered whether the toes were warm or numb. He moved them inside the moccasins and decided that they were numb.

He pulled the mitten on hurriedly and stood up. He was a bit frightened. He stamped up and down until the stinging returned into the feet. It certainly was cold, was his thought. That man from Sulphur Creek had spoken the truth when telling how cold it sometimes got in the country. And he had laughed at him at the time! That showed one must not be too sure of things. There was no mistake about it, it *was* cold. He strode up and down, stamping his feet and threshing his arms, until reassured by the returning warmth. Then he got out matches and proceeded to make a fire. From the undergrowth, where high water of the previous spring had lodged a supply of seasoned twigs, he got his firewood. Working carefully from a small beginning, he soon had a roaring fire, over which he thawed the ice from his face and in the protection of which he ate his biscuits. For the moment the cold of space was outwitted. The dog took satisfaction in the fire, stretching out close enough for warmth and far enough away to escape being singed.

When the man had finished, he filled his pipe and took his comfortable time over a smoke. Then he pulled on his mittens, settled the ear-flaps of his cap firmly about his ears, and took the creek trail up the left fork. The dog was disappointed and yearned back toward the fire. The man did not know cold. Possibly all the generations of his ancestry had been ignorant of cold, of real cold, of cold one hundred and seven degrees below freezing point. But the dog knew; all its ancestry knew, and it had inherited the knowledge. And it knew that it was not good to walk abroad in such fearful cold. It was the time to lie snug in a hole in the snow and wait for a curtain of cloud to be drawn across the face of outer space whence this cold came. On the other hand, there was no keen intimacy between the dog and the man. The one was the toil-slave of the other and the only caresses it had ever received were the caresses of the whiplash and of harsh and menacing throat-sounds that threatened the whiplash. So the dog made no effort to communicate its apprehension to the man. It was not concerned in the welfare of the man; it was for its own sake that it yearned back toward the fire. But the man whistled, and spoke to it with the sound of whiplashes, and the dog swung in at the man's heel and followed after.

The man took a chew of tobacco and proceeded to start a new amber beard. Also, his moist breath quickly powdered with white his mustache, eyebrows, and lashes. There did not seem to be so many springs on the left fork of the Henderson, and for half an hour the man saw no signs of any. And then it happened. At a place where there were no signs, where the soft, unbroken snow seemed to advertise solidity beneath, the man broke through. It was not deep. He wet himself halfway to the knees before he floundered out to the first crust.

He was angry, and cursed his luck aloud. He had hoped to get into camp with the boys at six o'clock, and this would delay him an hour, for he would have to build a fire and dry out his foot-gear. This was imperative at that low temperature—he knew that much; and he turned aside to the bank, which he climbed. On top, tangled in the underbrush about the trunks of several small spruce trees, was a high-water deposit of dry firewood—sticks and twigs, principally, but also larger portions of seasoned branches and fine, dry, last-year's grasses. He threw down several large pieces on top of the snow. This served for a foundation and prevented the young flame from drowning itself in the snow it otherwise would melt. The flame he got by touching a match to a small shred of birch bark that he took from his pocket. This burned even more readily than paper. Placing it on the foundation, he fed the young flame with wisps of dry grass and with the tiniest dry twigs. He worked slowly and carefully, keenly aware of his danger. Gradually, as the flame grew stronger, he increased the size of the twigs with which he fed it. He squatted in the snow, pulling the twigs out from their entanglement in the brush and feeding directly to the flame. He knew there must be no failure. When it is seventy-five below zero, a man must not fail in his first attempt to build a fire—that is, if his feet are wet. If his feet are dry, and he fails, he can run along the trail for half a mile and restore his circulation. But the circulation of wet and freezing feet cannot be restored by running when it is seventy-five below. No matter how fast he runs, the wet feet will freeze the harder.

All this the man knew. The old-timer on Sulphur Creek had told him about it the previous fall, and now he was appreciating the advice. Already all sensation had gone out of his feet. To build the fire he had been forced to remove his mittens, and the fingers had quickly gone numb. His pace of four miles an hour had kept his heart pumping blood to the surface of his body and to all the extremities. But the instant he stopped, the action of the pump eased down. The cold of space smote the unprotected tip of the planet, and he, being on that unprotected tip, received the full force of the blow. The blood of his body recoiled before it. The blood was alive, like the dog, and like the dog it wanted to hide away and cover itself up from the fearful cold. So long as he walked four miles an hour, he pumped that blood, willy-nilly, to the surface; but now it ebbed away and sank down into the recesses of his body. The extremities were the first to feel its absence. His wet feet froze the faster, and his exposed fingers numbed the faster, though they had not yet begun to freeze. Nose and cheeks were already freezing, while the skin of all his body chilled as it lost its blood.

But he was safe. Toes and nose and cheeks would be only touched by the frost, for the fire was beginning to burn with strength. He was feeding it with twigs the size of his finger. In another minute he would be able to feed it with branches the size of his wrist, and then he could remove his wet foot-gear, and, while it dried, he could keep his naked feet warm by the fire, rubbing them at first, of course, with snow. The fire was a success. He was safe. He remembered the advice of the old-timer on Sulphur Creek, and smiled. The old-timer had been very serious in laying down the law that no man must travel alone in the Klondike after fifty below. Well, here he was; he had had the accident; he was alone; and he had saved himself. Those old-timers were rather womanish, some of them, he thought. All a man had to do was to keep his head, and he was all right. Any man who was a man could travel alone. But it was surprising, the rapidity with which his cheeks and nose were freezing. And he had not thought his fingers could go lifeless in so short a time. Lifeless they were, for he could scarcely make them move together to grip a twig, and they seemed remote from his body and from him. When he touched a twig, he had to look and see whether or not he had hold of it. The wires were pretty well down between him and his finger-ends.

All of which counted for little. There was the fire, snapping and crackling and promising life with every dancing flame. He started to untie his moccasins. They were coated with ice; the thick German socks were like sheaths of iron halfway to the knees; and the moccasin strings were like rods of steel all twisted and knotted as by some conflagration. For a moment he tugged with his numb fingers, then, realizing the folly of it, he drew his sheath-knife.

But before he could cut the strings, it happened. It was his own fault or, rather, his mistake. He should not have built the fire under the spruce tree. He should have built it in the open. But it had been easier to pull the twigs from the brush and drop them directly on the fire. Now the tree under which he had done this carried a weight of snow on its boughs. No wind had blown for weeks, and each bough was fully freighted. Each time he had pulled a twig he had communicated a slight agitation to the tree—an imperceptible agitation, so far as he was concerned, but an agitation

**209**

sufficient to bring about the disaster. High up in the tree one bough capsized its load of snow. This fell on the boughs beneath, capsizing them. This process continued, spreading out and involving the whole tree. It grew like an avalanche, and it descended without warning upon the man and the fire, and the fire was blotted out! Where it had burned was a mantle of fresh and disordered snow.

The man was shocked. It was as though he had just heard his own sentence of death. For a moment he sat and stared at the spot where the fire had been. Then he grew very calm. Perhaps the old-timer on Sulphur Creek was right. If he had only had a trail-mate he would have been in no danger now. The trail-mate could have built the fire. Well, it was up to him to build the fire over again, and this second time there must be no failure. Even if he succeeded, he would most likely lose some toes. His feet must be badly frozen by now, and there would be some time before the second fire was ready.

Such were his thoughts, but he did not sit and think them. He was busy all the time they were passing through his mind. He made a new foundation for a fire, this time in the open, where no treacherous tree could blot it out. Next, he gathered dry grasses and tiny twigs from the high-water flotsam. He could not bring his fingers together to pull them out, but he was able to gather them by the handful. In this way he got many rotten twigs and bits of green moss that were undesirable, but it was the best he could do. He worked methodically, even collecting an armful of the larger branches to be used later when the fire gathered strength. And all the while the dog sat and watched him, a certain yearning wistfulness in its eyes, for it looked upon him as the fire-provider, and the fire was slow in coming.

When all was ready, the man reached in his pocket for a second piece of birch bark. He knew the bark was there, and, though he could not feel it with his fingers, he could hear its crisp rustling as he fumbled for it. Try as he would, he could not clutch hold of it. And all the time, in his consciousness, was the knowledge that each instant his feet were freezing. This thought tended to put him in a panic, but he fought against it and kept calm. He pulled on his mittens with his teeth, and threshed his arms back and forth, beating his hands with all his might against his sides. He did this sitting down, and he stood up to do it; and all the while the dog sat in the snow, its wolf-brush of a tail curled around warmly over its forefeet, its sharp wolf-ears pricked forward intently as it watched the man. And the man, as he beat and threshed with his arms and hands, felt a great surge of envy as he regarded the creature that was warm and secure in its natural covering.

After a time he was aware of the first far-away signals of sensation in his beaten fingers. The faint tingling grew stronger till it evolved into a stinging ache that was excruciating, but which the man hailed with satisfaction. He stripped the mitten from his right hand and fetched forth the birch bark. The exposed fingers were quickly going numb again. Next he brought out his bunch of sulphur matches. But the tremendous cold had already driven the life out of his fingers. In his efforts to separate one match from the others, the whole bunch fell in the snow. He tried to pick it out of the snow, but failed. The dead fingers could neither touch nor clutch. He was very careful. He drove the thought of his freezing feet, and nose, and cheeks, out of his mind, devoting his whole soul to the matches. He watched, using the sense of vision in place of that of touch, and then he saw his fingers on each side of the bunch, he closed them—that is, he willed to close them, for the wires were down, and the fingers did not obey. He pulled the mitten on the right hand, and beat it fiercely against his knee. Then, with both mittened hands, he scooped the bunch of matches, along with much snow, into his lap. Yet he was no better off.

After some manipulation he managed to get the bunch between the heels of his mittened hands. In this fashion he carried it to his mouth. The ice crackled and snapped when by a violent effort he opened his mouth. He drew the lower jaw in, curled the upper lip out of the way, and scraped the bunch with his upper teeth in order to separate a match. He succeeded in getting one, which he dropped on his lap. He was no better off. He could not pick it up. Then he devised a way. He picked it up in his teeth and scratched it on his leg. Twenty times he scratched before he succeeded in lighting it. As it flamed he held it with his teeth to the birch bark. But the burning brimstone went up his nostrils and into his lungs, causing him to cough spasmodically. The match fell into the snow and went out.

The old-timer on Sulphur Creek was right, he thought in the moment of controlled despair that ensued: after fifty below, a man should travel with a partner. He beat his hands, but failed in exciting any sensation. Sudden he bared both hands, removing the mittens with his teeth. He caught the whole bunch between the heels of his hands. His arm muscles not being frozen enabled him to press the hand-heels tightly against the matches. Then he scratched the bunch along his leg. It flared into flame, seventy sulphur matches at once! There was no wind to blow them out. He kept his head to one side to escape the strangling fumes, and held the blazing bunch to the birch bark. As he so held it, he became aware of sensation in his hand. His flesh was burning. He could smell it. Deep down below the surface he could feel it. The sensation developed into pain that grew acute. And still he endured it, holding the flame of the matches clumsily to the bark that would not light readily because his own burning hands were in the way, absorbing most of the flame.

At last, when he could endure no more, he jerked his hands apart. The blazing matches fell sizzling into the snow, but the birch bark was alight. He began laying dry grasses and the tiniest twigs on the flame. He could not pick and choose, for he had to lift the fuel between the heels of his hands. Small pieces of rotten wood and green moss clung to the twigs, and he bit them off as well as he could with his teeth. He cherished the flame carefully and awkwardly. It meant life, and it must not perish. The withdrawl of blood from the surface of his body now made him begin to shiver, and he grew more awkward. A large piece of green moss fell squarely on the little fire. He tried to poke it out with his fingers, but his shivering frame made him poke too far, and he disrupted the nucleus of the little fire, the burning grasses and tiny twigs separating and scattering. He tried to poke them together again, but in spite of the tenseness of the effort, his shivering got away with him, and the twigs were hopelessly scattered. Each twig gushed a puff of smoke and went out. The fire-provider had failed. As he looked apathetically about him, his eyes chanced on the dog, sitting across the ruins of the fire from him, in the snow, making restless, hunching movements, slightly lifiting one forefoot and then the other, shifting its weight back and forth on them with wistful eagerness.

The sight of the dog put a wild idea into his head. He remembered the tale of the man, caught in a blizzard, who killed a steer and crawled inside the carcass, and so was saved. He would kill the dog and bury his hands in the warm body until the numbness went out of them. Then he could build another fire. He spoke to the dog, calling it to him; but in his voice was a strange note of fear that frightened the animal, who had never known the man to speak in such way before. Something was the matter, and its suspicious nature sensed danger—it knew not what danger, but somewhere, somehow, in its brain arose an apprehension of the man. It flattened its ears down at the sound of the man's voice, and its restless, hunching movements and the liftings and shiftings of its forefeet became more pronounced; but it would not come to the man. He got on his hands and knees and crawled toward the dog. This unusual posture again excited suspicion, and the animal sidled mincingly away.

The man sat up in the snow for a moment and struggled for calmness. Then he pulled on his mittens, by means of his teeth, and got upon his feet. He glanced down at first in order to assure himself that he was really standing up, for the absence of sensation in his feet left him unrelated to the earth. His erect position in itself started to drive the webs of suspicion from the dog's mind; and when he spoke peremptorily, with the sound of whiplashes in his voice, the dog rendered its customary allegiance and came to him. As it came within reaching distance, the man lost his control. His arms flashed out to the dog, and he experienced genuine surprise when he discovered that his hands could not clutch, that there was neither bend nor feeling in the fingers. He had forgotten for the moment that they were frozen and that they were freezing more and more. All this happened quickly, and before the animal could get away, he encircled its body with his arms. He sat down in the snow, and in this fashion held the dog, while it snarled and whined and struggled.

But it was all he could do, hold its body encircled in his arms and sit there. He realized that he could not kill the dog. There was no way to do it. With his helpless hands he could neither draw nor hold his sheathknife nor throttle the animal. He released it, and it plunged wildly away, with tail between its legs, and still snarling. It halted forty feet away and surveyed him curiously, with ears sharply pricked forward. The man looked down at his hands in order to locate them, and found them hanging on the ends of his arms. It struck him as curious that one should have to use his eyes in order to find out where his hands were. He began threshing his arms back and forth, beating the mittened hands against his sides. He did this for five minutes, violently, and his heart pumped enough blood up to the surface to put a stop to his shivering. But no sensation was aroused in the hands. He had an impression that they hung like weights on the ends of his arms, but when he tried to run the impression down, he could not find it.

A certain fear of death, dull and oppressive, came to him. This fear quickly became poignant as he realized that it was no longer a mere matter of freezing his fingers and toes, or of losing his hands and feet, but that it was a matter of life and death with the chances against him. This threw him into a panic, and he turned and ran up the creek-bed along the old, dim trail. The dog joined in behind and kept up with him. He ran blindly, without intention, in fear such as he had never known in his life. Slowly, as he plowed and floundered through the snow, he began to see things again,—the banks of the creek, the old timber-jams, the leafless aspens, and the sky. The running made him feel better. He did not shiver. Maybe, if he ran on, his feet would thaw out; and, anyway, if he ran far enough, he would reach camp and the boys. Without doubt he would lose some fingers and toes and some of his face; but the boys would take care of him, and save the rest of him when he got there. And at the same time there was another thought in his mind that said he would never get to the camp and the boys; that it was too many miles away, that the freezing had too great a start on him, and that he would soon be stiff and dead. This thought he kept in the background and refused to consider. Sometimes it pushed itself forward and demanded to be heard, but he thrust it back and strove to think of other things.

It struck him as curious that he could run at all on feet so frozen that he could not feel them when they struck the earth and took the weight of his body. He seemed to himself to skim along above the surface, and to have no connection with the earth. Somewhere he had once seen a winged Mercury, and he wondered if Mercury felt as he felt when skimming over the earth.

His theory of running until he reached camp and the boys had one flaw in it: he lacked the endurance. Several times he stumbled, and finally he tottered, crumpled up, and fell. When he tried to rise, he failed. He must sit and rest, he decided, and next time he would merely walk and keep on going. As he sat and regained his breath, he noted that he was feeling quite warm and comfortable. He was not shivering, and it even seemed that a warm glow had come to his chest and trunk. And yet, when he touched his nose or cheeks, there was no sensation. Running would not thaw them out. Nor would it thaw out his hands and feet. Then the thought came to him that the frozen portions of his body must be extending. He tried to keep this thought down, to forget it, to think of something else; he was aware of the panicky feeling that it caused, and he was afraid of the panic. But the thought asserted itself, and persisted, until it produced a vision of his body totally frozen. This was too much, and he made another wild run along the trail. Once he slowed down to a walk, but the thought of the freezing extending itself made him run again. And all the time the dog ran with him, at his heels. When he fell down a second time, it curled its tail over its forefeet and sat in front of him, facing him, curiously eager and intent. The warmth and security of the animal angered him, and he cursed it till it flattened down its ears appeasingly. This time the shivering came more quickly upon the man. He was losing in his battle with the frost. It was creeping into his body from all sides. The thought of it drove him on, but he ran no more than a hundred feet, when he staggered and pitched headlong. It was his last panic. When he had recovered his breath and control, he sat up and entertained in his mind the conception of meeting death with dignity. However, the conception did not come to him in such terms. His idea of it was that he had been making a fool of himself, running around like a chicken with its head cut off—such was the simile that occurred to him. Well, he was bound to freeze anyway, and he might as well take it decently. With this new-found peace of mind came the first glimmerings of drowsiness. A good idea, he thought, to sleep off to death. It was like taking an anaesthetic. Freezing was not so bad as people thought. There were lots worse ways to die.

He pictured the boys finding his body next day. Suddenly he found himself with them, coming along the trail and looking for himself. And, still with them, he came around a turn in the trail and found himself lying in the snow. He did not belong with himself anymore, for even then he was out of himself, standing with the boys and looking at himself in the snow. It certainly was cold, was his thought. When he got back to the States he could tell the folks what real cold was. He drifted on from this to a vision of the old-timer on Sulphur Creek. He could see him quite clearly, warm and comfortable, and smoking a pipe.

"You were right, old hoss; you were right," the man mumbled to the old-timer of Sulphur Creek.

Then the man drowsed off into what seemed to him the most comfortable and satisfying sleep he had ever known. The dog sat facing him and waiting. The brief day drew to a close in a long, slow twilight. There were no signs of a fire to be made, and, besides, never in the dog's experience had it known a man to sit like that in the snow and make no fire. As the twilight drew on, its eager yearning for the fire mastered it, and with a great lifting and shifting of forefeet, it whined softly, then flattened its ears down in anticipation of being chidden by the man. But the man remained silent. Later, the dog whined loudly. And still later it crept close to the man and caught the scent of death. This made the animal bristle and back away. A little longer it delayed, howling under the stars that leaped and danced and shone brightly in the cold sky. Then it turned and trotted up the trail in the direction of the camp it knew, where were the other food-providers and fire-providers.

—*Jack London (1876-1916)*

# THE MASQUE OF THE RED DEATH

The "Red Death" had long devastated the country. No pestilence had ever been so fatal or so hideous. Blood was its Avatar and its seal—the redness and the horror of blood. There were sharp pains, and sudden dizziness, and then profuse bleeding at the pores, with dissolution. The scarlet stains upon the body, and especially upon the face of the victim, were the pest ban which shut him out from the aid and from the sympathy of his fellow-men; and the whole seizure, progress, and termination of the disease, were the incidents of half-an-hour.

But the Prince Prospero was happy and dauntless and sagacious. When his dominions were half-depopulated, he summoned to his presence a thousand hale and light-hearted friends from among the knights and dames of his court, and with these retired to the deep seclusion of one of his castellated abbeys. This was an extensive and magnificent structure, the creation of the prince's own eccentric yet august taste. A strong and lofty wall girdled it in. This wall had gates of iron. The courtiers, having entered, brought furnaces and massy hammers and welded the bolts. They resolved to leave means neither of ingress or egress to the sudden impulses of despair from without or of frenzy from within. The abbey was amply provisioned. With such precautions the courtiers might bid defiance to contagion. The external world could take care of itself. In the meantime it was folly to grieve or to think. The prince had provided all the appliances of pleasure. There were buffoons, there were improvisatori, there were ballet dancers, there were musicians, there was beauty, there was wine. All these and security were within. Without was the "Red Death."

It was toward the close of the fifth or sixth month of his seclusion, and while the pestilence raged most furiously abroad, that the Prince Prospero entertained his thousand friends at a masked ball of the most unusual magnificence.

It was a voluptuous scene, that masquerade. But first let me tell of the rooms in which it was held. There were seven—an imperial suite. In many palaces, however, such suites form a long and straight vista, while the folding doors slide back nearly to the walls on either hand, so that the view of the whole extent is scarcely impeded. Here the case was very different, as might have been expected from the duke's love of the *bizarre*. The apartments were so irregularly disposed that the vision embraced but little more than one at a time. There was a sharp turn at every twenty or thirty yards, and at each turn a novel effect. To the right and left, in the middle of each wall, a tall and narrow Gothic window looked out upon a closed corridor which pursued the windings of the suite. These windows were of stained glass whose color varied in accordance with the prevailing hue of the decorations of the chamber into which it opened. That at the eastern extremity was hung, for example, in blue, and vividly blue were its windows. The second chamber was purple in its ornaments and tapestries, and here the panes were purple. The third was green throughout, and so were the casements. The fourth was furnished and lighted with orange, the fifth with white, the sixth with violet. The seventh apartment was closely shrouded in black velvet tapestries that hung all over the ceiling and down the walls, falling in heavy folds upon a carpet of the same material and hue. But in this chamber only the color of the windows failed to correspond with the decorations. The panes here were scarlet —a deep blood-color. Now in no one of the seven apartments was there any lamp or candelabrum amid the profusion of golden ornaments that lay scattered to and fro or depended from the roof. There was no light of any kind emanating from lamp or candle within the suite of chambers; but in the corridors that followed the suite there stood opposite to each window a heavy tripod bearing a brazier of fire that projected its rays through the tinted glass and so glaringly illumined the room. And thus were produced a multitude of gaudy and fantastic appearances. But in the western or black chamber the effect of the firelight that streamed upon the dark hangings, through the blood-tinted panes, was ghastly in the extreme, and produced so wild a look upon the countenances of those who entered that there were few of the company bold enough to set foot within its precincts at all.

It was in this apartment also that there stood against the western wall a gigantic clock of ebony. Its pendulum swung to and fro with a dull, heavy, monotonous clang; and when the minute-hand made the circuit of the face, and the hour was to be stricken, there came from the brazen lungs of the clock a sound which was clear and loud, and deep, and exceedingly musical, but of so peculiar a note and emphasis that, at each lapse of an hour, the musicians of the orchestra were constrained to pause momentarily in their performance to hearken to the sound; and thus the waltzers perforce ceased their evolutions, and there was a brief disconcert of the whole gay company, and while the chimes of the clock yet rang it was observed that the giddiest grew pale, and the more aged and sedate passed their hands over their brows as if in confused reverie or meditation; but when the echoes had fully ceased a light laughter at once pervaded the assembly; the musicians looked at each other and smiled as if at their own nervousness and folly, and made whispering vows each to the other that the next chiming of the clock should produce in them no similar emotion, and then, after the lapse of sixty minutes (which embrace three thousand and six hundred seconds of the time that flies), there came yet another chiming of the clock, and then were the same disconcert and tremulousness and meditation as before.

But in spite of these things it was a gay and magnificent revel. The tastes of the duke were peculiar. He had a fine eye for colors and effects. He disregarded the *decora* of mere fashion. His plans were bold and fiery, and his conceptions glowed with barbaric lustre. There are some who would have thought him mad. His followers felt that he was not. It was necessary to hear, and see, and touch him to be *sure* that he was not.

He had directed, in great part, the moveable embellishments of the seven chambers, upon occasion of this great *fête*; and it was his own guiding taste which had given character to the masqueraders. Be sure they were grotesque. There were much glare and glitter and piquancy and phantasm—much of what has been since seen in *Hernani*. There were arabesque figures with unsuited limbs and appointments. There were delirious fancies such as the madman fashions. There were much of the beautiful, much of the wanton, much of the *bizarre*, something of the terrible, and not a little of that which might have excited disgust. To and fro in the seven chambers there stalked, in fact, a multitude of dreams. And these—the dreams—writhed in and about, taking hue from the rooms, and causing the wild music of the orchestra to seem as the echo of their steps, and, anon, there strikes the ebony clock which stands in the hall of the velvet; and then, for a moment, all is still, and all is silent save the voice of the clock. The dreams are stiff-frozen as they stand. But the echoes of the chime die away—they have endured but an instant—and a light, half-subdued laughter floats after them as they depart. And now again the music swells, and the dreams live, and writhe to and fro more merrily than ever, taking hue from the many tinted windows through which stream the rays from the tripods. But to the chamber which lies most eastwardly of the seven, there are now none of the maskers who venture; for the night is waning away; and there flows a ruddier light through the blood-colored panes; and the blackness of the sable-drapery appalls; and to him whose foot falls upon the sable carpet, there comes from the near clock of ebony a muffled peal more solemnly emphatic than any which reaches *their* ears who indulge in the more remote gaieties of the other apartments.

But these other apartments were densely crowded, and in them beat feverishly the heart of life. And the revel went whirlingly on, until at length there commenced the sounding of midnight upon the clock. And then the music ceased, as I have told; and the evolutions of the waltzers were quieted; and there was an uneasy cessation of all things as before. But now there were twelve strokes to be sounded by the bell of the clock; and thus it happened, perhaps, that more of thought crept, with more of

**215**

time, into the meditations of the thoughtful among those who revelled. And thus, too, it happened, perhaps, that before the last echoes of the last chime had utterly sunk into silence, there were many individuals in the crowd who had found leisure to become aware of the presence of a masked figure which had arrested the attention of no single individual before. And the rumor of this new presence having spread itself whisperingly around, there arose at length from the whole company a buzz, or murmur, expressive of disapprobation and surprise—then, finally, of terror, of horror, and of disgust.

In an assembly of phantasms such as I have painted, it may well be supposed that no ordinary appearance could have excited such sensation. In truth the masquerade license of the night was nearly unlimited; but the figure in question had out-Heroded Herod, and gone beyond the bounds of even the prince's indefinite decorum. There are chords in the hearts of the most reckless which cannot be touched without emotion. Even with the utterly lost, to whom life and death are equally jests, there are matters of which no jest can be made. The whole company indeed seemed now deeply to feel that in the costume and bearing of the stranger neither wit nor propriety existed. The figure was tall and gaunt, and shrouded from head to foot in the habiliments of the grave. The mask which concealed the visage was made so nearly to resemble the countenance of a stiffened corpse that the closest scrutiny must have had difficulty in detecting the cheat. And yet all this might have been endured, if not approved, by the mad revellers around. But the mummer had gone so far as to assume the type of the Red Death. His vesture was dabbled in *blood*—and his broad brow, with all the features of the face, was besprinkled with the scarlet horror.

When the eyes of Prince Prospero fell upon this spectral image (which with a slow and solemn movement, as if more fully to sustain its *rôle*, stalked to and fro among the waltzers) he was seen to be convulsed in the first moment with a strong shudder either of terror or distaste; but in the next his brow reddened with rage.

''Who dares?'' he demanded hoarsely of the courtiers who stood near him—''who dares insult us with this blasphemous mockery? Seize him and unmask him, that we may know whom we have to hang at sunrise from the battlements!''

It was in the eastern or blue chamber in which stood the Prince Prospero as he uttered these words. They rang throughout the seven rooms loudly and clearly—for the prince was a bold and robust man, and the music had become hushed at the waving of his hand.

It was in the blue room where stood the prince, with a group of pale courtiers by his side. At first, as he spoke, there was a slight rushing movement of this group in the direction of the intruder, who, at the moment was also near at hand, and now, with deliberate and stately step, made closer approach to the speaker. But, from a certain nameless awe with which the mad assumptions of the mummer had inspired the whole party, there were found none who put forth hand to seize him; so that unimpeded he passed within a yard of the prince's person; and while the vast assembly, as if with one impulse, shrank from the centers of the rooms to the walls, he made his way uninterruptedly, but with the same solemn and measured step which had distinguished him from the first, through the blue chamber to the purple—through the purple to the green—through the green to the orange—through this again to the white—and even thence to the violet, ere a decided movement had been made to arrest him. It was then, however, that the Prince Prospero, maddening with rage and the shame of his own momentary cowardice, rushed hurriedly through the six chambers, while none followed him on account of a deadly terror that had seized upon all. He bore aloft a drawn dagger, and had approached in rapid impetuosity, to within three or four feet of the retreating figure, when the latter, having attained the extremity of the velvet apartment, turned suddenly and confronted his pursuer. There was a sharp cry—and the dagger dropped gleaming upon the sable carpet, upon which, instantly afterwards, fell prostrate in death the Prince Prospero. Then,

**216**

summoning the wild courage of despair, a throng of the revellers at once threw themselves into the black apartment, and, seizing the mummer, whose tall figure stood erect and motionless within the shadows of the ebony clock, gasped in unutterable horror at finding the grave cerements and corpse-like mask which they handled with so violent a rudeness, untenanted by any tangible form.

And now was acknowledged the presence of the Red Death. He had come like a thief in the night; and one by one dropped the revellers in the blood-bedewed halls of their revel, and died each in the despairing posture of his fall; and the life of the ebony clock went out with that of the last of the gay; and the flames of the tripods expired; and darkness and decay and the Red Death held illimitable dominion over all.

—*Edgar Allan Poe (1809-1849)*

# THE SNAKE

It was almost dark when young Dr. Phillips swung his sack to his shoulder and left the tide pool. He climbed up over the rocks and squashed along the street in his rubber boots. The street lights were on by the time he arrived at his little commercial laboratory on the cannery street of Monterey. It was a tight little building, standing partly on piers over the bay water and partly on the land. On both sides the big corrugated-iron sardine canneries crowded in on it.

Dr. Phillips climbed the wooden steps and opened the door. The white rats in their cages scampered up and down the wire, and the captive cats in their pens mewed for milk. Dr. Phillips turned on the glaring light over the dissection table and dumped his clammy sack on the floor. He walked to the glass cages by the window where the rattlesnakes lived, leaned over and looked in.

The snakes were bunched and resting in the corners of the cage, but every head was clear; the dusty eyes seemed to look at nothing, but as the young man leaned over the cage the forked tongues, black on the ends and pink behind, twittered out and waved slowly up and down. Then the snakes recognized the man and pulled in their tongues.

Dr. Phillips threw off his leather coat and built a fire in the tin stove; he set a kettle of water on the stove and dropped a can of beans into the water. Then he stood staring down at the sack on the floor. He was a slight young man with the mild, pre-occupied eyes of one who looks through a microscope a great deal. He wore a short blond beard.

The draft ran breathily up the chimney and a glow of warmth came from the stove. The little waves washed quietly about the piles under the building. Arranged on shelves about the room were tier above tier of museum jars containing the mounted marine specimens the laboratory dealt in.

Dr. Phillips opened a side door and went into his bedroom, a book-lined cell containing an army cot, a reading light and an uncomfortable wooden chair. He pulled off his rubber boots and put on a pair of sheepskin slippers. When he went back to the other room the water in the kettle was already beginning to hum.

He lifted his sack to the table under the white light and emptied out two dozen common starfish. These he laid out side by side on the table. His preoccupied eyes turned to the busy rats in the wire cages. Taking grain from a paper sack, he poured it into the feeding troughs. Instantly the rats scrambled down from the wire and fell upon the food. A bottle of milk stood on a glass shelf between a small mounted octopus and a jellyfish. Dr. Phillips lifted down the milk and walked to the cat cage, but before he filled the containers he reached in the cage and gently picked out a big rangy alley tabby. He stroked her for a moment and then dropped her in a small black painted box, closed the lid and bolted it and then turned on a petcock which admitted gas into the killing chamber. While the short soft struggle went on in the black box he filled the saucers with milk. One of the cats arched against his hand and he smiled and petted her neck.

The box was quiet now. He turned off the petcock, for the airtight box would be full of gas.

On the stove the pan of water was bubbling furiously about the can of beans. Dr. Phillips lifted out the can with a big pair of forceps, opened it, and emptied the beans into a glass dish. While he ate he watched the starfish on the table. From between the rays little drops of milky fluid were exuding. He bolted his beans and when they were gone he put the dish in the sink and stepped to the equipment cupboard. From this he took a microscope and a pile of little glass dishes. He filled the dishes one by one with sea water from a tap and arranged them in a line beside the starfish. He took out his watch and laid it on the table under the pouring white light. The waves washed with little sighs against the piles under the floor. He took an eyedropper from a drawer and bent over the starfish.

At that moment there were quick soft steps on the wooden stairs and a strong knocking at the door. A slight grimace of annoyance crossed the young man's face as he went to open. A tall, lean woman stood in the doorway. She was dressed in a severe dark suit—her straight black hair, growing low on a flat forehead, was mussed as though the wind had been blowing it. Her black eyes glittered in the strong light.

She spoke in a soft throaty voice, "May I come in? I want to talk to you."

"I'm very busy just now," he said half-heartedly. "I have to do things at times." But he stood away from the door. The tall woman slipped in.

"I'll be quiet until you can talk to me."

He closed the door and brought the uncomfortable chair from the bedroom. "You see," he apologized, "the process is started and I must get to it." So many people wandered in and asked questions. He had little routines of explanations for the commoner processes. He could say them without thinking. "Sit here. In a few minutes I'll be able to listen to you."

The tall woman leaned over the table. With the eyedropper the young man gathered fluid from between the rays of the starfish and squirted it into a bowl of water, and then he drew some milky fluid and squirted it in the same bowl and stirred the water gently with the eyedropper. He began his little patter of explanation.

"When starfish are sexually mature they release sperm and ova when they are exposed at low tide. By choosing mature specimens and taking them out of the water, I give them a condition of low tide. Now I've mixed the sperm and eggs. Now I put some of the mixture in each one of these ten watch glasses. In ten minutes I will kill those in the first glass with menthol, twenty minutes later I will kill the second group and then a new group every twenty minutes. Then I will have arrested the process in stages, and I will mount the series on microscope slides for biologic study." He paused. "Would you like to look at this first group under the microscope?"

"No, thank you."

He turned quickly to her. People always wanted to look through the glass. She was not looking at the table at all, but at him. Her black eyes were on him, but they did not seem to see him. He realized why—the irises were as dark as the pupils, there was no color line between the two. Dr. Phillips was piqued at her answer. Although answering questions bored him, a lack of interest in what he was doing irritated him. A desire to arouse her grew in him.

"While I'm waiting the first ten minutes I have something to do. Some people don't like to see it. Maybe you'd better step into that room until I finish."

"No," she said in her soft flat tone. "Do what you wish. I will wait until you can talk to me." Her hands rested side by side on her lap. She was completely at rest. Her eyes were bright but the rest of her was almost in a state of suspended animation. He thought, "Low metabolic rate, almost as low as a frog's, from the looks." The desire to shock her out of her inanition possessed him again.

He brought a little wooden cradle to the table, laid out scalpels and scissors and rigged a big hollow needle to a pressure tube. Then from the killing chamber he brought the limp dead cat and laid it in the cradle and tied its legs to hooks in the sides. He glanced sidewise at the woman. She had not moved. She was still at rest.

The cat grinned up into the light, its pink tongue stuck out between its needle teeth. Dr. Phillips deftly snipped open the skin at the throat; with a scalpel he slit through and found an artery. With flawless technique he put the needle in the vessel and tied it in with gut. "Embalming fluid," he explained. "Later I'll inject yellow mass into the veinous system and red mass into the arterial system—for bloodstream dissection—biology classes."

He looked around at her again. Her dark eyes seemed veiled with dust. She looked without expression at the cat's open throat. Not a drop of blood had escaped.

The incision was clean. Dr. Phillips looked at his watch. "Time for the first group." He shook a few crystals of menthol into the first watch-glass.

The woman was making him nervous. The rats climbed about on the wire of their cage again and squeaked softly. The waves under the building beat with little shocks on the piles.

The young man shivered. He put a few lumps of coal in the stove and sat down. "Now," he said. "I haven't anything to do for twenty minutes." He noticed how short her chin was between lower lip and point. She seemed to awaken slowly, to come up out of some deep pool of consciousness. Her head raised and her dark dusty eyes moved about the room and then came back to him.

"I was waiting," she said. Her hands remained side by side on her lap. "You have snakes?"

"Why, yes," he said rather loudly. "I have about two dozen rattlesnakes. I milk out the venom and send it to the anti-venom laboratories."

She continued to look at him but her eyes did not center on him, rather they covered him and seemed to see in a big circle all around him. "Have you a male snake, a male rattlesnake?"

"Well, it just happens I know I have. I came in one morning and found a big snake in—in coition with a smaller one. That's very rare in captivity. You see, I do know I have a male snake."

"Where is he?"

"Why, right in the glass cage by the window there."

Her head swung slowly around but her two quiet hands did not move. She turned back toward him. "May I see?"

He got up and walked to the case by the window. On the sand bottom the knot of rattleshakes lay entwined, but their heads were clear. The tongues came out and flickered a moment and then waved up and down feeling the air for vibrations. Dr. Phillips nervously turned his head. The woman was standing beside him. He had not heard her get up from the chair. He had heard only the splash of water among the piles and the scampering of the rats on the wire screen.

She said softly, "Which is the male you spoke of?"

He pointed to a thick, dusty grey snake lying by itself in one corner of the cage. "That one. He's nearly five feet long. He comes from Texas. Our Pacific coast snakes are usually smaller. He's been taking all the rats, too. When I want the others to eat I have to take him out."

The woman stared down at the blunt dry head. The forked tongue slipped out and hung quivering for a long moment. "And you're sure he's a male."

"Rattlesnakes are funny," he said glibly. "Nearly every generalization proves wrong. I don't like to say anything definite about rattlesnakes, but—yes—I can assure you he's male."

Her eyes did not move from the flat head. "Will you sell him to me?"

"Sell him?" he cried. "Sell him to you?"

"You do sell specimens, don't you?"

"Oh—yes. Of course I do. Of course I do."

"How much? Five dollars? Ten?"

"Oh! Not more than five. But—do you know anything about rattlesnakes? You might be bitten."

She looked at him for a moment. "I don't intend to take him. I want to leave him here, but—I want him to be mine. I want to come here and look at him and feed him and to know he's mine." She opened a little purse and took out a five-dollar bill. "Here! Now he is mine."

Dr. Phillips began to be afraid. "You could come to look at him without owning him."

"I want him to be mine."

"Oh, Lord!" he cried. "I've forgotten the time. He ran to the table. "Three minutes over. It won't matter much." He shook menthol crystals into the second watch-glass. And then he was drawn back to the cage where the woman still stared at the snake.

She asked, "What does he eat?"

"I feed them white rats, rats from the cage over there."

"Will you put him in the other cage? I want to feed him."

"But he doesn't need food. He's had a rat already this week. Sometimes they don't eat for three or four months. I had one that didn't eat for over a year."

In her low monotone she asked, "Will you sell me a rat?"

He shrugged his shoulders. "I see. You want to watch how rattlesnakes eat. All right. I'll show you. The rat will cost twenty-five cents. It's better than a bullfight if you look at it one way, and it's simply a snake eating his dinner if you look at it another." His tone had become acid. He hated people who made sport of natural processes. He was not a sportsman but a biologist. He could kill a thousand animals for knowledge, but not an insect for pleasure. He'd been over this in his mind before.

She turned her head slowly toward him and the beginning of a smile formed on her thin lips. "I want to feed my snake," she said. "I'll put him in the other cage." She had opened the top of the cage and dipped her hand in before he knew what she was doing. He leaped forward and pulled her back. The lid banged shut.

"Haven't you any sense?" he asked fiercely. "Maybe he wouldn't kill you, but he'd make you damned sick in spite of what I could do for you."

"You put him in the other cage, then," she said quietly.

Dr. Phillips was shaken. He found that he was avoiding the dark eyes that didn't seem to look at anything. He felt that it was profoundly wrong to put a rat into the cage, deeply sinful; and he didn't know why. Often he had put rats in the cage when someone or other had wanted to see it, but this desire tonight sickened him. He tried to explain himself out of it.

"It's a good thing to see," he said. "It shows you how a snake can work. It makes you have respect for a rattlesnake. Then, too, lots of people have dreams about the terror of snakes making the kill. I think because it is a subjective rat. The person is the rat. Once you see it the whole matter is objective. The rat is only a rat and the terror is removed."

He took a long stick equipped with a leather noose from the wall. Opening the trap he dropped the noose over the big snake's head and tightened the thong. A piercing dry rattle filled the room. The thick body writhed and slashed about the handle of the stick as he lifted the snake out and dropped it in the feeding cage. It stood ready to strike for a time, but the buzzing gradually ceased. The snake crawled into a corner, made a big figure eight with its body and lay still.

"You see," the young man explained, "these snakes are quite tame. I've had them a long time. I suppose I could handle them if I wanted to, but everyone who does handle rattlesnakes gets bitten sooner or later. I just don't want to take the chance." He glanced at the woman. He hated to put in the rat. She had moved over in front of the new cage; her black eyes were on the stony head of the snake again.

She said, "Put in a rat."

Reluctantly he went to the rat cage. For some reason he was sorry for the rat, and such a feeling had never come to him before. His eyes went over the mass of swarming white bodies climbing up the screen toward him. "Which one?" he thought. "Which one shall it be?" Suddenly he turned angrily to the woman. "Wouldn't you rather I put in a cat? Then you'd see a real fight. The cat might even win, but if it did it might kill the snake. I'll sell you a cat if you like."

She didn't look at him. "Put in a rat," she said. "I want him to eat."

**221**

He opened the rat cage and thrust his hand in. His fingers found a tail and he lifted a plump, red-eyed rat out of the cage. It struggled up to try to bite his fingers and, failing, hung spread out and motionless from its tail. He walked quickly across the room, opened the feeding cage and dropped the rat in on the sand floor. "Now, watch it," he cried.

The woman did not answer him. Her eyes were on the snake where it lay still. Its tongue, flicking in and out rapidly, tasted the air of the cage.

The rat landed on its feet, turned around and sniffed at its pink naked tail and then unconcernedly trotted across the sand, smelling as it went. The room was silent. Dr. Phillips did not know whether the water sighed among the piles or whether the woman sighed. Out of the corner of his eye he saw her body crouch and stiffen.

The snake moved out smoothly, slowly. The tongue flicked in and out. The motion was so gradual, so smooth that it didn't seem to be motion at all. In the other end of the cage the rat perked up in a sitting position and began to lick down the fine white hair on its chest. The snake moved on, keeping always a deep S curve in its neck.

The silence beat on the young man. He felt the blood drifting up in his body. He said loudly, "See! He keeps the striking curve ready. Rattlesnakes are cautious, almost cowardly animals. The mechanism is so delicate. The snake's dinner is to be got by an operation as deft as a surgeon's job. He takes no chances with his instruments."

The snake had flowed to the middle of the cage by now. The rat looked up, saw the snake and then unconcernedly went back to licking its chest.

"It's the most beautiful thing in the world," the young man said. His veins were throbbing. "It's the most terrible thing in the world."

The snake was close now. Its head lifted a few inches from the sand. The head weaved slowly back and forth, aiming, getting distance, aiming. Dr. Phillips glanced again at the woman. He turned sick. She was weaving too, not much, just a suggestion.

The rat looked up and saw the snake. It dropped to four feet and back up, and then—the stroke. It was impossible to see, simply a flash. The rat jarred as though under an invisible blow. The snake backed hurriedly into the corner from which it had come, and settled down, its tongue working constantly.

"Perfect!" Dr. Phillips cried. "Right between the shoulder blades. The fangs must almost have reached the heart."

The rat stood still, breathing like a little white bellows. Suddenly it leaped in the air and landed on its side. Its legs kicked spasmodically for a second and it was dead.

The woman relaxed, relaxed sleepily.

"Well," the young man demanded, "it was an emotional bath, wasn't it?"

She turned her misty eyes to him. "Will he eat it now?" she asked.

"Of course he'll eat it. He didn't kill it for a thrill. He killed it because he was hungry."

The corners of the woman's mouth turned up a trifle again. She looked back at the snake. "I want to see him eat it."

Now the snake came out of its corner again. There was no striking curve in its neck, but it approached the rat gingerly, ready to jump back in case it attacked. It nudged the body gently with its blunt nose, and drew away. Satisfied that it was dead, the snake touched the body all over with its chin, from head to tail. It seemed to measure the body and to kiss it. Finally it opened its mouth and unhinged its jaws at the corners.

Dr. Phillips put his will against his head to keep it from turning toward the woman. He thought, "If she's opening her mouth, I'll be sick. I'll be afraid." He succeeded in keeping his eyes away.

The snake fitted its jaws over the rat's head and then with a slow peristaltic pulsing, began to engulf the rat. The jaws gripped and the whole throat crawled up, and the jaws gripped again.

Dr. Phillips turned away and went to his work table. "You've made me miss one of the series," he said bitterly. "The set won't be complete." He put one of the watch glasses under a low-power microscope and looked at it, and then angrily he poured the contents of all the dishes into the sink. The waves had fallen so that only a wet whisper came up through the floor. The young man lifted a trapdoor at his feet and dropped the starfish down into the black water. He paused at the cat, crucified in the cradle and grinning comically into the light. Its body was puffed with embalming fluid. He shut off the pressure, withdrew the needle and tied the vein.

"Would you like some coffee?" he asked.

"No, thank you. I shall be going pretty soon."

He walked to her where she stood in front of the snake cage. The rat was swallowed, all except an inch of pink tail that stuck out of the snake's mouth like a sardonic tongue. The throat heaved again and the tail disappeared. The jaws snapped back into their sockets, and the big snake crawled heavily to the corner, made a big eight and dropped its head on the sand.

"He's asleep now," the woman said. "I'm going now. But I'll come back and feed my snake every little while. I'll pay for the rats. I want him to have plenty. And sometime—I'll take him away with me." Her eyes came out of their dusty dream for a moment. "Remember, he's mine. Don't take his poison. I want him to have it. Goodnight." She walked swiftly to the door and went out. He heard her footsteps on the stairs, but he could not hear her walk away on the pavement.

Dr. Phillips turned a chair around and sat down in front of the snake cage. He tried to comb out his thought as he looked at the torpid snake. "I've read so much about psychological sex symbols," he thought. "It doesn't seem to explain. Maybe I'm too much alone. Maybe I should kill the snake. If I knew—no, I can't pray to anything."

For weeks he expected her to return. "I will go out and leave her alone here when she comes," he decided. "I won't see the damned thing again."

She never came again. For months he looked for her when he walked about in the town. Several times he ran after some tall woman thinking it might be she. But he never saw her again—ever.

—*John Steinbeck* (*1902-1969*)

# THE STRONGER

Characters

MRS. X, an actress, married
MISS Y, an actress, unmarried
A WAITRESS

SCENE: *The corner of a ladies' cafe. Two little iron tables, a red velvet sofa, several chairs. Enter MRS. X, dressed in winter clothes, carrying a Japanese basket on her arm.*

*MISS Y: sits with a half-empty beer bottle before her, reading an illustrated paper, which she changes later for another.*

MRS. X: Good afternoon, Amelia. You're sitting here alone on Christmas eve like a poor bachelor!

MISS Y: (*Looks up, nods, and resumes her reading.*)

MRS. X: Do you know it really hurts me to see you like this, alone, in a cafe, and on Christmas eve, too. It makes me feel as I did one time when I saw a bridal party in a Paris restaurant, and the bride sat reading a comic paper, while the groom played billiards with the witnesses. Huh, thought I, with such a beginning, what will follow, and what will be the end? He played billiards on his wedding eve! (*MISS Y starts to speak*) And she read a comic paper, you mean? Well, they are not altogether the same thing.

(*A WAITRESS enters, places a cup of chocolate before MRS. X and goes out.*)

MRS. X: You know what, Amelia! I believe you would have done better to have kept him! Do you remember, I was the first to say "Forgive him?" Do you remember that? You would be married now and have a home. Remember that Christmas when you went out to visit your fiancé's parents in the country? How you gloried in the happiness of home life and really longed to quit the theatre forever? Yes, Amelia dear, home is the best of all—next to the theatre—and as for children—well, you don't understand that.

MISS Y: (*Looks up scornfully.*)

(*MRS. X sips a few spoonfuls out of the cup, then opens her basket and shows Christmas presents.*)

MRS. X: Now you shall see what I bought for my piggywigs. (*Takes up a doll.*) Look at this! This is for Lisa, ha! Do you see how she can roll her eyes and turn her head, eh? And here is Maja's popgun.

(*Loads it and shoots at MISS Y.*)

MISS Y: (*Makes a startled gesture.*)

MRS. X: Did I frighten you? Did you think I would like to shoot you, eh? On my soul, if I don't think you did! If you wanted to shoot *me* it wouldn't be so surprising, because I stood in your way—and I know you can never forget that—although I was absolutely innocent. You still believe I intrigued and got you out of the Stora theatre, but I didn't. I didn't do that, although you think so. Well, it doesn't make any difference what I say to you. You will believe I did it. (*Takes up a pair of embroidered slippers.*) And these are for my better half. I embroidered them myself—I can't bear tulips, but he wants tulips on everything.

MISS Y: (*Looks up ironically and curiously.*)

MRS. X: (*putting a hand in each slipper*) See what little feet Bob has! What? And you should see what a splendid stride he has! You've never seen him in slippers!

**224**

(*MISS Y laughs aloud.*) Look! (*She makes the slippers walk on the table. MISS Y laughs loudly.*) And when he is grumpy he stamps like this with his foot. ''What! damn those servants who can never learn to make coffee. Oh, now those creatures haven't trimmed the lamp wick properly!'' And then there are draughts on the floor and his feet are cold. ''Ugh, how cold it is; the stupid idiots can never keep the fire going.'' (*She rubs the slippers together, one sole over the other.*)

*MISS Y:* (*Shrieks with laughter.*)

*MRS. X:* And then he comes home and has to hunt for his slippers which Marie has stuck under the chiffonier—oh, but it's so sinful to sit here and make fun of one's husband this way when he is kind and a good little man. You ought to have had such a husband, Amelia. What are you laughing at? What? What? And you see he's true to me. Yes, I'm sure of that, because he told me himself—what are you laughing at?—that when I was touring in Norway that brazen Frederika came and wanted to seduce him! Can you fancy anything so infamous? (*pause*) I'd have torn her eyes out if she had come to see him when I was at home. (*pause*) It was lucky that Bob told me about it himself and that it didn't reach me through gossip. (*pause*) But would you believe it, Frederika wasn't the only one! I don't know why, but the women are crazy about my husband. They must think he has influence about getting them theatrical engagements, but he is connected with the government. Perhaps you were after him yourself. I didn't use to trust you any too much. But now I know he never bothered his head about you, and you always seemed to have a grudge against him someway.

(*Pause. They look at each other in a puzzled way.*)

*MRS. X:* Come and see us this evening, Amelia, and show us that you're not put out with us—not put out with me at any rate. I don't know, but I think it would be uncomfortable to have you for an enemy. Perhaps it's because I stood in your way (*more slowly*) or—I really—don't know why—in particular.

(*Pause. MISS Y stares at MRS. X curiously.*)

*MRS. X:* (*thoughtfully*) Our acquaintance has been so queer. When I saw you for the first time I was afraid of you, so afraid that I didn't dare let you out of my sight; no matter when or where, I always found myself near you—I didn't dare have you for an enemy, so I became your friend. But there was always discord when you came to our house, because I saw that my husband couldn't endure you, and the whole thing seemed as awry to me as an ill-fitting gown—and I did all I could to make him friendly toward you, but with no success until you became engaged. Then came a violent friendship between you, so that it looked all at once as though you both dared show your real feelings only when you were secure—and then—how was it later? I didn't get jealous—strange to say! And I remember at the christening, when you acted as godmother, I made him kiss you—he did so, and you became so confused—as it were; I didn't notice it then—didn't think about it later, either—have never thought about it until—now! (*Rises suddenly.*) Why are you silent? You haven't said a word this whole time, but you have let me go on talking! You have sat there, and your eyes have reeled out of me all these thoughts which lay like raw silk in its cocoon—thoughts—suspicious thoughts, perhaps. Let me see—why did you break your engagement? Why do you never come to our house any more? Why won't you come to see us tonight?

(*MISS Y appears as if about to speak.*)

*MRS. X:* Hush, you needn't speak—I understand it all! It was because—and because—and because! Yes, yes! Now all the accounts balance. That's it. Fie, I won't sit at the same table with you. (*Moves her things to another table.*) That's the reason I had to embroider tulips—which I hate—on his slippers, because you are fond of tulips; that's why (*throws slippers on the floor*) we go to Lake Malarn in the summer, because you don't like salt water; that's why my boy is named Eskil—because it's·

your father's name; that's why I wear your colors, read your authors, eat your favorite dishes, drink your drinks—chocolate, for instance; that's why—oh—my God—it's terrible, when I think about it, it's terrible. Everything, everything came from you to me, even your passions. Your soul crept into mine, like a worm into an apple, ate and ate, bored and bored, until nothing was left but the rind and a little black dust within. I wanted to get away from you, but I couldn't; you lay like a snake and charmed me with your black eyes; I felt that when I lifted my wings they only dragged me down; I lay in the water with bound feet and the stronger I strove to keep up the deeper I worked myself down, down, until I sank to the bottom, where you lay like a giant crab to clutch me in your claws—and there I am lying now.

I hate you, hate you, hate you! And you only sit there silent—silent and indifferent; indifferent whether it's new moon or waning moon, Christmas or New Year's, whether others are happy or unhappy; without power to hate or to love; as quiet as a story by a rat hole—you couldn't scent your prey and capture it, but you could lie in wait for it! You sit here in your corner of the cafe—did you know it's called "The Rat Trap" for you?—and read the papers to see if misfortune hasn't befallen someone, to see if someone hasn't been given notice at the theatre, perhaps; you sit here and calculate about your next victim and reckon on your changes of recompense like a pilot in a shipwreck. Poor Amelia, I pity you, nevertheless, because I know you are unhappy, unhappy like one who has been wounded, and angry because you are wounded. I can't be angry with you no matter how much I want to be—because you come out the weaker one. Yes, all that with Bob doesn't trouble me. What is that to me, after all? And what difference does it make whether I learned to drink chocolate from you or someone else. (*Sips a spoonful from her cup*) Besides, chocolate is very healthful. And if you taught me how to dress—tant mieux!—that has only made me more attractive to my husband; so you lost and I won there. Well, judging by certain signs, I believe you have already lost him; and you certainly intended that I should leave him—do as you did with your fiancé and regret; but, you see, I don't do that—we mustn't be too exacting. And why should I take only what no one else wants?

Perhaps, take it all in all, I am at this moment the stronger one. You received nothing from me, but you gave me much. And now I seem like a thief since you have awakened and find I possess what is your loss. How could it be otherwise when everything is worthless and sterile in your hands? You can never keep a man's love with your tulips and your passions—but I can keep it. You can't learn how to live from your authors, as I have learned. You have no little Eskil to cherish, even if your father's name was Eskil. And why are you always silent, silent, silent? I thought that was strength, but perhaps it is because you have nothing to say! Because you never think about anything! (*Rises and picks up slippers.*) Now I'm going home—and take the tulips with me—*your* tulips! You are unable to learn from another; you can't bend—therefore, you broke like a dry stalk. But I won't break! Thank you, Amelia, for all your good lessons. Thanks for teaching my husband how to love. Now I'm going home to love him. (*Goes.*)

*August Strindberg (1849-1912)*

# RIDERS TO THE SEA
## A Play in One Act

Characters

*MAURYA, an old woman*
*BARTLEY, her son*
*CATHLEEN, her daughter*
*NORA, a younger daughter*
*MEN AND WOMEN*

*An Island off the west of Ireland.*
*Cottage kitchen, with nets, oilskins, spinning wheel, some new boards standing by the wall, etc. CATHLEEN, a girl of about twenty, finishes kneading cake, and puts it down on the pot-oven by the fire, then wipes her hands, and begins to spin at the wheel. NORA, a young girl, puts her head in at the door.*

*NORA:* (*In a low voice*) Where is she?

*CATHLEEN:* She's lying down, God help her, and may be sleeping, if she's able.

(*NORA comes in softly, and takes a bundle from under her shawl*)

*CATHLEEN:* (*Spinning the wheel rapidly*) What is it you have?

*NORA:* The young priest is after bringing them. It's a shirt and a plain stocking were got off a drowned man in Donegal.

(*CATHLEEN stops her wheel with a sudden movement, and leans out to listen*)

*NORA:* We're to find out if it's Michael's they are, sometime herself will be down looking by the sea.

*CATHLEEN:* How would they be Michael's, Nora? How would he go the length of that way to the Far North?

*NORA:* The young priest says he's known the like of it. "If it's Michael's they are," says he, "you can tell herself he's got a clean burial by the grace of God, and if they're not his, let no one say a word about them, for she'll be getting her death," says he, "with crying and lamenting."

(*The door which NORA half closed is blown open by a gust of wind.*)

*CATHLEEN:* (*Looking out anxiously*) Did you ask him would he stop Bartley going this day with the horses to the Galway fair?

*NORA:* "I won't stop him," says he, "but let you not be afraid. Herself does be saying prayers half through the night, and the Almighty God won't leave her destitute," says he, "with no son living."

*CATHLEEN:* Is the sea bad by the white rocks, Nora?

*NORA:* Middling bad, God help us. There's a great roaring in the west, and it's worse it'll be getting when the tide's turned to the wind. (*She goes over to the table with the bundle*) Shall I open it now?

*CATHLEEN:* Maybe she'd wake up on us, and come in before we'd done. (*Coming to the table*) It's a long time we'll be, and the two of us crying.

*NORA:* (*Goes to the inner door and listens*) She's moving about on the bed. She'll be coming in a minute.

*CATHLEEN:* Give me the ladder, and I'll put them up in the turf-loft, the way she won't know of them at all, and maybe when the tide turns she'll be going down to see would he be floating from the east.

**227**

(*They put the ladder against the gable of the chimney; CATHLEEN goes up a few steps and hides the bundle in the turf-loft. MAURYA comes from the inner room*)

MAURYA: (*Looking up at CATHLEEN and speaking querulously*) Isn't it turf enough you have for this day and evening?

CATHLEEN: There's a cake baking at the fire for a short space. (*Throwing down the turf*) and Bartley will want it when the tide turns if he goes to Connemara.

(*NORA picks up the turf and puts it round the pot-oven*)

MAURYA: (*Sitting down on a stool at the fire*) He won't go this day with the wind rising from the south and west. He won't go this day, for the young priest will stop him surely.

NORA: He'll not stop him, Mother, and I heard Eamon Simon and Stephen Pheety and Colum Shawn saying he would go.

MAURYA: Where is he itself?

NORA: He went down to see would there be another boat sailing in the week, and I'm thinking it won't be long till he's here now, for the tide's turning at the green head, and the hooker's[1] tacking from the east.

CATHLEEN: I hear someone passing the big stones.

NORA: (*Looking out*) He's coming now, and he in a hurry.

BARTLEY: (*Comes in and looks round the room; speaking sadly and quietly*) Where is the bit of new rope, Cathleen, was bought in Connemara?

CATHLEEN: (*Coming down*) Give it to him, Nora; it's on a nail by the white boards. I hung it up this morning, for the pig with the black feet was eating it.

NORA: (*Giving him a rope*) Is that it, Bartley?

MAURYA: You'd do right to leave that rope, Bartley, hanging by the boards. (*BARTLEY takes the rope*) It will be wanting in this place, I'm telling you, if Michael is washed up tomorrow morning, or the next morning, or any morning in the week, for it's a deep grave we'll make him by the grace of God.

BARTLEY: (*Beginning to work with the rope*) I've no halter the way I can ride down on the mare, and I must go now quickly. This is the one boat going for two weeks or beyond it, and the fair will be a good fair for horses I heard them saying below.

MAURYA: It's a hard thing they'll be saying below if the body is washed up and there's no man in it to make the coffin, and I after giving a big price for the finest white boards you'd find in Connemara. (*She looks round at the boards*)

BARTLEY: How would it be washed up, and we after looking each day for nine days, and a strong wind blowing a while back from the west and south?

MAURYA: If it wasn't found itself, that wind is raising the sea, and there was a star up against the moon, and it rising in the night. If it was a hundred horses, or a thousand horses you had itself, what is the price of a thousand horses against a son where there is one son only?

BARTLEY: (*Working at the halter, to CATHLEEN*) Let you go down each day, and see the sheep aren't jumping in on the rye, and if the jobber comes you can sell the pig with the black feet if there is a good price going.

MAURYA: How would the like of her get a good price for a pig?

BARTLEY: (*To CATHLEEN*) If the west wind holds with the last bit of the moon let you and Nora get up weed enough for another cock[2] for the kelp. It's hard set we'll be from this day with no one in it but one man to work.

---

[1]A single-masted fishing boat.

[2]A stack for burning seaweed into the ashes (kelp) useful as fertilizer.

**228**

*MAURYA:* It's hard set we'll be surely the day you're drownd'd with the rest. What way will I live and the girls with me, and I an old woman looking for the grave?

(*BARTLEY lays down the halter, takes off his old coat, and puts on a newer one of the same flannel*)

*BARTLEY:* (*To NORA*) Is she coming to the pier?

*NORA* (*Looking out*) She's passing the green head and letting fall her sails.

*BARTLEY:* (*Getting his purse and tobacco*) I'll have half an hour to go down, and you'll see me coming again in two days, or in three days, or maybe in four days if the wind is bad.

*MAURYA:* (*Turning round to the fire, and putting her shawl over her head*) Isn't it a hard and cruel man won't hear a word from an old woman, and she holding him from the sea?

*CATHLEEN:* It's the life of a young man to be going on the sea, and who would listen to an old woman with one thing and she saying it over?

*BARTLEY:* (*Taking the halter*) I must go now quickly. I'll ride down on the red mare, and the gray pony'll run behind me. . . . The blessing of God on you. (*He goes out*)

*MAURYA:* (*Crying out as he is in the door*) He's gone now, God spare us, and we'll not see him again. He's gone now, and when the black night is falling I'll have no son left me in the world.

*CATHLEEN:* Why wouldn't you give him your blessing and he looking round in the door? Isn't it sorrow enough is on everyone in this house without your sending him out with an unlucky word behind him, and a hard word in his ear?

(*MAURYA takes up the tongs and begins raking the fire aimlessly without looking round*)

*NORA:* (*Turning toward her*) You're taking away the turf from the cake.

*CATHLEEN:* (*Crying out*) The Son of God forgive us, Nora, we're after forgetting his bit of bread. (*She comes over to the fire*)

*NORA:* And it's destroyed he'll be going till dark night, and he after eating nothing since the sun went up.

*CATHLEEN:* (*Turning the cake out of the oven*) It's destroyed he'll be, surely. There's no sense left on any person in a house where an old woman will be talking forever.

(*MAURYA sways herself on her stool*)

*CATHLEEN:* (*Cutting off some of the bread and rolling it in a cloth; to MAURYA*) Let you go down now to the spring well and give him this and he passing. You'll see him then and the dark word will be broken, and you can say "God speed you," the way he'll be easy in his mind.

*MAURYA:* (*Taking the bread*) Will I be in it as soon as himself?

*CATHLEEN:* If you go now quickly.

*MAURYA:* (*Standing up unsteadily*) It's hard set I am to walk.

*CATHLEEN:* (*Looking at her anxiously*) Give her the stick, Nora, or maybe she'll slip on the big stones.

*NORA:* What stick?

*CATHLEEN:* The stick Michael brought from Connemara.

*MAURYA:* (*Taking a stick NORA gives her*) In the big world the old people do be leaving things after them for their sons and children, but in this place it is the young men do be leaving things behind for them that do be old.

(*She goes out slowly. NORA goes over to the ladder*)

*CATHLEEN:* Wait, Nora, maybe she'd turn back quickly. She's that sorry, God help her, you wouldn't know the thing she'd do.

*NORA:* Is she gone round by the bush?

*CATHLEEN:* (*Looking out*) She's gone now. Throw it down quickly, for the Lord knows when she'll be out of it again.

*NORA:* (*Getting the bundle from the loft*) The young priest said he'd be passing tomorrow, and we might go down and speak to him below if it's Michael's they are surely.

*CATHLEEN:* (*Taking the bundle*) Did he say what way they were found?

*NORA:* (*Coming down*) "There were two men," says he, "and they rowing round with poteen[3] before the cocks crowed, and the oar of one of them caught the body, and they passing the black cliffs of the north."

*CATHLEEN:* (*Trying to open the bundle*) Give me a knife, Nora, the string's perished with the salt water, and there's a black knot on it you wouldn't loosen in a week.

*NORA:* (*Giving her a knife*) I've heard tell it was a long way to Donegal.

*CATHLEEN:* (*Cutting the string*) It is surely. There was a man in here a while ago—the man sold us that knife—and he said if you set off walking from the rocks beyond, it would be seven days you'd be in Donegal.

*NORA:* And what time would a man take, and he floating?

(*CATHLEEN opens the bundle and takes out a bit of a stocking. They look at them eagerly*)

*CATHLEEN:* (*In a low voice*) The Lord spare us, Nora! isn't it a queer hard thing to say if it's his they are surely?

*NORA:* I'll get his shirt off the hook the way we can put the one flannel on the other. (*She looks through some clothes hanging in the corner*) It's not with them, Cathleen, and where will it be?

*CATHLEEN:* I'm thinking Bartley put it on him in the morning, for his own shirt was heavy with the salt in it. (*Pointing to the corner*) There's bit of a sleeve was of the same stuff. Give me that and it will do.

(*NORA brings it to her and they compare the flannel*)

*CATHLEEN:* It's the same stuff, Nora; but if it is itself aren't there great rolls of it in the shops of Galway, and isn't it many another man may have a shirt of it as well as Michael himself?

*NORA:* (*Who has taken up the stocking and counted the stitches, crying out*) It's Michael, Cathleen, it's Michael; God spare his soul, and what will herself say when she hears this story, and Bartley on the sea?

*CATHLEEN:* (*Taking the stocking*) It's a plain stocking.

*NORA:* It's the second one of the third pair I knitted, and I put up threescore stitches, and I dropped four of them.

*CATHLEEN:* (*Counts the stitches*) It's that number is in it. (*Crying out*) Ah, Nora, isn't it a bitter thing to think of him floating that way to the Far North, and no one to keen him but the black hags that do be flying on the sea?

*NORA:* (*Swinging herself round, and throwing out her arms on the clothes*) And isn't it a pitiful thing when there is nothing left of a man who was a great rower and fisher, but a bit of an old shirt and a plain stocking?

---

[3]A strong whiskey illegally brewed and sold.

CATHLEEN: (*After an instant*) Tell me is herself coming, Nora? I hear a little sound on the path.

NORA: (*Looking out*) She is, Cathleen. She's coming up to the door.

CATHLEEN: Put these things away before she'll come in. Maybe it's easier she'll be after giving her blessing to Bartley, and we won't let on we've heard anything the time he's on the sea.

NORA: (*Helping CATHLEEN to close the bundle*) We'll put them here in the corner.

(*They put them into a hole in the chimney corner. CATHLEEN goes back to the spinning wheel*)

NORA: Will she see it was crying I was?

CATHLEEN: Keep your back to the door the way the light'll not be on you.

(*NORA sits down at the chimney corner, with her back to the door. MAURYA comes in very slowly, without looking at the girls, and goes over to her stool at the other side of the fire. The cloth with the bread is still in her hand. The girls look at each other, and NORA points to the bundle of bread*)

CATHLEEN: (*After spinning for a moment*) You didn't give him his bit of bread? (*MAURYA begins to keen softly, without turning round*)

CATHLEEN: Did you see him riding down?

(*MAURYA goes on keening*)

CATHLEEN: (*A little impatiently*) God forgive you; isn't it a better thing to raise your voice and tell what you seen, than to be making lamentation for a thing that's done? Did you see Bartley, I'm saying to you.

MAURYA: (*With a weak voice*) My heart's broken from this day.

CATHLEEN: (*As before*) Did you see Bartley?

MAURYA: I seen the fearfulest thing.

CATHLEEN: (*Leaves her wheel and looks out*) God forgive you; he's riding the mare now over the green head, and the gray pony behind him.

MAURYA: (*Starts, so that her shawl falls back from her head and shows her white tossed hair. With a frightened voice*) The gray pony behind him.

CATHLEEN: (*Coming to the fire*) What is it ails you, at all?

MAURYA: (*Speaking very slowly*) I've seen the fearfulest thing any person has seen, since the day Bride Dara seen the dead man with a child in his arms.

CATHLEEN AND NORA: Uah.

(*They crouch down in front of the old woman at the fire*)

NORA: Tell us what it is you seen.

MAURYA: I went down to the spring well, and I stood there saying a prayer to myself. Then Bartley came along, and he riding on the red mare with the gray pony behind him. (*She puts up her hands, as if to hide something from her eyes*) The Son of God spare us, Nora!

CATHLEEN: What is it you seen?

MAURYA: I seen Michael himself.

CATHLEEN: (*Speaking softly*) You did not, Mother; it wasn't Michael you seen, for his body is after being found in the Far North, and he's got a clean burial by the grace of God.

MAURYA: (*A little defiantly*) I'm after seeing him this day, and he riding and galloping. Bartley came first on the red mare; and I tried to say, "God speed you,"

**231**

but something choked the words in my throat. He went by quickly, and "the blessing of God on you," says he, and I could say nothing. I looked up then, and I crying, at the gray pony, and there was Michael upon it—with fine clothes on him, and new shoes on his feet.

CATHLEEN: (*Begins to keen*) It's destroyed we are from this day. It's destroyed, surely.

NORA: Didn't the young priest say the Almighty God wouldn't leave her destitute with no son living?

MAURYA: (*In a low voice, but clearly*) It's little the like of him knows of the sea. . . . Bartley will be lost now, and let you call in Eamon and make me a good coffin out of the white boards, for I won't live after them. I've had a husband, and a husband's father, and six sons in this house—six fine men, though it was a hard birth I had with every one of them and they coming to the world—and some of them were found and some of them were not found, but they're gone now the lot of them. . . . There were Stephen, and Shawn, were lost in the great wind, and found after in the Bay of Gregory of the Golden Mouth, and carried up the two of them on the one plank, and in by that door.

(*She pauses for a moment, the girls start as if they heard something through the door that is half open behind them*)

NORA: (*In a whisper*) Did you hear that, Cathleen? Did you hear a noise in the northeast?

CATHLEEN (*In a whisper*) There's someone after crying out by the seashore.

MAURYA: (*Continues without hearing anything*) There was Sheamus and his father, and his own father again, were lost in a dark night, and not a stick or sign was seen of them when the sun went up. There was Patch after was drowned out of a curagh that turned over. I was sitting here with Bartley, and he a baby, lying on my two knees, and I seen two women, and three women, and four women coming in, and they crossing themselves, and not saying a word. I looked out then, and there were men coming after them, and they holding a thing in the half of a red sail, and water dripping out of it—it was a dry day, Nora—and leaving a track to the door.

(*She pauses again with her hand stretched out toward the door. It opens softly and old women begin to come in, crossing themselves on the threshold, and kneeling down in front of the stage with red petticoats over their heads*)

MAURYA: (*Half in a dream, to* CATHLEEN) Is it Patch, or Michael, or what is it at all?

CATHLEEN: Michael is after being found in the Far North, and when he is found there how could he be here in this place?

MAURYA: There does be a power of young men floating round in the sea, and what way would they know if it was Michael they had, or another man like him, for when a man is nine days in the sea, and the wind blowing, it's hard set his own mother would be to say what man was it.

CATHLEEN: It's Michael, God spare him, for they're after sending us a bit of his clothes from the Far North.

(*She reaches out and hands* MAURYA *the clothes that belonged to Michael.* MAURYA *stands up slowly, and takes them in her hands.* NORA *looks out*)

NORA: They're carrying a thing among them and there's water dripping out of it and leaving a track by the big stones.

CATHLEEN: (*In a whisper to the women who have come in*) Is it Bartley it is?

ONE OF THE WOMEN: It is surely, God rest his soul.

**232**

(*Two younger women come in and pull out the table. Then men carry in the body of* BARTLEY, *laid on a plank, with a bit of a sail over it, and lay it on the table*)

CATHLEEN: (*To the women, as they are doing so*) What way was he drowned?

ONE OF THE WOMEN: The gray pony knocked him into the sea, and he was washed out where there is a great surf on the white rocks.

(MAURYA *has gone over and knelt down at the head of the table. The women are keening softly and swaying themselves with a slow movement.* CATHLEEN *and* NORA *kneel at the other end of the table. The men kneel near the door*)

MAURYA: (*Raising her head and speaking as if she did not see the people around her*) They're all gone now, and there isn't anything more the sea can do to me. . . . I'll have no call now to be up crying and praying when the wind breaks from the south, and you can hear the surf is in the east, and the surf is in the west, making a great stir with the two noises and they hitting one on the other. I'll have no call now to be going down and getting Holy Water in the dark nights after Samhain,[4] and I won't care what way the sea is when the other women will be keening. (*To* NORA) Give me the Holy Water, Nora, there's a small sup still on the dresser.

(NORA *gives it to her*)

MAURYA: (*Drops Michael's clothes across Bartley's feet, and sprinkles the Holy Water over him*) It isn't that I haven't prayed for you, Bartley, to the Almighty God. It isn't that I haven't said prayers in the dark night till you wouldn't know what I'd be saying; but it's a great rest I'll have now, and it's time surely. It's a great rest I'll have now, and great sleeping in the long nights after Samhain, if it's only a bit of wet flour we do have to eat, and maybe a fish that would be stinking.

(*She kneels down again, crossing herself, and saying prayers under her breath*)

CATHLEEN: (*To an old man*) Maybe yourself and Eamon would make a coffin when the sun rises. We have fine white boards herself bought, God help her, thinking Michael would be found, and I have a new cake you can eat while you'll be working.

THE OLD MAN (*Looking at the boards*) Are there nails with them?

CATHLEEN: There are not, Colum; we didn't think of the nails.

ANOTHER MAN: It's a great wonder she wouldn't think of the nails, and all the coffins she's seen made already.

CATHLEEN: It's getting old she is, and broken.

(MAURYA *stands up again very slowly and spreads out the pieces of Michael's clothes beside the body, sprinkling them with the last of the Holy Water*)

NORA: (*In a whisper to* CATHLEEN) She's quiet now and easy; but the day Michael was drowned you could hear her crying out from this to the spring well. It's fonder she was of Michael, and would anyone have thought that?

CATHLEEN (*Slowly and clearly*) An old woman will be soon tired with anything she will do, and isn't it nine days herself is after crying and keening, and making great sorrow in the house?

MAURYA: (*Puts the empty cup mouth downwards on the table, and lays her hands together on Bartley's feet*) They're all together this time, and the end is come. May the Almighty God have mercy on Bartley's soul, and on Michael's soul, and on the souls of Sheamus and Patch, and Stephen and Shawn; (*Bending her head*) and may He have mercy on my soul, Nora, and on the soul of everyone is left living in the world.

---

[4]The equivalent of Allhallows. It falls on November 1 and marks the beginning of winter; it is celebrated with harvest rites and a Feast of the Dead.

*(She pauses, and the keen rises a little more loudly from the women, then sinks away)*

MAURYA: *(Continuing)* Michael has a clean burial in the Far North, by the grace of the Almighty God. Bartley will have a fine coffin out of the white boards, and a deep grave surely. What more can we want than that? No man at all can be living forever, and we must be satisfied.

*(She kneels down again and the curtain falls slowly)*

—John Millington Synge *(1871-1909)*

# HOW TO FIND INFORMATION ABOUT AN AUTHOR

To locate the background and other details of an author, it is helpful to know some basic facts about the person's life. One way to find some clues is to look at the cards listing the author's books in the *Card Catalog*.

1. The card giving the author's name on the top line often shows the **birth and death dates** right after the name.

2. The title of the book or the subject headings at the bottom of the card often reveals the author's **profession or interests**.

3. The place of publication typed after the book title is a clue to the **nationality** of the author.

Clues are also given on the book jacket, in the foreword of the book, or in the text of the book itself. Further information may be obtained in the library Reference Room in biographical dictionaries:

*For Living Authors*

    BIOGRAPHY INDEX (Ref Z 5301 B5)
    CONTEMPORARY AUTHORS (Ref Z 1224 C6)
    WHO'S WHO (Ref DA 28 W6) British Only
    WHO'S WHO IN AMERICA (Ref E 176 W642) U.S. Only
    WHO'S WHO OF AMERICAN WOMEN (Ref CT 3260 W5)
    CURRENT BIOGRAPHY (Ref CT 100 C8)

*For Authors No Longer Living*

    DICTIONARY OF AMERICAN BIOGRAPHY (Ref E 176 D563)
    DICTIONARY OF NATIONAL BIOGRAPHY (Ref DA 28 D4) British Only
    BIOGRAPHY INDEX (Ref Z 5301 B5)
    WHO WAS WHO IN AMERICA (Ref E 663 W54)

NOTE:

Use the older issues of CURRENT BIOGRAPHY, WHO'S WHO, and WHO'S WHO IN AMERICA for information about writers recently deceased.

*For Authors of Literature*

    AMERICAN AUTHORS, 1600-1900 (Ref PS 21 K8)
    BRITISH AUTHORS OF THE NINETEENTH CENTURY (Ref PR 451 K8 1936)
    BRITISH AUTHORS BEFORE 1800 (Ref PR 105 K9)
    CONTEMPORARY DRAMATISTS (Ref PR 106 V5)
    CONTEMPORARY NOVELISTS (Ref PR 737 V5)
    CONTEMPORARY POETS (Ref PS 324 C63)
    EUROPEAN AUTHORS 1000-1900 (Ref PN 451 K8)
    JUNIOR BOOK OF AUTHORS (Ref PN 1009 A1 K8 1951)
    LIVING BLACK AMERICAN AUTHORS (Ref PS 153 N5 S5)
    TWENTIETH CENTURY AUTHORS (Ref PN 771 K86)
    WORLD AUTHORS 1950-1970 (Ref PN 451 W3)

*For Authors With Other Occupations*

    AMERICAN MEN AND WOMEN OF SCIENCE (Ref Q 141 A47)
    DICTIONARY OF SCIENTIFIC BIOGRAPHY (Ref Q 141 D5)
    DICTIONARY OF AMERICAN SCHOLARS (Ref LA 2311 C32)
    WHO'S WHO IN AMERICAN POLITICS (Ref E 176 W6424)
    WHO'S WHO IN FINANCE AND INDUSTRY (Ref 3023 A2 W5)

*For Authors of Other Countries*

       DICTIONARY OF NATIONAL BIOGRAPHY (Ref DA 28 D4) British Only
       INTERNATIONAL WHO'S WHO (Ref CT 120 I 5)
       WEBSTER'S BIOGRAPHICAL DICTIONARY (Ref CT 103 W4)
       WHO'S WHO (Ref DA 28 W6) British Only
       WORLD BIOGRAPHY (Ref CT 120 W65)

SUGGESTIONS:

    1. Longer biographies of an author may be found in the Card Catalog under the name. Books *about* a person are filed after the books written *by* that person. The person's name is typed in capital letters to differentiate the person as subject of a book from the person as author.

    2. For additional material, look in the Card Catalog under such headings as:

       ARTISTS, AMERICAN       SCIENTISTS
       AUTHORS                 THEATER—U.S.
       GREAT BRITAIN—BIOGRAPHY   WOMAN—BIOGRAPHY

    3. For magazine articles about an author, consult the READERS' GUIDE TO PERIODICAL LITERATURE, THE HUMANITIES INDEX, or other indexes.

    4. Information about authors who have written very little or whose published work is very recent may be difficult to find. For these authors, try book reviews. These sometimes contain information about authors.

## HOW TO FIND BOOK REVIEWS

    A **review** is a notice of a current book published in a periodical. It announces a work, describes its subject, discusses its method and technical qualities, and examines its merit when it is compared with other similar works.

    A **critique**, on the other hand, is an essay or article which is more serious than a review. It is a critical examination of a literary work and attempts to explain and interpret. (See page 238.)

    Some special books in the Reference Room index book reviews published in magazines. To use these books the following information is needed:

    1. The full name of the **author**.
    2. The exact **title** of the book.
    3. The **year** the book was published. (Reviews usually appear soon after a book is published.)

       Note: Look for the date of publication or the copyright date on the front or back of the title page of the book. When more than one date is given, use the earliest date.

    This information may be found in the card catalog or in *Books In Print*.

*Special Book Review Indexes*

| | |
|---|---|
| REF<br>Z<br>1219<br>C95 | BOOK REVIEW DIGEST, 1905 to date. Locates reviews in more than 70 magazines and is kept up-to-date by monthly supplements. Entries are under author's name. Look first in the volume for the year the book was published. If the book is not listed, try the next annual volume. A short description of the book, references to magazines containing reviews, and quotations from some of those reviews will be found under the citation. |

| | |
|---|---|
| REF<br>Z<br>1035<br>A1<br>I 63 | INDEX TO BOOK REVIEWS IN THE HUMANITIES, 1961 to date. Published annually, listing reviews in the humanities. Includes history, biography, personal narratives, travel, and adventure. No quotations given. |
| REF<br>Z<br>1035<br>A1<br>B6 | BOOK REVIEW INDEX, 1965 to date. An index to reviews in about 200 periodicals. Important for the number of scholarly journals in the humanities and social sciences represented. Specialized scientific and technical periodicals are excluded. No quotations given. |

*Reviews of Books in General*

| | |
|---|---|
| SER OR REF<br>AI<br>3<br>R48 | READERS' GUIDE TO PERIODICAL LITERATURE, 1932 to date. Lists book reviews under name of author. New policy from 1976 issues is to group all book reviews at end of main body of text in a separate section headed "Book Reviews." Also lists movie reviews under "Moving Picture Plays—Criticisms—Single Works." Play reviews are listed under "Dramas—Criticisms" and full entries are under name of author. |
| SER<br>AI<br>3<br>P76 | POPULAR PERIODICALS INDEX, 1973 to date. This indexes magazines not covered by *Readers' Guide to Periodical Literature*. Reviews are listed under "Book Reviews." |

*Reviews of Books on Special Subjects*

APPLIED SCIENCE AND TECHNOLOGY INDEX (Ser Z 7913 I 7)
ART INDEX (Ser Z 5937 A78)
BIOLOGICAL AND AGRICULTURAL INDEX (Ser Z 5073 A46)
BUSINESS PERIODICALS INDEX (Ser Z 7164 C81 B983)
EDUCATION INDEX (Ser Z 5813 E23)
HUMANITIES INDEX (Ser AI 3 H85)
SOCIAL SCIENCE INDEX (Ser AI 3 S62)

Note: Book Review section since 1976 edition of each of these titles is now in a separate section at the back of the issue. Older issues list them in the "Bs" under "Book Reviews."

*Newspaper Indexes*

| | |
|---|---|
| SER<br>AI<br>21<br>N44 | NEW YORK TIMES INDEX, 1964 to date. Lists citations under "Book Reviews." |

*Reviews of Very New Books*

If the book is so new that reviews have not yet been listed in any of the general book reviewing indexes, you may find it reviewed in the latest numbers of current magazines regularly having book review sections, for example:

| | |
|---|---|
| ATLANTIC MONTHLY | NEW YORK TIMES BOOK REVIEW |
| HARPER'S | SATURDAY REVIEW |
| NEW YORK REVIEW OF BOOKS | TIMES LITERARY SUPPLEMENT |

# HOW TO FIND LITERARY CRITICISM OF SPECIFIC WORKS

A critical essay is usually written several years after the original publication and attempts to assess the importance of the work. Information needed for a search for criticism includes: Writer's name, title of work, country of its origin, and its literary genre (poem, novel).

The following sources can be used to find criticism buried in periodicals and books:

1. POETRY

*Poetry Explication* (Ref Z 2014 P7 K8). Covers British and American poetry. Indexes criticism printed in books and journals between 1925 and 1959.

*Index to Criticisms of British and American Poetry* (Ref Z 2014 P7 C6). Indexes criticism written between 1960 and 1971.

2. SHORT STORY

*Short Fiction Criticism* (Ref Z 5917 S5 T5). Indexes modern criticisms of short stories written from 1800 to 1958. Covers American, British, and Continental stories.

*Twentieth Century Short Story Explication* (Ref Z 5917 S5 W3). Indexes critical essays printed between 1900 and 1972. Covers stories of all countries and centuries.

3. DRAMA

*European Drama Criticism* (Ref Z 5781 P2). Covers classical to modern drama. Criticism written from 1900 to 1972.

*Modern Drama* (Ref Z 5781 A35). Covers 20th century drama and criticism.

*American Drama Criticism* (Ref Z 5781 P36). Covers only American plays. Indexes criticism written from 1890 to 1975.

*Guide to Critical Reviews* (Ref Z 5782 S342)
    Part I:   American Drama (20th century)
    Part II:   British and Continental Drama (1850-1960's)

*Dramatic Criticism Index* (Ref Z 5781 B8). Covers English, American, and foreign, from Ibsen to avant-garde.

*Drama Criticism* (Ref Z 5781 C66)
    Vol. 1: English and American drama, essays written between 1940 and 1966.
    Vol. 2: Classical and Continental, essays written between 1940 and 1970.

4. NOVEL

*English Novel* (Ref Z 2014 F4 B4). Includes novels written between 1578 and 1956. 20th century criticism.

*English Novel Explication* (Ref Z 2014 F5 P26). Criticism written between 1958 and 1975.

*American Novel* (Ref Z 1231 F4 G4). Novels written between 1789 and 1959. Criticisms written between 1900 and 1968.

*Contemporary Novel* (Ref Z 1231 F4 A34). British and American novels written between 1945 and 1969.

*Continental Novel* (Ref Z 5916 K4). Criticism written between 1900 and 1966. Includes French, Spanish, Portuguese, Italian, German, Scandinavian, Russian, and East European novels.

## OTHER SOURCES

### 1. CARD CATALOG

Look up *authors'* names in the card catalog to see if the library owns entire books devoted to their lives or work. Sometimes a particular literary piece will be discussed in a book of this kind. Check the index in the book for your title.

Criticism of short works such as poetry and short stories cannot be located by looking under *titles* in the card catalog. However, there may be entries in the card catalog under the author's name along with the title for books which deal with only one play or one novel, if it is a classic. (Example: MELVILLE, HERMAN. MOBY DICK.)

In addition, a search under certain *subject* headings in the card catalog can lead to more books which might contain useful information. Check the indexes of the books. Many of these books have been included in sources already consulted, but you might find a few not covered elsewhere. Some subjects to check are:

DRAMA—HISTORY AND CRITICISM    or AMERICAN, ENGLISH,
FICTION—HISTORY AND CRITICISM       FRENCH, etc. as appropriate
LITERATURE—HISTORY AND CRITICISM   to author's nationality
POETRY—HISTORY AND CRITICISM

### 2. *Essay and General Literature Index* (Ref AI 3 E752). Indexes essays within books and provides exact page references to criticism of an author's particular work. Look under author's name, then subdivision "About individual works." Titles will then be listed alphabetically.

### 3. *Reader's Index to "Twentieth Century Views"* Literary Criticism Series (Ref Z 6511 T86). Exact page references given for criticisms of individual works.

## SPECIAL COLLECTIONS

*Moulton's Library of Literary Criticism* (Ref PR 83 M73 1966).
     Covers English and American authors. 19th century criticism.

*The Critical Temper* (Ref PR 83 C764).
     Covers English and American literature up to 20th century.

*Contemporary Literary Criticism* (Ref PN 771 C59).
     Covers writers now living or who have died since 1960. Criticism written during past twenty-five years or so.

*A Library of Literary Criticism: Modern British Literature* (Ref PR 473 T4).

*A Library of Literary Criticism: Modern American Literature* (Ref PS 211 C8).

*American Writers* (Ref PS 129 A55).
     A collection of literary biographies. Gives lengthy discussion of lives, careers and works of major American writers, and includes lists of additional critical studies in books and periodicals.

# Index

**242**

**243**

**244**